T0318447

The Work of Communication

The Work of Communication: Relational Perspectives on Working and Organizing in Contemporary Capitalism revolves around a two-part question: "What have work and organization become under contemporary capitalism—and how should organization studies approach them?" Changes in the texture of capitalism, heralded by social and organizational theorists alike, increasingly focus on communication as both vital to the conduct of work and as imperative to organizational performance. Yet most accounts of communication in organization studies fail to understand an alternate sense of the "work" of communication in the *constitution* of organizations, work practices, and economies. This book responds to that lack by portraying communicative practices—as opposed to individuals, interests, technologies, structures, organizations, or institutions—as the focal units of analysis in studies of the social and organizational problems occasioned by contemporary capitalism.

Rather than suggesting that there exists a canonically "correct" route communicative analyses must follow, *The Work of Communication: Relational Perspectives on Working and Organizing in Contemporary Capitalism* explores the value of transcending longstanding divides between symbolic and material factors in studies of working and organizing. The recognition of dramatic shifts in technological, economic, and political forces, along with deep interconnections among the myriad of factors shaping working and organizing, sows doubts about whether organization studies is up to the vital task of addressing the social problems capitalism now creates. Kuhn, Ashcraft, and Cooren argue that novel insights into those social problems are possible if we tell different stories about working and organizing. To aid authors of those stories, they develop a set of conceptual resources that they capture under the mantle of *communicative relationality*. These resources allow analysts to profit from burgeoning interest in notions such as sociomateriality, posthumanism, performativity, and affect. It goes on to illustrate the benefits that investigations of work and organization can realize from communicative relationality by presenting case studies that analyze (a) the *becoming* of an idea, from its inception to solidification, (b) the emergence of what is taken to be "the product" in high-tech startup entrepreneurship, and (c) the branding of work (in this case, academic writing and commercial aviation) through affective economies. Taken together, the book portrays "the work of communication" as simultaneously about how work in the "new economy" revolves around communicative practice and about how communication serves as a mode of explanation with the potential to cultivate novel stories about working and organizing.

Aimed at academics, researchers, and policy makers, this book's goal is to make tangible the contributions of communication for thinking about contemporary social and organizational problems.

Timothy Kuhn is a Professor in the Department of Communication at the University of Colorado at Boulder, USA.

Karen Lee Ashcraft is a Professor in the Department of Communication at the University of Colorado at Boulder, USA.

François Cooren is a Professor in the Department of Communication at the Université de Montréal, Canada.

Routledge Studies in Management, Organizations and Society

This series presents innovative work grounded in new realities, addressing issues crucial to an understanding of the contemporary world. This is the world of organised societies, where boundaries between formal and informal, public and private, local and global organizations have been displaced or have vanished, along with other nineteenth century dichotomies and oppositions. Management, apart from becoming a specialized profession for a growing number of people, is an everyday activity for most members of modern societies.

Similarly, at the level of enquiry, culture and technology, and literature and economics, can no longer be conceived as isolated intellectual fields; conventional canons and established mainstreams are contested. **Management, Organizations and Society** addresses these contemporary dynamics of transformation in a manner that transcends disciplinary boundaries, with books that will appeal to researchers, student and practitioners alike.

Recent titles in this series include:

The Work of Communication

Relational Perspectives on
Working and Organizing in
Contemporary Capitalism

Timothy Kuhn, Karen Lee Ashcraft,
and François Cooren

Routledge
Taylor & Francis Group
NEW YORK AND LONDON

First published 2017 by Routledge

2 Park Square, Milton Park, Abingdon, Oxfordshire OX14 4RN
52 Vanderbilt Avenue, New York, NY 10017

Routledge is an imprint of the Taylor & Francis Group, an informa business

First issued in paperback 2019

Library of Congress Cataloging-in-Publication Data
A catalog record for this book has been requested

ISBN: 978-1-138-93015-5 (hbk)
ISBN: 978-0-367-24306-7 (pbk)

DOI: 10.4324/9781315680705

To Joan, Dick, Sophia, Ella, and Sam

To Peter D. and the many lives of Z

À Bruno, Sylvie et Mathieu, avec tout mon amour

Contents

Figures

Acknowledgments

We would like to express our sincere appreciation to all the agencies that have played important roles in the development of the ideas contained in the pages to follow. The participants we studied at Museomix and AmpVille, along with the airline pilots and aviation museum curators who shed light on occupational identity, were tremendously generous. And we are also grateful to the spaces we inhabited in these projects, the recording and computational devices we employed in data collection and analysis, the financial support of our universities and the social Research and Humanities Council of Canada (SSHRC 435–2013–0977), the infrastructure enabling our presence at the research sites, and the communication technologies that enabled the three of us to exchange ideas and the (nearly incalculable number of) drafts of these chapters. But back to people. We thank the graduate students who participated in a seminar as well as a colloquium at the University of Colorado Boulder, where we gave many of these ideas a "test run," and attendees at talks at Aalto University (Helsinki), Lund University (Sweden), University of Texas at Austin, Université de Montréal, St. Mary's University (Canada), and Massey University (New Zealand), as well as the ninth Organization Studies Summer Workshop (Greece).

We also are grateful for our colleagues, both at our universities and across the globe, for conversations that aided in the progress of these ideas, or for those who have read drafts of chapters: Will Barley, Gerald Bartels, Nicolas Bencherki, Boris Brummans, Chantal Benoit-Barné, Pascale Caïdor, Mathieu Chaput, Maurice Charland, Joëlle Cruz, Stan Deetz, Vincent Denault, Stephanie Fox, Lise Higham, Jody Jahn, Dan Kärreman, Matt Koschmann, Paul Leonardi, Thomas Martine, Frédérik Matte, Kirstie McAllum, Dennis Mumby, Amanda Porter, Linda Putnam, Jens Rennstam, Daniel Robichaud, Dennis Schoeneborn, Pete Simonson, Bryan Taylor, James Taylor, Jeff Treem, Elizabeth Van Every, and Consuelo Vásquez. And thank you to Dave Varley, Megan Smith, and Brianna Ascher at Routledge for their support and encouragement throughout the project.

1 Encountering Working and Organizing Under Contemporary Capitalism

Introduction

Viewed through history's rearview mirror, modernity has never seen a period when work wasn't undergoing dramatic change. Whether transformations in the workplace are seen as the result of demographic, technological, political, or competitive forces, shifting work arrangements have always drawn scholarly attention. The claims are everywhere: social critics, politicians, and management gurus proclaim a new era of capitalism, a "new economy" promising a working life characterized by either a utopian freedom and self-determination or a dystopian servitude produced by constant surveillance, competition, and insecurity (including the threat of job loss because of automation—a risk not only for so-called blue-collar workers) amid weak global economic growth (e.g., McDonough, Reich, & Kotz, 2010), with few pronouncements falling between those extremes.

By way of illustration, consider the consulting and accounting firm PwC's recent publication, *The Future of Work: A Journey to 2022* (Rendell & Brown, 2014). After noting that "disruptive innovations are creating new industries and business models" (1) and challenging readers—it targets human resource managers in for-profit enterprises—to consider what this means for their businesses, the report paints three scenarios, three prospective "worlds of work." What it calls the "Blue World" is where large multinational corporations dominate, where firms refine employee measurement and management efficiencies, and in which employees trade personal data for job security. In the "Green World," companies are portrayed as developing a social conscience and sense of responsibility such that firms offer ethical values and work-life balance in exchange for employee loyalty. Its "Orange World" speaks to the decline of large corporations and the ascendancy of small, nimble, networked, and technologically sophisticated firms. Here, job security disappears and in its place are the flexibility, autonomy, and attractiveness of new challenges that accompany the contract-based work of "portfolio careers." Of course, these worlds ignore a good deal of organizational forms, and all three are prevalent today; the lesson offered by the report, however, is

DOI: 10.4324/9781315680705-1

that constant and thoroughgoing change is on the horizon—change that threatens the viability of existing organizing practices.

To be sure, there are good reasons for skepticism about claims of grand, sweeping changes in the workplace, particularly when proffered by a company peddling its consulting services. One such reason is that we may be experiencing a break less radical than proposed. A key lesson offered by observers of capitalism over time (e.g., Boltanski & Chiapello, 2005) is that newness is ever present; there is always a contemporary set of unique arrangements that calls upon analysts and observers to develop conceptual schemes to illuminate, describe, and explain prevailing modes of production and accumulation. Capitalism modifies itself to respond to challenges to its legitimacy and, in so doing, protects itself from transformative change. Examining the mutable texture of capitalism is crucial for the field of organization studies, since what we take to be its key foci— work and organization—are being re-configured and re-understood in this "new economy."

A similar argument can be seen in Marxist discussions about work and labor, where the notion of "periodizations" speaks to changes in the economic, political, and ideological conditions, which may—or may *not*—be associated with shifts in the mode of production. As Fine and Harris (1979, p. 109) observe,

> The effects of the development of the forces and relations of production on the *form* of social relations within a mode [of production] define the transformation from one stage of a mode to another . . . such a periodisation will reveal itself through transformations in the methods of appropriating and controlling surplus value.

Given capitalism's fluidity and capacity to adapt, changes in patterns of social reproduction may well be indicative of deepening long-standing patterns rather than dramatic alterations in the underlying mode of production. In other words, it is probably impossible to determine, definitively, whether changes in the mode of production and accumulation are occurring.

An inability to substantiate claims of dramatic change occurs not merely because of capitalism's protean shape-shifting; nor is it because there exists no Archimedean point from which such a definitive statement about economic change could be advanced. Rather, the very notion of an economy existing "out there" as if objective and external to scholarly analysis is misguided. We—students and scholars of organization (a group we take to be the primary audience for this book)—attend to particular issues, write about them, teach them, present them as factual. In so doing, we tell a story about a "new economy" that is *performative* in its effects: It participates in the enactment of the reality it seeks to describe. We shall say more about performativity in Chapter 2, but in the main part of this chapter, we depict some of the most repeated stories told about sea changes in the terrain of working and organizing under contemporary capitalism.

Our Guiding Question and the Pursuit of Novelty

The aim of this book, then, is to examine how developments associated with contemporary capitalism—as well as the stories we tell about them, which are part of the developments themselves—bear consequences for how work is both accomplished and organized. Our particular concern is the extent to which customary frames and tools of scholarship in organization studies are up to the vital task of addressing social problems associated with shifts in capitalism. Rather than assessing those frames with a desire to judge their (in)adequacy, however, we ask in this chapter about what our stories are *doing*. Where are they leading, and where do they become stuck? Are there other fruitful stories to be told? Accordingly, our guiding question is this: *What have work and organization become under contemporary capitalism, and how should organization studies approach them?*

Addressing this question should begin, of course, with a consideration of how the field of organization studies has taken up capitalism, contemporary and otherwise. There are two dominant approaches. The first has been to treat capitalism as background, an uninterrogated frame for the conduct of work and organizing. Research of this sort often is functionalist in orientation, as seen in scholarship on entrepreneurship, for instance. Although there is a growing body of scholarship that critically examines entrepreneurship's antecedents and unintended consequences, the lion's share of research here considers the characteristics (of individuals, firms, and markets) associated with entrepreneurial success, processes through which new ventures emerge, and how states, communities, and even universities might foster greater entrepreneurial activity. This work tends to be guided by the assumption that entrepreneurship produces economic and social utility, often invoking the Schumpeterian notion of disruption, though it rarely examines that assumption's veracity (Shane, 2009). A market-based system of exchange, a system of economic relations, is the implied (but rarely interrogated) background upon which entrepreneurship unfolds; if it is invoked at all, it is to point to the ways the system enables and constrains the phenomenon of interest.

A second approach has been to suggest that capitalism generates the class distinctions upon which organizing proceeds (Roediger, 1999; Thompson, 1963). Here it is the economic system that produces social ordering, distinction, hierarchy, and distributions of resources that are unequal, but this system is understood as intimately bound up in the production and valorization of identities, communities, and forms of work. For instance, analysts have studied how the "working class" assimilates members into "blue-collar" values through cultural practices, forms of speech, and practices of (self-)discipline that produce group-based distinctions, construct subjectivities, and assert the superiority of the class against others (Lucas, 2011; Philipsen, 1975; Willis, 1977).

As plotlines, these broad approaches have borne significant fruit in the story of working and organizing. In this book, we build upon the solid foundation they have established, but our storytelling employs what we shall call *relational ontologies* to portray capitalism not as a figure lurking in the background, nor as an external force impelling particular forms of system organization, but as a participant inextricably bound up in socioeconomic practice. In other words, the perspectives we pursue (we shall offer three conceptualizations of what we term *communicative relationality*) are not offered to mend gaps created by other approaches, but because their distinctive conceptualizations offer inventive lines by which investigations might proceed. Relational ontologies have begun to garner significant attention in organization studies (Ganesh & Wang, 2015; Orlikowski, 2007; Vosselman, 2014), yet scholars—ourselves included—are struggling to elucidate the implications of this ontological turn for analyses of working and organizing, as well as the methodological claims it makes on our scholarship (see, e.g., Mutch, 2013). This book directly engages with these struggles in order to articulate concrete possibilities whereby relationality can facilitate novel ways of attending to social problems. In this way, we endeavor to tell a meaningfully different story about working and organizing as we (might) know it.

In this first chapter, we initiate pursuit of our guiding question—again, *what have work and organization become under contemporary capitalism, and how should organization studies approach them?* In the section to follow, we outline key stories scholars have told about the major transformations in working and organizing associated with contemporary capitalism. It is important to stress that, in framing scholarly accounts as "stories," we do not mean to belittle them. All theories put forth a narrative of things, and we do not take such narratives lightly. This book is simply more interested in their *production* rather than *truth* value. In other words, we are less concerned with the extent to which scholarly accounts correspond with some external reality and more concerned with how they participate in the making of certain realities and futures. This is *not* an abdication of facts in favor of relativism, as we shall see. Rather, it is an acknowledgment that shifts in capitalism are not somehow apart from the theories that punctuate their existence and occurrence. Theoretical stories contribute to the very developments they claim to study. This is precisely why we are so interested in them—in their possibilities *and* limitations, and in the promise of other stories to be told.

Our review of key stories pays particular attention to *communicative* forms of work. As we show next, work is increasingly about the analysis and manipulation of symbols, the interactive production of feelings, and the generation of images—forms of work that self-evidently revolve around actors engaging in communication with others. However, working and organizing are not merely symbolic: As we demonstrate, there is a wide (and shifting) array of forces at play, requiring an approach to studying them that foregrounds multiplicity, relationality, and transformation. This book is intended as a contribution to organization studies scholars' capacities to undertake studies of working and organizing when multiplicity, relationality, and transformation are configured as central features of the scene.

Conceptualizing "Work(ing)"

Before we encounter contemporary currents in working and organizing, we should clarify what we mean by "work." Certainly, *work*, as an activity, can take various forms and occurs in and through many domains; it has also been conceived differently depending on the historical circumstance of the writer. Unsurprisingly, then, definitions of work likewise abound. At an abstract level, work is about deeds, tasks, and instances of labor; it is "action or activity involving physical or mental effort and undertaken in order to achieve a result, esp. as a means of making one's living or earning money; labour; (one's) regular occupation or employment" (*Oxford English Dictionary*). It indexes the amount of effort necessary to complete a task or create an outcome; that outcome can involve providing the social/artificial world with things distinct from those found in our natural surroundings.

Work is, moreover, sometimes understood as "the creation of material goods and services, which may be directly consumed by the worker or sold to someone else" (Hodson & Sullivan, 1995, p. 3). In other words, though work is sometimes reduced to a noun—to the thing produced by activity—the term also implies *working*, the gerund indicating the action of bringing about deeds.

Other conceptions distinguish between forms of work. Bertrand Russell (1935/2004), somewhat playfully, held work to be of two kinds: "first, altering the position of matter at or near the earth's surface relative to other such matter; second, telling other people to do so" (p. 3). Still others distinguish work from play, suggesting that work is serious and solemn, whereas play is frivolous and joyful (e.g., Burke, 1981). Thomas (1999), seeking to capture the central elements of the range of conceptions depicted here, offers this encapsulation:

> Work has an end beyond itself, being designed to produce or achieve something; it involves a degree of obligation or necessity, being a task that others set us or that we set ourselves; and it is arduous, involving effort and persistence beyond the point at which the task ceases to be wholly pleasurable.
>
> (p. xiv)

Across definitions such as these, Daniels (1987) argues that work tends to be portrayed as (a) public, rather than private, activity; (b) requiring financial recompense, and (c) gendered, in that traditionally masculine activities are more likely to be considered work. All of these features, she argues, tend to relegate unpaid and invisible labor—not coincidentally, many activities coded as feminine—outside the realm of "work" (as "labors of love," for instance). In an effort to clarify what we mean by work while remaining open to the kind of activity to which Daniels draws attention, we depict work(ing) as *the practice of focusing labor toward the production of "objects" with value.* As the scare quotes suggest, objects may take many forms. Moreover, their value may be a matter of contestation; as we will show, value is rarely as simple as that which it is taken to be on its face.

Our aim in characterizing work(ing) this way is to suggest several important elements of contemporary renditions of work and working. This book seeks to understand the processes and products of working (as well as of organizing), acknowledging that work relies upon, and generates, objects that are simultaneously material and symbolic—objects that have the potential to participate in the (re)inscription of the relations of capitalism. Conceiving of work in this way is agnostic as to the sources of influence over the trajectory of the practice, being open to the multiplicity of forces initiating, pushing, and benefiting from work (or, perhaps, considering these issues topics for examination). As we address in the next sections (and in more detail in Chapter 3), we see communication as axial to understanding working, but only if we avoid the common relegation of communication to the realm of the *merely* symbolic, interactional, and imaginative. We shall argue, instead, that communication is the force that *constitutes* working (and organizing), which also, in turn, constitutes economic realities.

The Story of the New Economy in Studies of Work and Organization

What stories about the contemporary socioeconomic scene are told in the organization studies literature? To what factors do analysts point, and what consequences, in the sense of social problems, do they note? And, importantly, what are the assumptions about communicating and organizing that mark their thinking? A point to which we turn at the end of this chapter is that organization studies should think carefully about how it conceives of such "factors," because these conceptual foundations matter for our epistemological and methodological engagement with working and organizing.

The story is often abbreviated as *neoliberalism*, the ideology that subsumes social and political life into the capitalist logic of accumulation and, according to many analysts, does so in deterministic fashion: "Neoliberalism transmogrifies every human domain and endeavor, along with humans themselves, according to a specific image of the economic. All conduct is economic conduct; all spheres of existence are framed and measured by economic terms and metrics" (Brown, 2015, p. 10). Whereas some argue that neoliberalism is the antithesis of (pure) capitalism, the term tends to direct attention to the reduced role of the state and the increased power of the market in contemporary governance brought on by right-leaning

Western governments, particularly of the Reagan-Thatcher variety (though, as Harvey [2005] notes, its seeds were planted several decades earlier), which sought to ease restrictions on capital flows and to make privatized enterprises out of what had previously been public services.

Neoliberalism is not only about the production of new subjects and their conduct; it also heralds an enlarged corporate power in public life, one in which corporations have been the beneficiaries (and often coauthors) of laws, policies, and rights that previously had been the sphere of persons and publics, and governments have learned to operate like commercial firms (Coates, 2015). Neoliberalism is a loose and shifting signifier, and a detailed historical account of its origins, emergence, and variations is beyond our scope here. Yet we note that neoliberalism's preference for capital over labor, management over trade unions, individuals over communities, work over welfare, and markets over governments animates the stories told about contemporary capitalism.

With respect to working and organizing, one consequence of neoliberalism is the rise of the "entrepreneurial self," a subject who pursues enterprise—monitoring the self, building personal skills, and displaying individual productivity, both within and beyond the boundaries of the organization—not only because work increasingly demands it but also because entrepreneurialism has become situated as the source of personal meaningfulness (Pinchot, 1985). The protagonists in the neoliberal story are rational actors who are granted the right to pursue their economic self-interest by using property as they see fit, and the entrepreneurial self is an archetype of this brand of individualization (Brökling, 2015).

Tales of entrepreneurial success are contemporary heroes' journeys (Watt, 2016; Whelan & O'Gorman, 2007) in which the individual doggedly pursues a vision, overcoming a hostile marketplace (and often governmental impediments) to achieve renown and financial prosperity. The notion of difference is present here: Those who distinguish themselves as courageous and technologically sophisticated entrepreneurs are worthy of praise, whereas those who are unable to do so, or who are not imaginative enough, are left behind in the neoliberal world. The valorization of this sort of entrepreneur tells us at least as much about the contemporary economic scene as it does about the characters involved.

Although these developments point to important changes in capitalism, using neoliberalism as synecdoche—as a covering term for an array of related processes—risks missing the various and complex relations of power, struggles over meaning, and forms of contingency that mark working and organizing. We thus unpack these more nuanced plotlines in what follows.

Post-Fordism and the Organization of Work

Early efforts to tell the story of change in working and organizing coined the term *post-Fordism* to describe how workplaces were moving from large and vertically integrated economies of scale (as in Henry Ford's factories) to networks of small and agile enterprises connected through more informal means of control. The change, which began in the 1970s and has been noted in several cultural contexts beyond the for-profit firm (Kumar, 1995), was made possible by

> the growing significance of global competition, freedom to locate in different parts of the world (in order both to cheapen production and on the other side to access distinctive new knowledge), and new forms of innovation that undermined the sort of long-term planning characteristic of the large managerial hierarchies.
>
> (du Gay & Morgan, 2013, p. 16)

This picture is certainly changing, but it has shaped thinking about the distribution of work for decades. The concept of management participated as well: The task of managing became not simply one of planning, coordinating, and controlling production, but of a constant search for flexibility and cost-efficiency—a stance that separated production from particular persons and places while simultaneously creating the conditions for the ascendancy of finance in organizational decision making.

Consumption, too, was key to the shift. As mass consumption declined and market segmentation rose, Baudrillard (1998) noted the ascendancy of a "consumer society" where people defined themselves through their consumption choices. Aligning with this, Schulz and Robinson (2013) show that, after WWII, consumers became less interested in purchasing power and more concerned with choice and feelings of well-being achieved through consumption. Although many have suggested that the consumer society shifts emphasis from production to consumption, emphasizing consumption alone misses an important element of the story. Specifically, a consumer society creates a need for flexible specialization in *production*. An important consequence of this flexible specialization has been the development of a global division of labor, where production of goods occurs in low-wage countries, largely in Asia and the global South, while marketing, accounting, management, consulting, and other high-wage activities are located in richer northern countries. Flexible specialization and globally distributed production were enabled, many commentators suggest, by technological developments that allowed design, distribution, and communication to be easy, cheap, and located anywhere (e.g., A. Friedman, 2000).

In the developed world, the technological advances that ushered in post-Fordism created a division of labor that separated intellectual and manual work (Florida, 1991; Pleios, 2012). The new information and communication technologies meant that workers' time and activity could now be *flexible* such that they could work whenever and wherever necessary. Workers—but also consumers and firms—who benefit from these post-Fordist changes are those who can be mobile, whose bodies and minds can move easily (Sennett, 1998); they thus create a differential between themselves and those who are slower and sedentary.

Considering such a disparity in benefit created by a post-Fordist capitalism—not to mention the well-known disparities in wealth and income across the globe (Spinello, 2014)—an obvious question is why has the world seen so little in the way of resistance or generation of alternatives (Crouch, 2011)? One response has been that resistance becomes more hidden, subaltern; resistance may not look like the large-scale social movement of which (post-)Marxists dream, but alternative subjectivities and subtle moments of creative interrogation are opened up in post-Fordist work (Ashcraft, 2005; Mumby, 2005).

A second response—and another way to tell the story of contemporary capitalism—is seen in Boltanski and Chiapello's aforementioned *The New Spirit of Capitalism*. Hearkening back to Max Weber, they define a spirit as the ideology that justifies engagement in capitalism, capable of supplying not merely technical logics, but *moral* justifications for participants; these motivations "inspire entrepreneurs in activity conducive to capital accumulation" (2005, pp. 8–9). Capitalism's shifting spirit (they note three distinct versions) affords actors justifications for their actions, furnishing them with beliefs about the creation of the common good generated from capitalistic practices.

Boltanski and Chiapello emphasize that the spirit is not merely about defending an economic order; it is at least as much about securing commitment and attraction to it. The spirit secures commitment by presenting participation as stimulating, exciting, and secure—as the site for a free realization of a stable self over time and space such that capitalism is seen not only as an acceptable but also as a *desirable* order of things. Because these spirits are embedded in rules of conduct, language, institutions, practices, and cognitions, they are difficult to challenge, and even when challenges hit their mark, capitalism finds new bases upon which to mount its justifications (cf. Jessop & Sum, 2006).

The Project as Iconic

Boltanski and Chiapello demonstrate their thinking on the self-sustaining logic of capitalism with an analysis of its present spirit, one that aligns with many of the claims of post-Fordism. The contemporary spirit curbs the assumption that large firms comprise the standard conception of capitalism, vaulting the *project* to a position of conceptual centrality instead. Projects activate a section of a network for the duration of a shared task; once the job is completed, the links stay alive but less active, as seen in the "adhocracy" (Bennis & Slater, 1964), and the freelance work associated with the "gig economy" and its digitally enabled mobility (Fish & Srinivasan, 2011; Storey, Salaman, & Platman, 2005).

In a project regime, firms hire employees on short-term and flexible arrangements, often as independent contractors who complete a task in a

defined time period. Although labor markets establish wage rates, this flexibility is seen as desirable for organizations, since firms can more quickly
adapt to economic fluctuations without the burden that long-term employment relationships imply. Individuals, then, rather than firms, assume risk.
Gerald Friedman (2014, p. 171) sums up the individual-organization relationship thusly, "There is no more connection between the worker and the
employer than there might be between a consumer and a particular brand
of soap or potato chips."

Those workers, in turn, measure their (and others') activity in terms of their
success attracting (and consuming) gigs—success that depends crucially on
extending and "capitalizing" on personal networks. They are, consequently,
constantly on the lookout for additional projects through their networks:

> What matters is to develop activity—that is to say, never to be short of a
> project, bereft of an idea, always to have something in mind, in the pipe-
> line, with other people whom one meets out of a desire to do something.
> (Boltanski & Chiapello, 2005, p. 110)

Those who are busy are esteemed, but, beyond that, it is those who cultivate a sense for valuable ideas, projects, and people who have real status in this world. Developing communication skills that lend themselves
to effortless adaptability, inquiry, enthusiasm, and self-promotion are
therefore crucial for actors inhabiting this world. They also must rely on
computerized networking technologies; these factors also become part of
the network. And because such networks run on information and a com-
munitarian ethic, actors prevent each other from hoarding information
and closing off networks.

As a mode of capitalist production, the project claims to produce social
benefit by encouraging integration into networks, enhancing employ-
ability and self-determination, and fostering a sense of meaningfulness
rarely found in large bureaucracies (Peters, 1999). Project-based capitalism, consequently, is self-sustaining in its ability to marshal a set of connections that bring particular objects and subjects into existence; these
objects and subjects create a world that portrays both personal value and
social benefit as arising from this version of economic order.

The Rise of the Knowledge Economy

Associated with the move to project-based work is the rise of what has
become known as the "knowledge economy" or "information society"—
terms introduced to highlight how data, information, and knowledge, as
opposed to machinery, land, and physical labor, are now regarded as the
primary elements of capitalist production and accumulation (Castells,
1996; Drucker, 1992; Thrift, 2005). Especially in the post-industrial
Western world, the value of a worker often appears as a feature of the

mind and not the body, and organizations of many sorts seek to attract, manage, and build storehouses of knowledge (Adler, 2001).

As Powell and Snellman (2004) mention, however, the notion of a "knowledge economy" can refer to increased attribution of economic value to either (a) certain sorts of work and occupations that qualify as knowledge-intensive, such as STEM (science, technology, engineering, and math) fields, service-based work, and finance jobs, or (b) intra-organizational processes of learning, continuous innovation, and creativity. And although there are significant debates about the extent to which the knowledge economy, like post-Fordism, is a cause or an effect of advances in information and communication technologies (Lilley, Lightfoot, & Amaral, 2004), as well as about whether the increased emphasis on knowledge has created fundamentally different forms of work than in the past (Kochan and Barley, 1999), few deny the power of the proclamations of a new economic order revolving around knowledge (OECD, 1996).

Knowledge, in this line of thinking, is considered an "intangible" asset—one that participates in the production of value for both individuals and organizations, but upon which it is difficult to place a price. Prices are difficult to establish because knowledge cuts across functions and does not apply only in discrete units of time, making it less amenable to standard models of accounting despite being celebrated as the primary source of competitive advantage in contemporary firms (Grant, 1996; Spender, 1996). Thus because knowledge is not a typical commodity, and because it is seen to "stick" to its locations (Szulanski, 2003), actors have a vested interest in guarding what they and their organizations "possess" (Teece, 1998) as well as in managing others' impressions of their knowledge (Alvesson, 2001; Treem, 2012).

Communicative Knowledge

Literature on knowledge work is often characterized by claims about the broad sweep of this work and its increasing cultural centrality in Western economies, but critics suggest that developments in informational capitalism are more likely to produce low-level service jobs, particularly those in interactive service work, than the technologically adept symbolic analysts typically taken as characteristic of knowledge workers. When the "service encounter" becomes a key source of organizations' operational focus, employees' technical abilities are prized less than their aesthetic and social competence. Embodied communication practices thus become key to working, and organizations are increasingly aestheticized (Bryman, 2004; Korczynski, Shire, Frenkel, & Tam, 2000; Kuhn & Jackson, 2008; Thompson, Warhurst, & Callaghan, 2001; Witz, Warhurst, & Nickson, 2003). The notion of difference, mentioned earlier in the introduction of entrepreneurship, enters here as well: Only particular forms of knowledge work are valorized, only particular bodies are associated with service work (work that is often dismissed, as we did earlier in this paragraph, as "low level"), and only particular sorts of activity are acceptable to "contract out" to contingent workers (Rennstam & Ashcraft, 2014).

The question of how to manage workers whose labor is less explicitly connected to their bodies also arose with the post-Fordist knowledge economy. The story told about knowledge workers suggests that they seek challenge and meaning in their work, and that they reject traditional command-and-control approaches to management. Shaping hearts and minds in the organizational interest, accordingly, became central to how management saw its task. Somewhere around the 1980s (though see Barley & Kunda, 1992; Ouchi, 1980), managers recognized the need to encourage knowledge workers to identify with organizational cultures—for workers to see themselves as engaged not only in an economic exchange but also in a moral and emotional relationship. Knowledge workers were then understood as members of communities rather than as occupying a position in an impersonal bureaucracy, and normative and ideological control, as well as making the workplace an enjoyable experience, became managerial imperatives (Alvesson, 2000; Fleming & Sturdy, 2011). Difference enters here as well: Strong identification and the conception of work as a personal relationship are encouraged with only particular workers; others not fitting the mold are subject to the post-Fordist model of contingency and flexibility (Gossett, 2002).

Accompanying the rise of a post-Fordist economy has been the importance of what Rennstam and Ashcraft (2014) call *communicative knowledge*. Communicative knowledge, for them, is a form of knowing located not merely in brains, bodies, routines, or texts (cf. Blackler, 1995) but as also (and inherently) *in* and *about* interaction. Communicative knowledge

> generates interactive experiences that attend to the (often strategic) use of symbols, but the experience cannot be reduced to the symbolic. Instead, communicative knowledge resides in practice, 'between' the knower and its object of knowledge . . . [it] entails the merging of presence, physicality, situational familiarity and sensitivity, practical know-how, and action—embodied capacities honed through practice over time. Interaction here becomes a craft, trade, or even art unto itself—a social task that is also technical.
>
> (pp. 10–11)

Although communication, as a form of knowledge and knowing, has typically been relegated to a secondary status in management and organization studies thinking, it is increasingly understood as a key site of value production (Mumby, 2016; Witz et al., 2003).

In a following section (on precarious and immaterial labor), we shall augment this interest in communicative knowledge, but, for the time being, our point is that capitalism revolves more around communication than ever before, and one important upshot of this is that pinpointing *the* point at which value production occurs becomes more challenging than ever before.

The Knowledge of the Crowd

An additional line of inquiry connecting with knowledge is literature on crowdsourcing. *Crowdsourcing* is a model of organizing and accomplishing work that begins with a call to a large (and often reasonably undifferentiated) group; using Internet-enabled information and communication technologies, the crowd generates responses to the call. As an approach to managing complex tasks, crowdsourcing uses online communities—it employs the "wisdom of the crowd"—to foster scientific breakthroughs, generate responses to persistent organizational problems, and gather citizen input in community planning.

Some uses of crowdsourcing are relatively straightforward, such as when "the crowd" is asked to process large data sets, as is the case with Amazon's Mechanical Turk (Irani, 2015). Other uses are more about knowledge creation, as when the phenomenon in question is spatially and conceptually distributed and crowds are needed to generate maps, as when organizations seek to assemble information scattered around the Internet or residents of a city provide information about infrastructure problems that need repair (Brabham, Ribisl, Kirchner, & Bernhardt, 2014). And what Brabham (2012, 2013) calls *peer-vetted creative production* describes the crowdsourcing case where there exists no correct answer to the problem at hand; the aim is instead to generate and assess new ideas or to ascertain the level of support for an organization's idea (or marketing campaign).

The individuals who comprise the crowd rarely receive financial remuneration for their work (some, such as the individuals populating Mechanical Turk, are paid relatively paltry sums), raising the question of personal motivations and the specter of exploitation. We shall return to this theme next in a discussion of digital "free labor"; our argument here is that the story of knowledge production in the "new economy" is not merely one of prizing individual knowledge workers organized in professional-service firms. The story is, instead, a complex one in which technologies, communication practices, communities, firms, and knowledge expropriation intersect in the pursuit of solutions to pressing problems.

Financialization and Algorithmic Culture

Contemporary capitalism takes this valorization of knowledge further, framing an ever-wider array of elements as assets to be evaluated and exchanged in the pursuit of profit. The term often employed to describe such changes is *financialization*, and those telling the story of the new economy using this notion refer to both (a) the dominance of securities markets and the financial sector's speculative activities in the governance of Western countries and (b) "the processes and effects of the growing power of financial values and technologies on corporations, individuals, and households" (French, Leyshon, & Wainwright, 2011, p. 799). The term thus embraces a wide array of activity:

> Financialization . . . includes everything from the growth in size and scope of finance and financial activity in our economy to the rise of debt-fueled speculation over productive lending, to the ascendancy of shareholder value as a model for corporate governance, to the proliferation of risky, selfish thinking in both our private and public sectors, to the increasing political power of financiers and the CEOs they enrich, to the way in which a "markets know best" ideology remains the status quo, even after it caused the worst financial crisis in seventy-five years.
> (Foroohar, 2016, p. 5)

Ushered in by market-oriented policy changes encouraged by devotees of the Chicago School of economics, including securities and bank deregulation, monetary devaluation, separation of corporate ownership and control, and tax reform (Nussbaum, 1997), financialization became palpable in organizations when investors began to demand continual appreciation in the value of their investments.

For publicly traded corporations, financialization framed value as encompassed by (or reduced to) the stock price; this framing fit well with the portfolio conception of the firm and the associated agency theory, which saw lines of business as cash flows (Jensen & Meckling, 1976; Krippner, 2011). Managers' tasks became the configuration and maximization of those cash flows, and their interests became aligned with investors' goals; maximizing shareholder value—the shareholder value thesis—quickly became a prime managerial directive (Lazonick & O'Sullivan, 2000; Stout, 2012). Managers learn, often in business schools, to minimize costs, restructure internal labor practices and relations, and continually reorganize to attract investment capital in ways that give an unquestioned priority to shareholders' interests (Froud, Haslam, Johal, & Williams, 2000).

Writers on financialization point to the influence of investment bankers concentrated in global financial centers, such as Wall Street and the City of London and created by some of the world's top universities, in the shaping of a widespread attention to short-term stock returns. In her ethnography of Wall Street bankers, Karen Ho makes the connection unambiguous:

> Through their middlemen roles as financial advisors to major U.S. corporations as well as expert evaluators of and spokespeople for the stock and bond markets, investment bankers work to transfer and exchange wealth from corporations to large shareholders (and their financial advisors), hold corporations accountable for behavior and

values that generate short-term value, and generate debt and securities capital to fund these practices.

(2009, p. 5)

The raw materials for investment bankers' work, then, are assets that can be securitized (i.e., made into tradable securities), and a key consequence of that work is the promulgation of the aforementioned shareholder value thesis. The logic is justified by references to the workings of "the market," an abstraction of prices and exchanges portrayed as both separate from any given workplace practice and as embodying a form of rationality, of "natural" inevitability (Davis, 2009; Fox, 2009). That market, despite its contributions to global economic instability (Dore, 2008), is increasingly portrayed as superior to governments in the ability to provide both liberty and opportunity (Peck, 2010).

Beyond managers and bankers, financialization alters "shop-floor" labor processes because it gives license to managers to reduce labor costs (especially wage levels and head counts) and engage in the sort of restructuring moves that foster worker insecurity in the service of demonstrating short-term profits (Cushen & Thompson, 2016). The story analysts tell about financialization in and around organizations, then, is one in which finance, originally developed as a tool to facilitate business, became businesses' driving force, making firms and their managers beholden to parties with little interest in the production of goods and services—parties disconnected from the accomplishment of work.

Moving beyond workplaces, financial centers, and corporate boardrooms, individuals' lives have become financialized in terms of the expansion of consumer (including mortgage and student) debt, the securitization of that debt, the move from defined-benefit to defined-contribution retirement plans, the privatization of welfare, and the decreased impediments to speculating on securities markets. The financial system depends on the cultivation of consumption needs and converts those needs into reliable revenue streams, including interest on the debt incurred by individuals and households to meet those needs. This debt production means that individuals' subjectivities revolve around consumption and investment—in other words, subjectivities are disciplined by financial markets—far more than in times past (Allon, 2010; Erkturk, Froud, Johal, Leaver, & Williams, 2007; Langley, 2008; Leyshon & Thrift, 2007).

One of the more fascinating elements of financialization, as practiced in financial centers, is its reliance on large sets of data, along with mathematical formulas (algorithms) to make sense of those data. Decisions about workforce scheduling, setting prices, trading securities, monitoring citizens' electronic messaging, estimating the size of a market, and setting rates on insurance (among many other things) are now the province of algorithms, which can consider much more data, be more sensitive to contingencies, and choose more quickly than could any human (Mayer-Schönberger & Cukier, 2013).

One concern, of course, is about privacy, with increasing efforts to create massive data sets. The more significant issue for social critics, however, is governance: The use of fast networked computers running sophisticated algorithms shapes what counts as knowledge in organizing—but that knowledge is shielded from interrogation because the values guiding the algorithms are rarely reconstructed, reflected upon, and argued through (Bidhé, 2010; Flyverbom & Rasche, 2015). Big data, and the algorithms that process those data, present themselves as "the market," yet they "are selective in the sense that they employ a set of implicit and seldom discussed values that determine how information should be interpreted and visualized, and how prices should be calculated" (Arvidsson & Peitersen, 2013, p. 12). Consequently, choices become framed as purely technical and mathematical concerns, and less so as moral issues. This is not to imply that humans are (or ever were) more judicious or moral than algorithms, but that considering only what can be quantified limits actors' capacity to challenge the status quo and insert alternative considerations into the dominant models of working and organizing (Totaro & Ninno, 2014, 2016). And to the extent that management of organizations is increasingly accomplished by and through the application of algorithms to big data (Schild, 2017), the problems and possibilities they afford should draw the attention of those who study work and organization.

A striking example of financialization's impact on work is the prevalence of algorithmic scheduling in retail work. Increasingly, workers in retail and service jobs are scheduled in a "just-in-time" manner—a notion borrowed from inventory control production processes developed in Japan (and particularly associated with Toyota). Algorithms built on sales patterns, forecasts for customer traffic, and other data apply the same logics to employees, seeking to yield maximum flexibility while minimizing labor costs. Because most retail workers are paid hourly, these algorithms track customer demand, modifying employees' work schedules as often as needed to maintain lean staffing.

Algorithmic scheduling can reduce staffing costs dramatically—and because many retailers operate with razor-thin profit margins, managers often see these systems as survival tools—but other costs are borne by the employees whose work hours are subject to the algorithmically empowered passion for schedule optimization. Workers often receive work schedules with little advance notice, and they are expected to be always available for subsequent shifts; when working, they can be dismissed early if the algorithm suggests fewer staff are needed than had been anticipated. Planning for life outside work, managing family demands, and receiving a stable paycheck are all threatened for those who work under such systems.

Here again is an example of how the conditions of work appear rather different to those in different social locations: Hourly retail workers are subject to algorithmic scheduling systems, while so-called knowledge workers are largely ignorant of their existence. For the beneficiaries of financialized capitalism, "flexibility" may mean working from home or shifting hours to accommodate non-work needs; for low-wage retail workers, however, it often implies instability and risk. Financialization's provision of algorithms and large data sets to managers seeking greater profitability produces a work world in which work/non-work negotiations become significantly more challenging for low-wage workers. The point is not that the technologies alone produce these outcomes—indeed, scheduling algorithms could be employed to generate greater predictability—but, appropriated under a set of workplace logics associated with financialization, these algorithms generate significant burdens for those whose work is subject to them.

Branding and the Extension of Organization

The rise of both the knowledge economy and financialization suggest a shift in the sort of assets considered key to the production of value. When value is not tied directly to "objective" characteristics of a product, intangible features become emphasized. However, because those features are interpretations, they are part of an ongoing negotiation—a struggle over meanings. In other words, a brand is not merely the image of a product created by a corporation's advertising; it is the set of associations and feelings publics experience with respect to the target in question. Moreover, branding has moved past a desire to create product distinctiveness and customer loyalty and has become about the generation of consumer needs via the seduction of the consumer (Olins, 2003).

Branding, and brand management, is increasingly about creating shared symbolic experiences and a common identity (Arvidsson, 2005). Scholarly analyses of branding activity tend to highlight the importance of "intangibles" such as images, symbols, and aesthetic associations in the creation of value, where a product or company cultivates affective relations with consumers, employees, and other stakeholders. In the marketing literature, these elements are often explicitly divorced from "tangible" elements: For instance, Keller and Lehmann (2006, p. 741) define intangibles as "aspects of the brand image that do not involve physical, tangible, or concrete attributes or benefits . . . [that] transcend physical products"; likewise, Ailawadi and Keller (2004, p. 333) observe that "brands are being positioned on the basis of their intangibles and attributes and benefits that transcend product or service performance."

We shall argue in this book that such simple divisions between tangible and intangible elements is misguided—and that interesting lines of inquiry open up when we reject the division—but for the present purposes, our point is that the branding literature tells the story of the new economy by portraying branding as not only about differentiating products but also about crafting identities. Consumers increasingly inhabit identities that respond to, and even require, brands: "The process of branding impacts the way we understand who we are, how we organize ourselves in the world, what stories we tell about ourselves" (Banet-Weiser, 2012, p. 5).

From these constructed identities emerge brand communities where members organize around their affinity for, and identification with, the brand (Schau, Muñiz, & Arnould, 2009). Recognition that identity is increasingly linked to brands also leads marketers to target not only consumers but also employees as potential members of brand communities and as producers of the organizational image (Kärreman & Rylander, 2008; Mumby, 2016; Rennstam, 2013). Branding, thus, is both a business strategy and a model of subjectification.

Branding is about building the value of a product, service, or organization, and this work demonstrates that value exceeds what analysts have typically thought of as "work." Production and consumption have long been considered distinct in both spatiotemporal location and with respect to value (i.e., production creates a good's value, whereas consumption depletes it; production is what paid laborers do, whereas consumption is what people do after they've purchased the product), but this distinction no longer holds. Instead, branding increasingly is the domain of "prosumers" (Toffler, 1980; Ritzer & Jurgenson, 2010) who participate in the "co-creation" of brand value. These prosumers may be found on social media discussing their attraction for the brand and their kinship with other prosumers (Bertilsson & Cassinger, 2011); they supply the "free labor" of content contributions to social media sites (e.g., customer ratings or personal posts) (De Kosnik, 2013; Terranova, 2000).

This vision of branding represents a significant break from traditional-media conceptions of marketing because it can "put consumers to work":

> Co-creation represents a dialogical model that no longer privileges the company's vision of production and thus what constitutes, in the jargon of the marketing profession, "customer value." Therefore, rather than putting customers to work as more or less unskilled workers to further rationalize (Fordist) production processes and their focus on predictability, calculability, and efficiency, co-creation instead aspires to build ambiences that foster contingency, experimentation, and playfulness among consumers. From this perspective, customers are configured as uniquely skilled workers who, for the production of value-in-use to occur, must be given full rein to articulate their inimitable requirements and share their knowledge.
>
> (Zwick, Bonsu, & Darmody, 2008, p. 166)

Co-creation is based on the concept that communication occurs in a complex, constant, and instantaneous network of interactions among a wide array of actors, often in online contexts. As the Zwick et al. excerpt demonstrates, marketers see the consumers populating this communication network as a source of continually updated socio-cultural knowledge to be exploited (Tapscott & Williams, 2006). Value production thus occurs increasingly in the "social factory," beyond what has traditionally been taken to be the point of production; as Mason (2015, p. 33) asserts, "once every human being can generate a financial profit just by consuming—and the poorest can generate the most—a profound change begins in capitalism's attitude toward work."

Observers of this form of co-creation—what Cova, Dalli, and Zwick (2011) call "collaborative capitalism"—frequently assert that this free labor is a form of exploitation. Prosumers are generally not paid for the work they contribute to the building of these brands; instead, their creativity and participation are marshaled for the financial benefit of the corporations that own the brands. Consumers' communicative practices produce information, and information is the key resource in branding. Sometimes consumers are well aware of the model of value generation and choose to participate without compensation because they enjoy participation, they seek to develop new skills, or they are generating a portfolio of work to be used in the pursuit of future employment (Cova & Dalli, 2009).

In other instances, it is not so conscious, such as when consumers use corporation-provided ("free") resources to shop, network, search, and chat online. In these cases, their contributions are captured for the benefit of the brand, but "they do not freely choose to exchange their personal information for convenience but do so under conditions structured by the private ownership of network resources and the attendant low level of awareness about actual tracking practices" (Andrejevic, 2013, p. 157). It is possible, then, that a reliance on publics for the production of value carries with it the possibility that those publics will introduce additional, and even conflicting, criteria of evaluation regarding economic exchange (Arvidsson & Peitersen, 2013). The question of exploitation, then, is about the openness of branding to alternative conceptions of value, whether the domains of leisure and work are still distinct in contemporary capitalism, and the degree to which choice is a meaningful concept in a consumer society.

Venture Labor, Precarious Labor

Earlier, in our presentation of financialization, we discussed how a drive for short-term results is underwritten by (what appears to be) an unassailable discourse of the market. Not only has this drive shifted the models of capital accumulation; it has also created a pattern of financial crisis and widening socioeconomic inequality that have made working and organizing in all sectors of the economy considerably more uncertain—one of the key problems with which analyses of contemporary capitalism are (or should be) concerned (Marens, in press). Freelance work, intermittent work, and jobs based on short-term contracts (as well as those without contracts at all) often provide both low pay and little certainty about the future (Kalleberg, 2009). Enabled by both flattened organizational structures and nation-states' trade agreements, labor is often the target of outsourcing, which is typically justified in terms of reducing costs, boosting profits, and, thereby, enhancing shareholder value.

Shareholders and executives tend to benefit from outsourcing, whereas workers experience insecurity—even if it is merely threatened (Collinson, 2003).

One stance on insecurity is outlined by Gina Neff's (2012) ethnography of Internet-based creative and culture industries in New York City's Silicon Alley. Among these "knowledge workers," an ethic of individualism had taken hold over the past few decades—one in which flexible, short-term, and project-based work came to be seen as standard. This individualism created greater insecurity; Neff labels their strategy for positioning themselves in relation to work as *venture labor*:

> Venture labor is the explicit expression of entrepreneurial values by nonentrepreneurs. Venture labor refers to an investment by employees into their companies or how they talk about their time at work as an investment. When people think of their jobs as an investment or as having a future payoff other than regular wages, they embody venture labor.
>
> (p. 16)

Workers in the culture industry were thus expected to be continually self-monitoring and self-reflexive and to be the sole engineers of their careers—and thus also to be the site of blame for shortcomings.

Interestingly, Neff found that the risk accompanying insecurity was understood by workers as *desirable*—evidence of challenging and fulfilling work. A key problem with this model of working and organizing was that the social capital cultivated by workers tended to benefit their companies, but did little to protect individuals during economic downturns such as the 2001 bursting of the dot-com bubble. In other words, venture labor was a resource to build companies—companies that promised substantial wealth accumulation for knowledge workers. However, when the economic winds shifted, workers found themselves with little control over their workplaces or their financial futures.

A second perspective employs the term *precarity* to name the condition of instability associated with forms of labor that are flexible, contingent, invisible, or easily moved. However, there is more to the notion:

> Precarity signifies both the multiplication of precarious, unstable, insecure forms of living and, simultaneously, new forms of political struggle and solidarity that reach beyond the traditional models of the political party or trade union. This *double meaning* is central to understanding the ideas and politics associated with precarity; the new moment of capitalism that engenders precariousness is seen as not only oppressive but also as offering the potential for new subjectivities, new socialities and new kinds of politics.
>
> (Gill & Pratt, 2008, p. 3)

In other words, precarity is a perilous condition that follows acute social and material vulnerability. Precarity is amplified as multiple vectors of vulnerability and violence collide with one another, such as those stemming from relations of race, class, gender, sexuality, ability, nation, citizenship, migration and immigration, religion, and other forms of dispossession. Put differently, while we are all relationally precarious, in that our very bodies and selves are bound in ties of social and material interdependence, precarity—as used here—is a hazardous mode of (wobbly, barely) living that is magnified in particular forms of labor, performed by particular bodies, in particular places, and under particular forms of duress (Butler, 2004; Puar, 2012). In colloquial terms, there is the inescapable precariousness of making a life, and then there is precar*ity*, wherein making even a volatile life is, inescapably, a dicey daily endeavor. Importantly, however, the routine strains of precarity are also a potential source of reflection on and resistance to the relations of contemporary capitalism.

One inspiration for the dual sides of precarity—as insecure living that can breed a new politics—is rooted in work associated with the body of thought known as Autonomist Marxism, an offshoot of Marxism developed in the 1960s and '70s, particularly in Italy. The focus of Autonomists is often on what they call *immaterial labor*: that which develops affective, cognitive, or cultural meanings rather than transforming physical materials. As Lazzarato (1996, p. 133) portrays it, "immaterial labour involves a series of activities that are not normally recognized as 'work'—in other words, the kinds of activities involved in defining and fixing cultural and artistic standards, fashions, tastes, consumer norms and, more strategically, public opinion."

Although it is possible to fault this work for neglecting material and contingent work in its attention to immaterial labor (Dyer-Witheford, 2001), it can also be said that by recognizing work that aligns with, and creates, cultural standards, Autonomists show how immaterial labor depends upon the *general intellect*. The general intellect was Marx's term for the common knowledge of a society that must be developed outside of the point of production but is brought into it through the vehicle of workers' embodied interaction—what Williams and Connell (2010) refer to as "looking good and sounding right." Communication, then, is not merely that which one does during a job; it is the site of value production and, thus, of capitalism's reproduction (Carlone, 2008; Greene, 2004).

The second inspiration for the dual conception of precarity emanates from Autonomist Marxism's belief in labor's capacity to alter capitalist relations apart from political parties and labor unions. Autonomists assert that solidarity among precarious workers is possible; that they can reflect on their shared positioning (even if it does not appear shared at first) and find common cause. Doing so will aid them in recognizing the power to *refuse* work and, concomitantly, to choose forms of engagement in the social detached from (and even in opposition to) capital—in this sense, refusal, seen as freedom, concerns less the uncompensated labor of the prosumer than the freedom *from* work—a freedom from the belief that work is the primary path to economic security and self-actualization (Beverungen, Otto, Spoelstra, & Kenny, 2013).

Lazzarato claims, "It is by sympathy, mutual assistance, collaboration and confidence that creation takes place" (2004, p. 206). Autonomists suggest that the creative forms of organizing they proffer would be immune from capture by capitalist logics of appropriation and accumulation such that it would not be merely work, but *life*, that would be autonomous from capitalist relations of production (Hardt & Negri, 2000).[1] Notwithstanding its rousing force, this stance has drawn significant criticism from those who foreground how concrete relations of difference (e.g., race, nation, sexuality) *matter* to relations of precarity, which are invariably lived out in particular bodies, not by mythic generic subjects. For instance, McRobbie (2010) roundly critiques Autonomist analyses for rendering gender invisible and ignoring feminists' accomplishments, as well as setbacks on the very scores Autonomists appear to romanticize.

Skepticism, Critique, and New Directions

The preceding section presented a story of the "new economy" by describing not the unfolding of its plot over time, but its central themes, origins, and consequences. The story tends to be one of dramatic change in the way working and organizing proceed. Two issues are relevant at this point in our discussion. The first is about accuracy, or what we earlier called *truth* value: Is there evidence that these changes are actually occurring? The second is about analytical frameworks and their *production* value: How do tales of radical change explain the emergence and influence of the "new economy," and what do they suggest we do next?

Suspicions About the Scope of Change

In several quarters, there is doubt about the facticity of the changes presented earlier, some skepticism that precarity, branding, post-Fordist organizing, project-based work, and immaterial labor are as significant to the global economy as the authors surveyed earlier claim. For instance, there is reason to believe that, at least in the U.S., the prevalence of the "gig economy" has been overstated. The trend toward freelance work, sometimes also called the 1099[2] economy, may not have grown to the extent commonly reported. Using figures from the U.S. Bureau of Labor Statistics, Dourado and Koopman (2015) and Grose and Kallerman (2015) found modest gains over time for 1099s as compared to W-2s, and that gains in 1099s now outpace those for W-2s, but that the rise is not as stark as those proclaiming its economic dominance would have us believe.

Fox (2015) suggests that poor methodology is largely responsible for the assertion of supremacy, but acknowledges that change is afoot, perhaps currently on the fringes of the labor market. Countering this claim is work by economists Lawrence Katz and Alan Krueger, who are, at the time of this writing, developing a paper from data displaying a sharp rise in "alternative work arrangements" in the U.S., from 9.3% of all employment in 1995, to 10.1% in 2005, and up to 15.8% in 2015—23.6 million workers. Katz and Krueger hold that this increase in nontraditional work, which includes the gig economy, accounts for the vast majority of net employment growth in the country (Wile, 2016; see also G. Friedman, 2014).

In the sociological literature, a similar debate swirls around social theorists' assertions about the very story of the "new economy." Some take aim at Sennett's (1998, 2006, 2008) depiction of the contemporary workplace—specifically, its demands for short-termism (e.g., temporary and project-based work), flexibility, and mobility—which, in his telling, foment insecurity and degrade work experiences. Those features of work, Sennett argues, damage workers' character, craft, relationships, and even their communities such that "changes in modern work have eroded both the critical grasp of workers on what they do, and a clear view of the place of work in the larger social structure" (Sennett, 2005, p. 131).

Critics, however, contend that the transformation of work has not been at all as dramatic as theorists such as Sennett imply. Reacting to Sennett's anecdotal approach, along with the case study approach used by many others, Fevre (2007) and Doogan (2005, 2009) examined government-collected data on employment in the UK, EU, USA, and Canada, and found no evidence of a dramatic growth in transitory or insecure employment, though Green (2009) found greater insecurity for women, minorities, and older workers. Something similar can be seen in Johnson, Wood, Brewster, and Brookes's (2009) 12-year survey of human resources professionals in 22 European countries. They found evolution and change in the workforce in line with the claims earlier, yet they also noted that the transformation was rather uneven and that nation, sector, and organization size mattered a great deal. Investigations such as these challenge the sweeping claims of the sort presented earlier; furthermore, the authors of such studies submit that claims of widespread insecurity can further discipline workers, making them feel more vulnerable than is necessary and, in turn, leading them to accept state policies and organizational practices unfavorable to their interests.

These allegations about the lack of empirical evidence for the pervasiveness of the gig (i.e., 1099) economy and of Sennett's vision of a new model of capitalism are important and demand further investigation. Specifically, they force scholars to clarify the place of ideology in their portrayals of working and organizing under contemporary capitalism. A crude way of putting this is to ask if our interest is in how work "actually" proceeds (the scare quotes signaling skepticism about the objectivity implied in such analyses), or if instead there is another story to be told about working.

Our interests tend toward the latter, so we align with authors such as Tweedie (2013), who suggests that the anti-Sennett analyses tend to miss both the social locations in which the transformed work practices are their sharpest (e.g., high-profile firms, entrepreneurial sites) in their use of census data. Tweedie also suggests these analyses miss one of the key points of the attention to work under new capitalism: that the loss of a job, and the loss of income it generates, is only one of many possible forms of insecurity associated with work. Collinson (2003) suggests that insecurity likewise derives from individuals' attachment to particular notions of the self, particularly those associated with work. And of course, relations of difference noted earlier, such as nation and citizenship status, race, religion, ability, gender, and sexuality—to name a few—matter profoundly to the insecurities of work as well.

Yet critiques such as Tweedie's run the risk of missing how stories that find traction, regardless of empirical evidence or other indicators of truth value, enjoin workers (as well as those about to enter the labor force) to orient to these new "realities." That is, the ideology, as cultural force, is portrayed as so pervasive that it must inevitably shape how people approach working and organizing. In other words, workers have been told repeatedly that career is a personal responsibility, that achievement is a product of self-discipline, and that continual enterprise is essential to being a competitive workplace commodity (du Gay, 1996; Grey, 1994; Vallas & Cummins, 2015). As noted earlier, theoretical stories cannot be taken lightly precisely because those that find footing act on the world they claim merely to study, enacting and enforcing the realities of which they speak.

Critique of Existing Frameworks for Understanding

Assuming, then, that the aforementioned changes to working and organizing under contemporary capitalism are worthy of attention, one might wonder how the authors surveyed here might explain *why* such transformations are occurring—to return to the terminology mentioned earlier, when telling the story of the "new economy," to what actors and factors do they turn in developing explanations? Culling from the discussion earlier, we can identify the following, offered in no particular order:

> *Work flexibility, Chicago School of economics, securities and bank deregulation, monetary devaluation, separation of corporate ownership and control, tax reform, portfolio conception of the firm, shareholder value thesis, consumer debt, retirement (in)security, welfare privatization, big data, branding, globalization (including the global division of labor), bodily mobility, technological change (especially in information and communication technologies, but also automation), decline of trade unions, crowdfunding, welfare reform, project work and the gig economy, class, capital liberalization, knowledge, individualization, agency theory, general intellect, personal networks, post-Fordism, "the" market, labor, entrepreneurs, investment bankers, consumption/prosumption, algorithms, service work, communicative labor (and knowledge), neoliberalism, brand communities, risk, precarious labor . . .*

This set of factors is obviously multifarious, dense, even dizzying. And that's the point: Attempting to trace causes and effects through this byzantine, recursive, and shifting array of elements—elements that writers also see as occurring at different levels of analysis—should lead one to doubt the possibility of generating any single and straightforward story.

Given our interest in considering what working and organizing have become under contemporary capitalism, such a list is not terribly helpful, because it fails to help navigate through the thicket of factors. The question, then, becomes what sort of framework would be suitable to access such a complex arrangement of elements involved in accomplishing contemporary capitalism.

One route would be to identify the "real" structures operating beneath the surface of the factors mentioned earlier—a reduced set of forces generating the observed changes in working and organizing (Fleetwood, 2014; Thompson & Harley, 2012). Moves like these—often associated with the versions of critical realism associated with Roy Bhaskar and Margaret Archer—assume that working and organizing can be explained with reference to underlying causal (generative) mechanisms. As with Fevre's, Doogan's, and Johnson et al.'s analyses of the "real" landscape of work, there is an implied objectivism in the analyses—one characterized by both an assumption of causality and the assurance of epistemological certainty in determining the character of that causality. Explanations such as these can be attractive until one recognizes that they leave little room for contingency, contestation, or creativity; they constrain a consideration of agency and the emergence of alternatives in our examinations of, and interventions into, working and organizing.

A second path would be to draw upon tools complicated enough to match the intricacy of the world they endeavor to grasp. This is the domain of models of the social world that endeavor to capture a long list of variables and combine them in computer programs that can manage the large data sets and produce probabilistic claims about likely trajectories. Computer modeling of complex economic systems is common in economic science (Foster & Metcalfe, 2001; Markose, 2005) and has gained adherents in the social sciences as well (Axelrod & Cohen, 1999; Harvey & Reed, 1997); they tend to be interested in balancing the ability to include a wide range of factors, exploitable by advanced computing power, with producing parsimonious models of the social and organizational phenomena (Corman, 1996). Other approaches in this second path are more inductive in that they attempt to analyze naturally occurring data, such as the wealth of talk produced in organizational life, through the application of heuristics techniques, linguistic tools, and data reduction tools (Contractor, Wasserman, & Faust, 2006; Corman, Kuhn, McPhee, & Dooley, 2002).

A third route would be to suggest that the various disciplines and lines of thought each offer unique and insightful views of the set of factors. Fields oriented toward "macro" issues would examine issues different from those focusing on the "micro," economically minded scholars would take up topics different from those of interest to humanistically oriented thinkers. On this path, intellectual communities assert the value of their distinct "perspectives" or "takes" on working and organizing in late capitalism (Leonardi, 2017), and somewhere in the conversation, a commentator inevitably introduces the parable of the blind men and the elephant to both chastise the analysts and suggest the presence of a "real" object waiting to be discovered if only scholars would follow a path to overcome the obstacle of disciplinary fragmentation (March, 2005; Zorn, 2002).

An Alternative Approach

A fourth possibility is to start with the suggestion that both the search for simple underlying causes and the effort to create complex systems models are the product of scholars looking in the wrong places and asking the wrong questions. Once again, we mean "wrong" in the sense that they yield predictable traps, or that we continually find ourselves stuck in familiar ways when we follow their lead. Specifically, all three of those responses separate the world from scholars' and practitioners' efforts to understand it. In those approaches, subject and object are split such that the scholarly task becomes one of mapping theory onto (an external and unquestioned) reality. The criterion of research quality in both those approaches is one of *correspondence*, where models that *fit*, that mirror the (putatively) objective external world, are desirable (for critiques, see Deetz, 2003; Rorty, 1979).

In the plotlines of contemporary capitalism, some of the elements in our long list noted earlier are portrayed as agents, some as conditions, some as tools, and some as outcomes. Some are framed as human and others nonhuman. Some are seen as material and others symbolic or ideational. In an alternative framework, such preordained, a priori assignments of roles and positions do not hold. Beginning with a recognition that those elements exist and are associated with one another only in and through working and organizing, a key break is to foreground a different unit of analysis. The scholarship presented earlier tends to rely on units of analysis familiar to many social scientists: individuals, organizations, and networks.

The question with which we began, in contrast, was not about individuals, organizations, or networks, but about work*ing* and organiz*ing*—the gerund signifying our commitment to shifting analytical attention from traditional units of analysis to practice, activity, and accomplishment. The market is a composite of practices, entrepreneurship is a set of practices, and financialization is an array of linked practices; if analysts endeavor to understand *how* markets, entrepreneurship, and financialization work, if they seek to generate novel insights into the operations of these phenomena, they will be hamstrung if they allow the notion of empirical correspondence, and an ever-growing set of elements, to guide their examinations. By foregrounding practice—and specifically communicative practice—as a means of contrast, we see the possibility of framing routinized action as the ongoing, continually reconstructed product of an array of forces that gain status as elements, as *agencies*, only through their connections with other elements in the carrying off of the activity in question.

This fourth view, which is thoroughly *relational* in orientation, is the story we are eager to tell in this book, for we find it especially conducive to writing new plotlines for attending to social problems. Relationality is an ontological move that begins with the claim that it is less helpful to posit substances—to assume the existence of bounded entities that predate the interactions in which they engage—than it is to suggest that the elements of the long list noted earlier are participants in, and simultaneously products of, practices. Relationality posits that what is commonly taken to be actors and factors creating contemporary capitalism—individuals, organizations, markets, public policies, structures, as well as the very figure of the "new economy"—emerge from, and are performed in, communication (when communication is understood as a dynamic practice). Efforts to understand a phenomenon such as financialization should resist assuming that actors draw upon policies and tools to create a financialized world; a relational analysis would instead start with the personal and organizational *practices* that grant priority to monetary instruments.

Further, this orientation denies any subject/object split, refusing to portray the various (and often taken-for-granted) participants in working and organizing as *either* discursive or material, tangible or intangible, human or nonhuman. In place of those dichotomies, relationality highlights agential hybridity, multiplicity, interdependency, and indeterminacy in suggesting that the identification of participants is an epistemological choice that must always be grounded in a comprehension of a practice. Barad (2012, p. 32) explains what relational ontologies aim to offer:

> The point is not merely to include nonhuman as well as human actors or agents of change but rather to find ways to think about the nature of causality, agency, relationality, and change without taking those issues to be foundational or holding them in place.

Relationality, then, is not a claim that the social and the material are connected, but that the demarcations "social" and "material" are *effects of practices*—including the practice of scholarly writing. It is also a recognition that all agency, all acting, occurs *conjointly*. Reconfiguring our conceptions of the division between the human and the nonhuman also carries potential ethical implications: If the nonhuman cannot be rendered solely an inanimate "thing" in the service of human interests, if we instead understand practice to be the product of entanglements of agencies, then we may well be forced to revisit the ethical principles guiding action (Dale & Latham, 2015). This is the project of Chapter 2, in which we present conceptions of relationality to analyze not only their onto-epistemological assertions but also their capacity to contribute novelty to investigations.

Communication, as we shall present it in Chapter 3, can augment a shift of this sort. In the work presented earlier, communication (when it's attended to at all) is usually relegated to that which *occurs in the conduct of* working and organizing; it is seen as just one process among many necessary in re-producing a pre-existing and objective economic sphere. We shall make a bolder claim: that working and organizing—and, thus, "doing" capitalism—*is* communication. We shall suggest that a reworking of our guiding question is in order such that it becomes *how are we to conceive of communication such that it can magnify our insights on working and organizing in contemporary capitalism?* In Chapter 3, we argue that if a view of communication grounded in relationality is to play a heuristic role, scholars must marshal a conception of communication rich enough to illuminate (and reframe) the practices of contemporary capitalism.

The remainder of the book illustrates how scholarship might pursue these multiple visions. We present three case studies to demonstrate both how analysts might proceed when seeking to examine working and organizing in the "new economy" grounded in a relational ontology. The first, in Chapter 4, is a study of the becoming of an idea in the context of a creative event, from its inception to its prototypification. The second, in Chapter 5, is an examination of the multiplicity of "the product" in high-tech startup entrepreneurship. The third, in Chapter 6, offers an examination of academic publishing and commercial aviation. We follow these studies with a concluding chapter that draws out the implications of the approach we term communicative relationality for organization studies in terms of the methodological approaches they employ, the claims they make, and the implications they bear for organization studies' explorations of working and organizing under late capitalism.

Notes

1. Although this is an alluring vision for many, some communication scholars harbor important concerns about its treatment of communication. Autonomists, especially Hardt and Negri (2004), rely on what appears to be a simplistic version of interest representation in locating that common cause. Communication is portrayed as necessary to recognize shared interests and to build networks that can support an alternative form of the commons (Brophy, Cohen, & de Peuter, 2016). Communication, in this perspective, is that which (a) merely expresses persons' pre-existing meanings and experiences, and (b) is oriented toward commonality, neglecting the inevitability of (and even, perhaps, desirability of) difference (Dempsey & Carlone, 2014). As we shall illustrate next, such a conception of communication is a significant limitation on the utility of the theory.
2. The concept "1099" refers to the U.S. tax forms that (are intended to) capture income earned by organizations' employees through salaries, wages, and tips—those associated with sporadic and contract work—as opposed to more traditional employees who use a form called the W-2 to report salaried workers, those with (putatively) more stable employment.

2 Relationality

Cultivating Novelty in Explorations of Working and Organizing

The scene established in the previous chapter is undoubtedly a messy one, marked by a dizzying catalog of phenomena that are finding circulation in the "new economy." We concluded that this tangle of developments resists the drive for stable explanations based on coherent system logics. A tangle of this order (*dis*order?) calls for approaches that respect and work *with*, rather than against, its unruly and elusive character. But what kind of approach can do so and still shed light on contemporary problems of working and organizing?

Whereas the first chapter took up our initial question of what work and organization have become in contemporary capitalism, this chapter addresses the second half of our guiding inquiry: How can organization studies approach this complex scene in novel and productive ways? Our specific aim is to introduce novel modes of (re)thinking and (re)making the worlds of working and organizing, which converge under the sign of "relationality."

We begin by briefly contextualizing the rise of relationality in and around the "linguistic turn" as manifest in organization studies. The idea is not to belabor histories elaborated by others (e.g., Aakhus et al., 2011; Faulkner & Runde, 2012; Iedema, 2007; Leonardi & Barley, 2010), but to position relationality as a radical continuation of long-nurtured seeds of thought—not some kind of snub of the "newly old" from the smug "next new." To ease readers into the dense waters of relational thinking, we then present five provocations that motivate most relational approaches. Finally, we focus in on specific streams of relationality. Our intent is neither to recommend one over the others nor to produce some sort of theoretical confluence. Instead, we seek to enhance encounters and open conversations across channels. Chapter 3 follows this effort with visions of communication as a relational practice, which, we argue, can usefully amplify insights generated by the theorizing described in this chapter.

The Emergence of Relationality

Over the past few decades, organization theory has witnessed the ascendancy of what is often called a *linguistic turn*.[1] Beginning in the 1930s and building on conceptual insights engendered by phenomenology and

DOI: 10.4324/9781315680705-2

hermeneutics, theorists began to argue that the very existence of persons, experiences, organizations, and objects is dependent upon language. Meaning slowly became understood as the center of the social world, accompanied by recognition that processes of meaning formation are always linguistic. This view was accompanied by a rejection of the long-standing Cartesian divide between subject and object, where cognition was seen as the site of (subjective) experience, of the interpretation and experience of an (objective) external world.

The presence of a subject-object split led to questions about how organized action could proceed given the potential proliferation of subjective meanings; one response was to posit *intersubjectivity*—the creation of more or less shared meanings between persons. Although the guises assumed by the notion of intersubjectivity depend on how the social surround is conceived (i.e., whether it is background to interaction or whether it is intimately bound up in all experience and action) and where meaning is to be "located" (i.e., in cognitions, in language, or in socio-cultural forms), most versions of the concept draw ontological divisions between the domain of the individual and the domain of the collective, retaining the subject/object divide (Grossberg, 1982).

The linguistic turn, in contrast, sought to transcend this dualism by suggesting that what we typically relegate to categories of "subject" or "object" are the result of linguistic distinctions and the power relationships written into them such that discourse could now be understood as *constituting* social reality rather than merely *representing* it (Deetz, 2003). The explanatory devices employed in social science also came into question, since methods of investigation could no longer be understood as generating a "scientific" distance from the phenomena of investigation—phenomena that were now understood as existing in a complex hermeneutic with the conduct of science (Giddens, 1976; Rorty, 1979). The linguistic turn's rejection of subject/object dualisms was more than simply a truth claim about the centrality of language; it was a wholesale attack on the conduct of social science.

In organization studies, the linguistic turn's influence led to the suggestion that organizations are best understood as ongoing discursive constructions rather than ontologically independent entities. Discourse and communication could then be objects of study in their own right, ushering in an interest in elements such as narratives, metaphors, and rhetoric. As an outgrowth, it encouraged scholars to attend to (local) processes of meaning creation as well as to the ways in which these processes advantaged some interests over others. Yet the emphasis on discourse tended to relegate what had previously been considered *objects* to secondary positions. It is not that objects disappeared from analysis; the concern is that objects were defined in discursive terms.

Whether they were classes, texts, corporations, identities, technologies, norms, ethnicities, spaces, cognitions, discourses, traits, institutions, or motivations, objects typically were understood as abstractions, as attributes of either individual or collective actors, or as relevant only to the extent that they entered humans' conversations (Ashcraft, Kuhn, & Cooren, 2009; Barad, 2003; Fleetwood, 2005). The linguistic turn's aim of transcending subject/object divisions too often turned the material into the symbolic, refusing to consider the thingness of things, the mattering of the material. Relationality, as a broad ontological and epistemological project, aims to redress that reduction—and, simultaneously, offers a radical push beyond orthodox conceptions of theorizing.

Introducing Relationality: Five Premises

In 1997, Emirbayer's "Manifesto for a Relational Sociology" assembled decades of relevant theory toward a trajectory now condensed as "relationality" (or relational ontologies). As with any articulation of major turns in thought, the lineage traced there is one of many possible ways to tell this intellectual history, each version of which invites particular futures. Because we seek to keep the future of organization studies open and brimming with multiple potentialities, to the extent possible we avoid privileging any one tale of ancestry here. We ask instead, what are the most pivotal claims about the world to which relationality subscribes? In that spirit, we pose five provocations—incitements that provide loose operating principles, or *non*-foundational premises, for those engaged in relational analyses of work and organization. (The reason for the "non" there will soon become clear.)

1. From Substantialism to Relationality in Conceptualizing Entities: An Ontological Reversal (or, at Least, a Turn)

A useful starting place for thinking relationally is this: things are not pre-bounded entities that exist before they come into contact with humans. Rather, ever-unfolding contact produces "things" as they are. In other words, the substance and boundaries that appear to distinguish something as a coherent unit arise, gather steam and stabilize (or not), and only exist within particular relations that are constantly (re)enacted. When and as relations change, this something becomes a different thing, or perhaps fades away altogether. It is worth noting that it does not simply *seem* like a different thing; it is not simply represented or symbolically constructed differently. Rather, it *is* a different thing, made or produced—that is to say, actually constituted—differently. To abridge once again, entities *only exist* in relation.

For a vivid illustration that also enacts this first premise, consider how the linguistic relations that enable this very discussion are at the same time complicating a fuller appreciation of the reversal it proposes. Specifically, English sentence construction demands an entity-subject (such as I or it) presented as self-evidently discrete, preceding any movement by or upon it, a stable center of being and action. Indeed, Western thinking is marked by a long history of preoccupation with entities, more interested in their essential properties than their conditions of possibility. Minimized by this habitual "thingification" (Barad, 2003, p. 812) are the complex, swirling, and often precarious matrix of relations (e.g., grammatical rules and embodied practices of speaking and writing) that generate and sustain "I" and "it" as demarcated units, subject and object.

Thus the linguistic relations vital to forming and exchanging thoughts provide a partial infrastructure such that they support some thoughts more readily than others. In particular, linguistic relations reinforce a substantialist ontology and hinder the ontological reversal attempted here by insisting on the "re-presentation" (as in representation, over and over) of fixed entities with an independent existence as subjects and objects of action. A more conducive linguistic infrastructure would be needed in order to address the variable relations giving rise to such stabilities. The perspectives featured later in this chapter seek to initiate just that.

Each of the theoretical developments reviewed below adhere to some version of this first premise, although they use different terms to make the point. Emirbayer (1997), for example, refers to the relational production of unit-things as "transaction," which he contrasts with "self-action" and "interaction" orientations that presume a priori the separation of subject and object. Writing from the meeting of feminism and theoretical physics, Barad (2003) prefers the term "intra-action," contrasted with "interaction," to denote how amorphous phenomena get parsed into recognizable, acting elements through "agential cuts." More on meaningful nuances among these and other vocabularies will follow, but, for now, the point is that these diverse developments can be drawn together by a relational rather than a substantialist ontology.

Relationality is commonly described, especially in anthropology, as taking an "ontological turn," by which we mean a redirection of concern toward the status of the real (and not only how we come to know it, or epistemology), as well as a shift toward novel ways of conceiving ontology, to which we turn next. Although it can be helpful initially to grasp this turn as cast here—an ontological *reversal* in which relations produce things rather than the other way around—caution is also advised. As we will soon see, there is no neat reversal, where cause and effect simply switch positions, to be had.

2. The Real as Enacted, Multiple, and Flat

A relational ontology prioritizes the ever-evolving "relations" that make possible and recognizable the very stuff of the world. But what can we say, more concretely, of these relations? Three initial points will suffice for introductory purposes. First, relations in this view are a buzzing hive of activity—an "assemblage" of ongoing performances or enactments—rather than a steady state or solid structure.

Second, relations are arbitrary trajectories of practice, the "realization" of some possibilities out of innumerable others. Although their enactment tends to develop habitual, territorial defenses that perpetuate some patterns down the line, they could always be accomplished otherwise, and they frequently veer off course. Relations teem at once with predictability, volatility, excess, and surprise, and it is only clear in retrospect—and even then, only provisionally—which of those features might win out for a time. The potentialities of a particular mode of relation are therefore never exhausted (even when the inhabitants they support may feel so). Because "things" can be—and, across space and time, *are*—done in many ways, it makes more sense to speak of ontolog*ies*: plural and shape-shifting enactments of the real rather than entities in possession of essential and enduring character.

To put the second point plainly, the "nature" of things is multiple. This does not simply mean that there are many ways to *look at* something—a thing that still remains the same thing as it is observed and known from multiple angles (think of the proverbial elephant example, mentioned in the preceding chapter). Rather, it means that there are many ways to *do* something—that is, to make that thing real such that it becomes a different thing altogether (Mol, 1999; Mol & Law, 2004), even if its manifold performances are held together with linguistic string (e.g., as an *it* or an *I*).

It is worth underscoring the difference between multiplicity as invoked here and other affirmations of plural reality, such as that in much social constructionism. In Linstead and Pullen's (2006) terms, relationality entails a "multiplicity of difference and dispersion" (p. 1293) or proliferation, rather than a "multiplicity of the same" (p. 1306). We might say that things "come to pass" in just about every sense: Entities (a) happen or arrive in practice, (b) are transient and changing from scene to scene, yet also (c) "pass" as stable, independent units. "Things" occur as verbs yet pose as nouns, slipping into a next moment or passing away altogether.

Third, relationality surrenders a depth ontology in favor of what is commonly called a flat (or flattened) ontology. Certain imagery evoked thus far becomes significant—for example, a preference for traversing surfaces (e.g., "down the line," "across space and time," "from scene to scene") rather than diving deep to discover anchors or looking to an ideology floating above and imposing itself on practice. If, as wagered thus far, the real is *done* rather than *discovered*—or done *as* discovered (i.e., knowledge practices enact the very relations they seek to capture)—then the hope of finding *underlying* explanatory properties or mechanisms begins to fade. No wizard hides behind the curtain, and no pearls of essence lay buried at the bottom of the ocean. To be clear, the claim is not simply that we can never finally know these truths; the claim is that they are not "out there" at all. Only vectors of ordinary practice can explain the relations in which we find ourselves.

The pivotal task of knowing shifts (and, for now, we can still say, *reverses*) accordingly: away from the search for deep ontological origins that explain social action and toward the explanation of such apparent "roots" through description of the ontological practices that bring them to life. Some of the most persistent dualisms guiding social analysis, such as agency-structure and individual-society, come under suspicion here, as do any "top-down versus bottom-up" views of the social world. A "flatland" view emerges in their place: What if the roiling surfaces of practice are all there is (Latour, 2005)?

3. The Real as Social and Material, or Sociomaterial

In the preceding paragraph, we referenced "human" activity as the enduring object of "social" analysis. A relational ontology interrogates such terms and concludes, as with agency-structure and individual-society mentioned earlier, that the binaries on which they rest—social-material, human-nonhuman, culture-nature, mind-body, and so on—cannot be taken for granted. These dualisms too should be understood as relational productions that create the world in partial ways with profound consequences.

One specific excess of the linguistic turn is a tendency to elevate the significance of the social and cultural realm—especially, that of human symbol use and meaning—over the material and physical realm, as a response to deterministic modes of materialism that once diminished the social. We might say that the muscle of materiality, in all its human and nonhuman variety, was left to atrophy while the muscle of human discourse developed. The pendulum swung in the other direction.

Accompanying the ontological turn, then, is a material turn often abridged as "new materialisms" (e.g., Coole & Frost, 2010). This movement rekindles interest in objects and artifacts, space and place, tools and instruments, bodies and embodiments, currencies and economies, but it does so in a particular way. Namely, it treats the material not as a reality external to or independent of the social, which impinges on the social, but, rather, as an integral *participant, along with* the social, in performing the relations that make the world as it is. New materialisms do not merely push the pendulum back toward materiality, in other words. They draw on and enrich the linguistic turn's effort to transcend the dualism of subject and object, asserting that new visions and vocabularies of the social-material relation are crucial to understanding the diverse players that/who take part in practices of the real.

New materialisms go well beyond affirmation that materiality is relevant, that humans use physical as well as discursive means to navigate the world, or that material things possess capabilities of their own. Such claims are problematic because they preserve linguistic relations that affirm substantialist ontology as outlined earlier (e.g., already discrete entities that interact). New materialisms offer a more ambitious reworking that refuses to treat as a given the division of social and material, and, instead, reframes this pervasive dualism as a particular enactment of relations—a consequential way of parsing the world. In this view, discursive and material realities are always staged together, fully indivisible until they are *made* to appear detached in and through specific practices. To be clear, they are not braided (i.e., distinct but intertwined; the same could be said for the term "entangled"), but are two sides of the same coin (Martine & Cooren, 2016). The demarcation of social from material is an *effect* of ongoing performances of the real (including those of scholarly writing, such as this).

It does not make sense, therefore, to continue referencing material and social worlds as necessarily apart. These separate worlds do not exist except as practices insist so, for example, through continued reference. New materialism thus challenges what Alfred North Whitehead (1920) denounced as the *bifurcation of nature* (see also Latour, 2013)—an ontological stance premised on the division of what Locke (1690/1959) would have called "secondary qualities" such as discourse, meaning, and affect from "primary qualities" such as rocks, technologies, and buildings. In relational ontology, any assumption that fundamental bifurcations like this—culture and nature, symbolic and physical, human and nonhuman, and mind and body—have an external existence outside of the practices that summon them is ill advised. Materiality and relationality are intractable aspects of *everything* that exists (Barad, 2003, 2007; Langley & Tsoukas, 2010; Martine & Cooren, 2016).

Indeed, even ostensibly immaterial and evanescent phenomena must somehow become *materialized in order to matter*. For instance, an idea "flashes" across one's register, transforms into words on paper, or circulates through embodied presentations. Anything that exists, by definition, takes on material dimension, in that it has to be made through relation to other "things." It does not follow that all things are similarly or equally material, of course; we might envision or experience materialization in kinds, degrees, and gradations. It does mean, however, that nothing completely *im*material can exist.

Taking a closer look at the phrasing emphasized earlier—"materialized in order to matter"—we begin to see how relational ontologies capitalize on quirks of language, such as the dual meaning of matter as stuff *and* significance, to chip away at the substantialist tilt of current linguistic relations from within. No longer an inert noun, matter at its "stuff-iest" is nonetheless *materialized* (i.e., made real) as a verb in practice. And *mattering* (i.e., the process of becoming some*thing* that makes a difference) is what unites material and symbol: both machines and values must take forms to exert influence on a scene.

Such playful and often-repeated invocations of "matter" work to unsettle the engrained divide of social and material, as does the term "sociomaterial," coined to perform their inseparability. These creative linguistic practices also illustrate, and enact, the materiality of symbol and vice versa such that it is impossible to materialize relational ontology without altering the linguistic relations (themselves materialized in concrete practices such as this writing) that can make it matter.

If symbols are another sort of stuff, and any stuff can signify, the question is not whether discourse or materiality would win some mythic wrestling match, but how it is that they are staged as separate and opposing contenders in the first place, and how they can be rendered otherwise. MacLure (2013) explains that "words collide and connect with things on the same ontological level, and therefore, language cannot achieve the distance and externality that would allow it to represent—i.e., to stand over, stand for and stand in for—the world" (p. 660). Earlier, we referred to symbols and stuff as joint players, or co-participants, in making the real. Next, we elaborate what these terms hint: the implications for agency when the social and material collapse into one another.

4. Agency as Hybrid, Distributed, and Interrupted: Humanism Humbled

The enmeshment of social and material, a premise abridged hereafter as sociomateriality, carries major repercussions for conceptions of action and the human subject. For now, we focus on two points especially pertinent to the perspectives that follow. First, agency becomes a hybrid and distributed phenomenon. We say hybrid because action *is* sociomaterialization, or mattering precisely as defined earlier: jumbles of symbol and stuff coming to "matter" in both senses of the term. Hybrid too because the so-called human and nonhuman are caught up in relations of (inter) dependence; they simply cannot exist, much less exert influence, on their own. Creature desire and will, for instance, relies on bodies, environments, and technologies for its formation, as well as for any hope of pursuit and execution. Moreover, such efforts are routinely distracted and derailed (i.e., interrupted) by other more and less creaturely forces, which leads to the claim that agency is distributed.

Agency is dispersed in this sense: As sociomaterialization, action entails a multiplicity of hybrid forces at work in concrete practice. Hence agency cannot be understood as the possession of any single element. After all, a "single element" needs its relation with others in order to *be* such an element, and thus certainly in order to move toward particular trajectories. "It is not quite right, then, to say that either humans or non-humans 'have' or 'possess' agency; rather, [agency] is the product of the marshaling of multiple elements of an assemblage in the performative and relational generation of action" (Kuhn & Burk, 2014, p. 154). Relations teem with agentive forces whose names, forms, directions, collisions, and fates are thoroughly interdependent and indeterminate (Cooper, 2005; Cooren, 2010; Lynn, 1992). Put simply, no one and no*thing* act alone, or know quite what will happen for their encounter (Latour, 1996).

The second implication for agency may already be obvious; namely, the absolute centrality, autonomy, and potency of the human subject cannot be maintained in relational ontology. For one thing, human consciousness, symbol use, and negotiations of meaning are decentered. As Fenwick (2010) observes, relational ontology moves "away from a primary preoccupation with human meaning including meanings attributed to such objects, as we see in hermeneutic, narrative, or symbolic approaches" (pp. 104–105). Instead of treating meaning as a purely social construction or possession of encultured human actors, relational ontologies treat meaning as a particular kind of matter located within practice (a point we elaborate in Chapter 3.) Indeed, the human capacity for all manners of independent activity, but especially for imposing "our" will on the world as primary agents, is denied by relational ontology. Further eroding the sovereignty of the subject, relationality casts the "human" itself, and its ostensive distinction from the "nonhuman," as the constantly enacted effect of a particular relational matrix.

None of this is to say that humans do not exist or act but, rather, to reposition the human as one sort of sociomaterial vessel for agency that is continually produced as such. Returning to our earlier phrasing, humans can be seen as co-participants among a diverse team of players that contribute to producing the real. And humans rely on the mercy of these "others" for their very existence, much less their efficacy, as do the "others" in return.

The radical and sweeping implications of relationality now come into view. For the moment, consider only these potential ethical ramifications: If the nonhuman cannot be rendered as inanimate things appropriated in the service of human interests, if we understand practice to be a dance among multiple agencies, then ethical principles as we know them become inadequate (Cooren, 2016; Dale & Latham, 2015). Recognizing that we inhabit a network of agencies could imply, for instance, that human impulses for control over nonhuman things should be tempered by new conceptions of community that enable "things" to be and to have a say, so to speak (Introna, 2009). When we displace the human from center stage, we are better positioned to reconsider pressing biopolitical and bioethical issues associated with the Anthropocene, such as climate change, genetically modified organisms, and synthetic life (Coole & Frost, 2010).

5. Causality in/as Action

The final premise returns to our early caution about understanding relationality as an ontological *reversal*: from already-existing things that form relations with each other (i.e., substantialism) to relations that produce "things" as such. As we have colored in our portrait of relationality, this neat picture of turnaround has grown muddy. For example, if relations yield "things" as their enacted effects, rather than the other way around, how are we to understand the action in which these so-called effects engage, or how things act back on their *constitutive* relations? What kind of causality, if any, is this?

To clarify the problem, it might help to condense the usual linguistic relations of causality, over which relationally inclined tongues have tripped a thousand times. In much of the social sciences and even humanities, humans, for the most part, carry out action, or at least human action is the main show. The activity of other living and mobile creatures is largely relegated to the "natural" sciences, attesting to how disciplined divisions of knowing enact the bifurcation of culture and nature, human and nonhuman. Individual humans are regarded as the primary acting units, a societal atom of sorts, though people act in collectives as well. Human (and most creature) action is generally motivated, driven if not determined by cause, and a host of factors can fit this bill: intentions, instincts, desires and passions, personality, or other psychological drivers, environmental, and structural forces, to name just a few. Causality proceeds in a linear fashion, wherein cause stimulates action, which leads to effect—rinse and repeat.

In this view, effects are "consequents" or outcomes that serve up a next set of circumstances to which human action responds, causes are "antecedent" factors that narrow options for response, and agency is the opportunity, however constrained, to select among options for action. In sum, agency and action are the purview of the human, cause and effect are locked in necessary sequence, and effects are inert.

Or are they? Have we not long asked, in innumerable ways, how circumstance forms people, or how products of our own making act back on us? Of course we have (as countless iterations of Frankenstein tales would suggest). Even then, however, action remains conceived as the capacity of coherent entities or systems, such as "the market" (or other robotic monsters), which become anthropomorphized as actors of a sort. Effects, *as* effects, do not act.

In blunt terms, the language game of causality as we know it does not allow easy reference to action without a motivated agent who comes first and assumes primary responsibility for the action, even when succumbing to cause. Yet this is precisely what we need in order to sustain the relational model of agency emerging in the previous premise: action without *an* agent, action *as* cause, agencies *born* of action, agency as effect *and* action. Specifically, relational ontology requires linguistic relations that can articulate causality in terms of (a) simultaneous rather than linear links between cause and effect; (b) indeterminate and organic, rather than deterministic and mechanistic, links between cause and effect; and (c) hybrid agencies in constant formation *through* action, rather than stable, personified units *with*, or in prior possession of, agency. It is a tall order, but one that occupies all of the perspectives to follow.

Butler (2015), for example, summarizes the challenge for a relational conception of subjectivity and causality this way:

> We tend to make a mistake when, in trying to explain subject formation, we imagine a single norm acting as a kind of "cause" and then imagine the "subject" as something formed in the wake of that norm's action . . . The task is to think of being acted on and acting as simultaneous, and not only as a sequence. Perhaps it is a repeated predicament: to be given over to a world in which one is formed even as one acts or seeks to bring something new into being (pp. 5–6). . . . This is not a matter of discovering and exposing an origin or tracking

a causal series, but of describing what acts when I act, without precisely taking responsibility for the whole show.

(p. 16)

The relational quest does not ask us to surrender causality altogether; on the contrary, it seeks alternative causalities that perform the features mentioned earlier (see also Barad, 2003). Emirbayer (1997, p. 307) and proposes novel forms of "action language" that locate cause in practices (e.g., bargaining, or the matrix of action that constitutes struggling over resources) rather than discrete agents and forces (e.g., human stakeholders and interests). Similarly, others suggest description of concrete networks of activity that reveal a rich array of human and nonhuman actors, treated synonymously with "causes," that point practice in certain directions (Latour, 2013). These are but a few of many ongoing efforts to rework causality in relational terms.

Relationality Meets Contemporary Capitalism: The Promise of Initial Encounters

None of the "matters" considered thus far are settled. We present the five premises noted earlier as suggestive, but by no means exhaustive, starting points for distinguishing relationality as a promising yet still nascent approach. As portrayed here, relationality emanates from, and endeavors to redress the excesses of, the linguistic turn. It is worth underscoring for those still in doubt: relationality learns a great deal, and departs significantly, from the various strands of social constructionism (or constructivism) with which some readers might be more familiar.

Equipped with these introductory impressions of relational ontology, we are better prepared to return to the question of *how organization studies can approach this complex scene in novel and productive ways.* Relationality offers a promising alternative, if for no other reason than its insistence upon, and comfort with, complicated and dynamic scenes such as that set in Chapter 1. The notion that buzzing hives of sociomaterial activity—rather than primarily human efforts to construct meaning or, conversely, externally existing nonhuman causes—constantly enact "things" as they are signals a different mode of engagement with the tangle of late-capitalist phenomena evoked earlier.

Namely, we can release persistent images such as that of capitalism as an overarching structure with (over)determined effects, a global network of market fiefdoms, an economic force upon separate spheres such as culture and politics, a clash of humanistic and economic interests, and so on. We can relinquish capitalism as a thing altogether—a noun nearing proper proportions, an ideal type or abstract form, a coherent entity or system-subject, the devil or the savior. Instead, we can begin to see "it" as the continuously emerging enactment of market relations, in concrete practices performed by diffuse assemblages of heterogeneous participants, caught up in interdependent, contingent, and always indeterminate relations—a mouthful, to be sure, but one made more digestible through the preceding introduction.

Characterizing the value of a relational ontology in a different context (science and technology studies), Woolgar, Coopmans, and Neyland (2009) celebrates the propensity of such thinking "to cause trouble, provoke, be awkward," to deflate grandiose theoretical and methodological tools and mechanisms with accountability to specific empirical cases and practices, and to "take revered and standardized ideas and concepts . . . and convert them into objects of study" by emphasizing "the processual, situated and contingent bases for the terms" (pp. 21–22). They conclude that relationality is "a radical intellectual challenge, not merely a political preference or a practical obligation" (p. 22).

Our goal with this book is to commence a reciprocal challenge—that is, a challenge both *of* and *to* relationality. On the one hand, we aim to collaborate with readers in performing a radical intellectual exercise of relationality with respect to work and organizing today, while at the same time, we seek to expand the capacity of relationality to engage with specific problems of work and organizing amid late capitalism in ways that *matter* (i.e., are tangible and meaningful). Toward these mutual aims, we now dip our toes in four specific streams of relationality.

Renderings of Relationality

As the aforementioned section displays, relationality does not merely respond to the discursive emphasis of linguistic turn (or, rather, appropriations of the turn in organization studies) with an insistence upon the powers of material things. Relational ontologies do not insist that objects, spaces, bodies, and the like *have* or *possess* particular capabilities; such a view leads right back to the sorts of deterministic and mechanistic accounts of action that scholars have long sought to avoid. What are needed, then, are ambitious reconceptualizations of social theory based on the five premises, or principles, developed earlier. Social theory has witnessed the emergence of several such reconceptualizations over the past couple of decades, and this section provides a sampling.

Specifically, we present four approaches to—theories of, sensitivities about, or vocabularies for—relationality particularly suitable for making sense of contemporary forms of working and organizing. We overview performativity, a posthumanist version of performativity and sociomateriality, Actor-Network Theory, and affect theory.[2] Our ordering of these is not a signal of preference, but is a recognition that (a) some version of performativity is a key component of each of the perspectives, so beginning there can assist in interpretation of subsequent models, (b) these views evince a rough trajectory from a relative emphasis on discursivity to an increasing sociomateriality, and (c) affect theorizing breaks with the systems-oriented thinking manifest in some of the preceding lines of thought (e.g., economic performativity and

Actor-Network Theory) such that presenting those approaches first enables a starker contrast, aiding the clarity in our depiction.

Performativity

Relational ontologies harbor an overarching interest in *how* questions, asking about the concrete activities through which particular realities are generated, sustained, and changed. A first stream of thought in this vein suggests that the question of accomplishment—the *how* of working and organizing—can only be answered with respect to the ways that speech acts participate in the production of practice. Because much of the work following in this line of thinking draws on Austin's (1962) conception of performative utterances, the thinking is often captured under the broad mantle of *performativity* theorizing (Gond, Cabantous, Harding, & Learmonth, 2015).

Utterances, for Austin, are performative[3] in the sense that they bring about some state of reality—they do not merely reflect or represent an already-existing word. For many, this may seem an obvious point—Wittgenstein (1953/2009, p. 155) preceded Austin with the recognition that language is not merely representational, that "words are also deeds"—but Austin struck a chord as providing novel insight into the beyond-representational character of communication (Loxley, 2007). Performativity theorizing thus starts from the position that language and communication are productive, generative, and active processes, neither epiphenomenal nor inert.

Derrida and Butler

Derrida uses Austin to found his alternative conception of speech acts. Derrida (1988) separates intention and performance, arguing that performatives can break from the context of their utterance and, in so doing, can perform novel (and unintended) acts in situations beyond the original speaker's control (Cooren, 2000, 2009, 2010). This is important for thinking about performance because, argues Derrida, neither the performative context nor the meaning can be predetermined. He asserts that the term "communication" appears to have a standard, accepted referent: one of transmission of meaning from a sender to a receiver. The problem, of course, is that there are many meanings of "communication"—many signified for the signifier. "Communication," therefore, is polysemic, and this polysemy threatens the notion of communication commonly understood as transmission. Participants in communication manage polysemy by establishing (usually unarticulated) expectations about how interaction proceeds and what counts as communication in a given context. This is very similar to Austin's claim about performative utterances, which are more likely to be successful—in his phrase, felicitous—if their use is *conventional* in terms of (a) a procedure upon which participants agree, (b) the persons, words, and circumstances involved, and (c) the effect(s) of the act.

As Austin, Derrida (1988) was interested in cases in which performative utterances fail, when they do not achieve the impact their authors intended. Austin, however, excluded from his analysis cases in which an utterance was "etiolated": When it was not used seriously, when it was designed for entertainment (as when an actor recites lines on the stage), or when it occurs in artistry like a poem. One of Derrida's great innovations is to assert not merely that these cases should indeed be included in our conceptions of speech acts, but that these are endemic to social life. For Derrida, there is no absolute distinction between acting (performing) a role on the stage and in everyday life; the words, intentions, and interpretations are never our own, but instead have been written for us. We inhabit and quote, we are parasitical.

For Derrida, speech—and, in particular for him, writing (but even speech is a form of writing)—is *iterable*: It repeats previous moves, but never in duplicate. The significance of iterability is that it reproduces meaning, and it does so *each time in a new* context that can never be absolutely circumscribed—showing that context matters less for meaning transmission than we might have assumed. When we speak or write—anytime we engage in a form of symbol exchange in an effort to shape meaning—we engage in citation (lifting words out of a sequence and placing them in a new setting). So he concludes that communication is possible, but only if communication is considered transactions that presuppose repetition-with-difference, quotation, and re-insertions, without (contextual) boundaries. Insights like this led scholars to understand the multifarious character of communication: They highlighted the possibility of utterances serving several (potentially conflicting) purposes, the ambiguity of symbol use, and the instability of meaning.

Judith Butler's (1997) version of performativity builds on Derrida's claim about speech acts' power being founded on iterability. For Butler, each utterance acquires the authority of those that have gone before, and adds something of its own, at once constituting a subject and claiming authority over it. As descriptions (utterances) circulate, they break with context and become available for deployment elsewhere—and this is where a space for revision and resistance lies. Butler's interests turn to gender as a form of subjectification via performativity, where she breaks from Austin's (1962) assumption that the person precedes the statement she or he utters. Butler (1993) defines performativity as "that reiterative power of discourse to produce the phenomena that it regulates and constrains" (p. xii). Moreover, the repetition associated with iterability is not engineered by the subject, but is the condition of (im)possibility for the subject's very becoming. Gender, following this thinking, is "a corporeal style, an act as it were, that is both intentional and performative, where 'performative' suggests a dramatic and contingent construction of meaning" (Butler, 2000, p. 177). That construction of meaning is shaped, at every turn, by the authoritative expectations of the social surround. The subject, in Butler's thinking, is thus not the only source of action; it is also the effect of performance; "subject" refers not only to what one is but also to what one does.

Butler argues that what we take to be personal characteristics (such as gender) are not simply intrinsic features of individuals; they are *also* culturally produced as people draw upon "ambient understandings of what is implied by masculinity and femininity and repeatedly rehearsing these in their everyday practices" (Guerard, Langley, & Seidl, 2013, p. 571). The features of subjectivity are, accordingly, ongoing projects, achieved through practices of working where they are repeatedly enacted. Yet these activities generate chains of consequences that are not readily predictable.

Performative "success" occurs not when intention and outcome align, 'but only because that action echoes prior actions, and accumulates the force of authority through the repetition or citation of a prior and authoritative set of practices" (Butler, 1997, p. 51). Yet *failure* is a particular interest for Butler. Because every performance is iterable, it is also open to all sorts of failures, especially when it comes to subjectivities. Drawing on Derrida (1988), she holds that if subjects cannot control signification and the effects of language, subversion of norms is always a possibility, even aside from actors' intentions. Importantly, this also means that every performance can be the site of invention, making uncertainty, contingency, and transgression constitutive features of performative operations.

Analysts must therefore look at how "things" of all sorts are (re)produced in ongoing fashion, because they are always amenable to alteration. Licoppe (2010) explains that the risk of failure—that an expected action, or an expected subject position, will *not* be produced—"is not just a contingent characteristic of the situation but a constitutive feature of performative operations. It is because the ensuing actions may fail that performative operations produce reality" (p. 172). Butler's argument is that *reproduction* is (im)possible; it is this very impossibility that simultaneously creates spaces of possibility and displays the constitutive logic of speech acts with respect to the social and organizational realm.

To what extent does Butler's vision of performativity aid our thinking of materiality and relationality? Butler's interest is in the performative accomplishment of subjectivity, the active becoming of gendered bodies, and her focus tends to be on individual persons. Although this focus on the individual, discursive, and cultural has been a criticism of her work (Lloyd, 1999), she argues that it forces us to recognize the agency of language as a participant in the always-emergent process of subjectivation. And, for Butler, language is intimately connected with the material: "Language and materiality are fully embedded in each other, chiasmic in their interdependency, but never fully collapsed into one another" (Butler, 1993, p. 69).

At the same time, Butler refuses to reduce performativity to discourse:

> Just as no prior materiality is accessible without the means of discourse, so no discourse can ever capture that prior materiality; to claim that the body is an elusive referent is not the same as claiming that it is only and always constructed. In some ways, it is precisely

to claim that there is a limit to constructedness, a place, as it were, where construction necessarily meets its limit.

(Butler, in Meijer & Prins, 1998, p. 278)

Her view thus makes materiality a key concern in the recognition of the inherently linguistic and embodied character of gender performativity. Although she has directed less attention to conceptions of materiality beyond the body, her theorizing provides a rich vein from which to mine insights about the performativity of subjectivity. And, more recently, her work has extended beyond gender to the performativity of organizing (Butler, 2015) and the economy (Butler, 2010). Of the latter, she notes that what we take to be "the" economy "only becomes singular and monolithic by virtue of the convergence of certain kinds of processes and practices that produce the 'effect' of the knowable and unified economy" (p. 147).

Callon's Economic Performativity

Derrida's and Butler's work suggests an important distinction between performance and the (still-emerging) notion of performativity. A *performance* is an event, signified by a noun; its only life is in the present (Phelan, 1998). *Performativity*, in contrast, is about the production of meaning in the present that endures beyond its moment of articulation (La Berge, 2015). A second relational conception of performativity builds on this notion of enduring meaning, arguing that it is impossible to divorce speech acts from the sociomaterial world in which they occur; it holds that performative utterances (i.e., illocution and perlocution) depend upon a framework of agencies and meanings that enable statements to produce their effects.

Michel Callon has led inquiry into what has come to be called *economic performativity*, a view investigating how economic theories and models are not merely representations of an external world—they *create* the very phenomena, such as markets, they describe (Cardwell, 2015; Vollmer, Mennicken, & Preda, 2009). This perspective draws on a few categories by which performativity is said to operate (MacKenzie, 2007). First is *generic* performativity, which occurs when actors take up economic concepts and theories and use them in their everyday action. *Effective* performativity, second, is when such forms of appropriation make a difference in economic processes. Third is *Barnesian*, or strong, performativity (Barnes, 1983), where the use of economic theory actively impinges on social practice in ways that lead those practices to align ever more closely with the assumptions and predictions of the theory (the associated notion of "counter-performativity" speaks to the possibility of a theory's adoption by actors leading to its *decreased* resemblance to observable practice). If models are to make themselves "true" in this performative sense, they have to be embedded in discourses and tools utilized by actors in the conduct of practice (Healy, 2015).

Analyses making claims about the Barnesian form of performativity with respect to organization studies concepts make the same moves as they do in economics, showing how models and tools are appropriated to make a theory harmonize with social practice. For instance, Carter, Clegg, and Kornberger (2010) show how Porter's (1980) Five Forces model of corporate strategy did not, when it was first written, *reflect* strategic practice; it instead shaped how strategists talk and think and, over time, strategizing changed to fit the model. A similar claim characterizes Cabantous and Gond's (2011) assessment of rational choice theory, a conception of the world that pervades organizational life because it underlies decisional tools such as SWOT analyses.

Callon's thinking on performativity bears the imprint of his long association with Actor-Network Theory in his claim that realities (including economic realities) are accomplished because of the workings of a complex set of linked human and nonhuman elements (Callon, 1998, 2008; Callon & Muniesa, 2005; Gherardi, 2016; MacKenzie & Millo, 2003; Muniesa, 2014). Borrowing a term from Deleuze and Guattari (1987), Callon describes this complex set as an *agencement*. Although *agencement* has often been translated into English as *assemblage*, the term is drawn from the French verb *agencer*, which suggests "articulating, arranging, disposing, and setting" (Cochoy, Trompette, & Araujo, 2016, p. 3). At the same time, however, *agencer* implies a consideration of organizing practices that create, and simultaneously depend upon, particular configurations of human and nonhuman elements. As Phillips (2006, p. 108) puts it, "*agencement* designates the priority of neither the state of affairs nor the statement but of their connection, which implies the production of a sense that exceeds them and of which, transformed, they now form parts."

Given the interest in economic issues, Callon and his followers are attracted to the study of *calculation*, the activity often taken to be a form of rational accounting for value. Calculation relies on detaching and arranging objects from one another, ordering and displaying them in (physical or conceptual) space, manipulating and transforming them, and then extracting a result.[4] The detaching, arranging, ordering, and displaying involved in calculation are inherently communicative practices in that they are concerned with the production of actions and meanings through the positioning of (human and nonhuman) participants in the conduct of a practice. The *agencement*, then, is a distributed "calculative agency," as the relationships between the participants are what is understood to be acting. The character of the participants, moreover, breaks down conventional distinctions between the social and the material:

> Calculative agencies are not human individuals but collective hybrids, "centres of calculation" (Latour, 1987). These agencies are equipped with instruments; calculation does not take place only in human minds, but is distributed among humans and non-humans.
> (Callon & Muniesa, 2005, p. 1236)

Agency, moreover, is a feature of the *distribution* of participants; it is the arrangement as a whole that engages in a practice. Beunza and Stark

(2004) used a similar model in their study of arbitrage trading, suggesting that the trading room can be considered a laboratory where humans and instruments conduct experiments to test a market. Calculative agency, in these accounts, is thus not an entity; it is a *practice* that brings a network of (human and nonhuman) elements together and activates it for particular purposes. The point of drawing attention to the *agencement* as a calculative agency is not merely to question the rationality, but to provide a tool to grasp the multiplicity of participants tangled together in the production and attribution of value.

Economic Performativity in Organization Studies

The model of the *agencement*, as a calculative device, does not imply a macro-level collective entity, nor does it smuggle human intent into the frame. Analysts using these notions suggest that the *agencement* establishes the conditions by which particular elements (or conjunctions of elements) become defined as agents with the capacity to engage in calculation: economists (MacKenzie, Muniesa, & Siu, 2007), traders of commodities and financial devices (MacKenzie & Millo, 2003; Zaloom, 2006), and algorithms (Muniesa, 2004, 2011). Yet the performativity of language and communication is never far removed, as in Holmes's (2014) study of central banks:

> The communicative dynamics operating within the field of monetary policy are far more consequential [than communicative practices in natural science laboratories] insofar as markets themselves, as I will argue, are a function of language . . . [bankers'] statements are not merely expressing an interpretative account or commentary, they are making the economy itself as a communicative field and as an empirical fact.
>
> (p. 5)

De Goede (2005) makes a similar point in her study of the rise and practice of finance, which she depicts as a discursive domain made possible through performative practices. As both Holmes and De Goede argue, economic domains often seen as "objective," as distinct from human action, are instead dependent on it. These are not efforts to fold the economic into the social, but are claims that the economic is materialized in the performative relationships between the myriad components of an *agencement*.

In this version of performativity, then, interest is in how (economic) propositions and practices (such as monetary policy and finance) reflexively construct the contexts to which they refer—just as we suggested in our portrayal of the *story* of the new economy in Chapter 1. Generally using ethnographic and interview-based methods, analysts also consider how those propositions draw upon devices and infrastructures, and thus also seek to attend to the material as elements of the *agencements* (Roscoe & Chillas, 2014). Rather than assuming that propositions (or economists, or algorithms) *possess* agency to construct that context, however, these scholars highlight communication, though rarely labeling it as such, in making sense of how action occurs: "the capacity to give meaning to action is linked to the reflexive ability of an *agencement*, and is tied to the establishment of feedback loops that allow consequences to be linked to specific actions" (Araujo & Kjellberg, 2015, p. 4).

There exist several penetrating critiques of this work. Cardwell (2015), for instance, argues that, in its focus on the pragmatic accomplishment of economies, the perspective is inherently conservative, lacking any political stance or ability to challenge economists' views of the world. Butler (2010) similarly critiques Callon's view of performativity because it provides no route to interrogate the interests underlying economic formations. She suggests that economic performativity is concerned with either (a) the notion that economic realities are neither natural nor preordained or (b) the illocutionary force of bringing economic reality into being. Both concerns, she argues, portray a totalizing and subject-less conception of the economic.

Butler sees in economic performativity theory little room for contingency, creativity, or (to return to Butler's version of performativity) cases in which economic theory *fails* to bring about the economic reality it envisages:

> If the theory presumes efficacity, then it fails to see that breakdown is constitutive of performativity (performativity never fully achieves its effect, and so in this sense "fails" all the time; its failure is what necessitates its reiterative temporality, and we cannot think iterability without failure). Its moments of breakdown are also important for another version of "critique."
>
> (p. 153)

Butler encourages, then, an attention to what Austin (1962) would have called *misfires*, cases in which performances undermine the very model or theory that is supposed to drive them (Fleming & Banerjee, 2015). Callon, who employs the term *overflows* to address a similar theme (Callon, 1998), views such transgressions as *external* to performative communication—for him, overflows are outcomes that can be managed outside of the performative act, by an agency external to the *agencement* under consideration. In contrast, Butler sees misfires or overflows as occurring *within* the performative act (Nyberg & Wright, 2016) such that analysts should examine *in situ* processes of working and organizing to understand the possibility of both transgression and change.

Both Butler and Cardwell, then, want to encourage those who draw upon economic performativity to think about the *political* value of particular economic configurations. Butler and Carwell hold that Callon's (2010) conception of the political is limited to emphasizing the contingency of any performative truth claim, but that a more productive approach is to situate the political within performativity itself. Thus, they accuse Callon's economic performativity of neglecting its opportunity to challenge the legitimacy of the markets within and through which working and organizing operate.

Posthumanist Performativity and Sociomateriality

A third version of performativity—a version of performativity distinct enough to merit its own section heading—is associated with the "agential realism" of Karen Barad and her interpreters in organization studies. Drawing on quantum physics and feminist studies of science, Barad (2003) presents a *posthumanist* version of performativity, which means that, for her, action should not be reduced to what human beings do (with words or without words). Strongly influenced by the material turn, Barad argues that matters of practices or doings *always* concern *nonhumans*. However, as we shall show next, she questions the usefulness of the uncomplicated distinction between human and nonhuman.

Barad defends what she calls a "performative understanding of discursive practices" (Barad, 2003, p. 802), which she contrasts with representationalism, understood as "the belief in the ontological distinction between representations and that which they purport to represent; in particular, that which is represented is held to be independent of all practices of representing" (p. 804). Her approach, borrowing from Foucault and Butler, instead pursues the *material nature of discursive practices*, asserting that discourse must always be materialized in specific practices (see premise three). This materialization is not inscription (as in writing on a surface), but as the set of associations that, over time, produce the effect of boundedness and fixity.

When Barad (2003) defends what she calls a "performative understanding of discursive practices" (p. 802), she specifies that

> Performativity, properly construed, is not an invitation to turn everything (including material bodies) into words; on the contrary, performativity is precisely a contestation of the excessive power granted to language to determine what is real. Hence, in ironic contrast to the misconception that would equate performativity with a form of linguistic monism that takes language to be the stuff of reality, performativity is actually a contestation of the unexamined habits of mind that grant language and other forms of representation more power in determining our ontologies than they deserve.
>
> (p. 802)

Barad's contribution has been read as an attempt to go beyond the linguistic turn, which she associates with an attempt to turn everything into a matter of language. This conception of the material discursive is tied to her concern about the bifurcation of the natural and the social (a division Whitehead also denounced almost a century ago). As she famously said, "Language matters. Discourse matters. Culture matters. There is an important sense in which the only thing that does not seem to matter anymore is matter" (p. 801). *Making matter matter* means, for Barad, that matters of concern have to be, analytically speaking, taken seriously.

Intra-Action

These matters of concern are likely to be manifold. For instance, when a manager introduces a just-in-time scheduling regime into a retail environment, the statement is inseparable from the algorithm running the program, the assumed calculable objectivity of money and profitability, the demand for "lean" operations shaping the decision, the temporal challenges experienced by workers, the physical location of the workplace, and the embodied character of the work—among many other features. In a case such as this, Barad's interest is in "intra-action," a term signaling for Barad the mutual and entangled constitution of discourse and matter in the conduct of practice. For her, the more common term, *inter*action, "presumes the prior existence of independent entities/relata" (p. 815) because "inter" means "among," "between," or "in the midst of." In contrast, Barad defines *intra*-action as "the mutual constitution of entangled agencies" (2007, p. 33); that is, agencies emerge through their intra-action (intra means "within"), and only within a practice. In other words, the distinction between agencies has to be understood *relationally* and never unconditionally. For Barad, intra-action calls upon analysts to not focus on what actors do, think, or say, but to "what provides them with their actions and intentionality, namely what is already assumed as appropriate and legitimate ways of acting by the circulating flow of agency through material-discursive practices" (Hultin & Mähring, in press, p. 7).

An important upshot of intra-action is that the traditional distinction between ontology and epistemology is broken. When we deny the strict division of the social and the material, we also deny the historical moralism contained in the nature/culture divide—along with the assumption that nature has interests and desires that mesh well with our own (Barad, 2012).

What the term "intra-action" helps us understand is that properties are always relational, which means that properties are never absolutely *proper* (Bencherki & Cooren, 2011; Derrida, 1993). They emerge (or emerged from) relations with other beings (where "beings," again, is not limited to the human). Understanding knowledge work in contemporary capitalism, by way of example, cannot imply simply the attention to either an abstract set of concepts taken to be knowledge, nor can it be to actors' image management strategies; for posthumanist performativity, neither knowledge nor persons precede relations—*all relations* must be taken into account.

The task, in turn, is to examine how particular components of practice emerge and become considered, from *within* the practice, distinct elements—and, further, how particular distinct elements are granted supremacy over others. So the question is less about what sorts of knowledge is valuable than it is about tracing the particular material-discursive practices through which particular elements of the scene become considered knowledgeable, and how the associated agency impacts subsequent practice. There can be, therefore, autonomy, individuality, separability, but it is always relative and emergent in practice (Piette, 2016). In other words, autonomy, individuality, and separability are always the result of the iterable or repeatable character of what a specific being or entity performs (for instance, we remember who we are because memories are, by definition, the materialization of intra-actions—that, is ways by which past relations keep materializing themselves to us).

Two terms that Barad (2003, 2007) also uses to talk about this relative autonomy, individuality, or separability are the "agential cut" and the "phenomenon." An *agential cut*, which is produced by a specific intra-action, materializes a given *phenomenon*—a practice, a differential pattern of mattering—where specific properties can be determined. The agential cut generates a separation between, for instance, "subject" and "object" and posits a relationship between the elements. In this way, Barad's relational ontology does not lead to indeterminacy and solipsism, as it allows securing a form of ontological and semantic *objectivity*, especially when the same apparatus is reinstated. For instance, much of the "gig economy"—think ride-sharing services like Uber or Lyft—relies on persons who either cannot (or who choose not to) find more stable sources of work or who seek supplemental income through working temporary "gigs." The practice of generating a ride-sharing economy is a complex one, and making sense of it requires several agential cuts. These cuts include framing the worker as a site of decision/choice, but also can include laws allowing these companies to consider drivers as subcontractors (and thus to reduce interdependencies), the presence of consumer debt, the possession of a vehicle, the development of apps and the widespread use of smartphones upon which they run, the existence of a clientele dissatisfied with other forms of transportation, the manifestation of cashless payment services, and the ability to use public infrastructure at low cost. Many agencies are at play in what could seem to be a simple scene; Barad's claim is that they have no independent (autonomous, individual, separable) existence until they are *made to* have an independent existence—they are not distinct agencies until they are made to be. And that "making" is the work of agential cuts, effected when specific properties, beings, characteristics, or traits are selected *in phenomena*. Agential cuts thus occur in, and are properties of, practices; they are not reducible to human intention or action.

Posthumanist Performativity in Organization Studies

Barad thus offers a relational ontology that insists on the performative dimension of discursive-material relations. In organization studies, this thinking has been mobilized most notably by Wanda Orlikowski (2007) and her colleague Susan Scott (Orlikowski & Scott, 2008, 2014, 2015) to analyze questions related to technologies' adoption, diffusion, and use in organizational contexts.

Thinking the world relationally indeed helps us rethink the way we traditionally conceive of machineries, tools, and technologies in organizational settings. In her landmark essay published in 2007, Orlikowski reminds us that the literature on technology suffers from the same divide that we already denounced at the beginning of this chapter—i.e., the divide between, on one side, the so-called material world, which is almost systematically identified with the world of technologies, tools, and artifacts (e.g., Leonardi, 2012; Leonardi & Barley, 2008) and the so-called social world, which is also almost systematically associated with the word of meanings, discourses, and cultures. In other words, whenever investigations of technology speak of materiality, they immediately think of machines, computers, or algorithms (and sometimes tables, rocks, or rooms), though Barad argues that materiality, understood as mattering, is *constitutive of anything that exists* (including discourse, ideas, and emotions). Orlikowski (2007) shows that this mistake is reproduced by scholars who tend to have opposing views about the way to deal with technology adoption, diffusion, and use: on one side is what she calls the *techno-centric* perspective (usually associated with functionalism), which analyzes and insists on the effects of technology on human action, on the other side is what she calls the *human-centered perspective* (usually associated with social constructionism), which highlights the way people not only make sense of technology but also interact with it (see also Leonardi, 2012).

Even if they disagree about *what matters* in technology adoption, diffusion, and use, these two opposing views thus share the same ontological bias, which consists of arbitrarily separating the material and social worlds. Orlikowski (2007) thus proposes to transcend this divide by proposing what she calls, echoing Mol (2002) and Suchman (2007), a *sociomaterial*[5] perspective, which she explicitly identifies with Barad's (2003, 2007) agential realism, Latour's (2005) Actor-Network Theory, and Pickering's (1995) material agency.

Organizational practices are *sociomaterial* to the extent that they mark "the constitutive entanglement of the social and material in everyday organizational life" (Orlikowski, 2007, p. 1438). The word "entanglement" is important in her demonstration, as it is borrowed directly from Barad's stance on the *entanglement of matter and meaning*. Instead of asking *what is influencing what*, Orlikowski invites us to analyze what emerges from specific apparatuses, devices, and phenomena, knowing that this emergence can express a form of stability and constancy, and therefore a form of objectivity.

Using the Google search engine and mobile communications as illustrations, she convincingly shows what emerge from these sociomaterial assemblages. Speaking of the search engine, Orlikowski (2007) notes that:

> The Google search engine is computer code that was produced and is maintained by software engineers, that executes on computers (configured with particular hardware and software elements), and whose

operation depends on the millions of people who create and update web pages every day, and the millions of people who enter particular search terms into it. The result is a constitutive entanglement of the social and the material.

(p. 1440)

In other words, the divide between the social and the material would not make any sense to the extent that it would become impossible to "separate technology from human affairs" (p. 1445).

Instead of focusing on individualities and separateness, Orlikowski and Scott (2008, 2014, 2015) encourage analysts to focus on what they call, echoing Barad, *material-discursive practices*. This means that no attempt is ever made to analyze "the discursive effects of the material, and the material effects of the discursive" (Orlikowski and Scott, 2015, p. 698) as studying such effects would reproduce the arbitrary separation between meaning and matter. On the contrary, Orlikowski and Scott focus on *materialization processes* (as described in our premise three): that is, "how materializations make a difference in the enactment of reality in practice" (p. 700).

An illustration of this position is their comparison between the two apparatuses of hotel valuation mobilized by the United Kingdom Automobile Association (AA), on one side, and TripAdvisor, on the other side. While AA uses what they call a formulaic valuation apparatus, made of "formal standards, objectified criteria, and trained expertise, while excluding consumer opinion and multiple experiences" (p. 887), Trip Advisor uses an algorithmic valuation apparatus, made of "open ended consumer opinion, content aggregation, flexible parameters, and reprogrammable criteria while excluding professional classifications and formal measures" (p. 887). In keeping with Barad's notions of intra-action and agential cuts, these two apparatuses are understood as producing two different types of hoteliers, two different types of guests, and, of course, two different types of valuations; performativity is the *enactment* of relations, boundaries, and valuations. As they point out,

> The different practices producing guest comments and TripAdvisor reviews configure guests and hoteliers differently. Guests who have read TripAdvisor reviews about a hotel prior to staying at it have more detailed knowledge about others' experiences with the hotel. Many feel empowered by this information to request particular rooms and services, and to demand upgrades or discounts on threat of possible negative reviews. Hoteliers in a world of TripAdvisor no longer see a guest walking through the door; they see a potential reviewer.
>
> (p. 703)

As we see with this excerpt, it would indeed make no sense to analyze the discursive effects of the material, and the material effects of the discursive, as the TripAdvisor apparatus is, like any apparatus, the expression of an entanglement where discourse and materiality appear inextricably related.

Beyond Orlikowski and Scott, the organization studies field has seen a few other efforts to deploy posthumanist performativity theorizing in the study of working and organizing. For instance, Nyberg (2009) studied an Australian call center, showing how practice involved a myriad of agencies, but that agential cuts occurring during customer calls opened up different possibilities for action. Hultin and Mähring's (in press) investigation of an emergency room in a Nordic university hospital shows how sensemaking was distributed in a circulating flow of agency that linked humans and nonhumans; they concluded that what "made sense" in organizing always *emerged* from material-discursive practices. And in a case study of an organization devoted to using computing to increase the social inclusion of disabled persons, Dale and Latham (2015) argue,

> Materialities and the ways in which they have come to be constituted as phenomena (Barad, 2007) *produce* the disabled body, since although it is the individual human body which is perceived as not being able to do certain things, it is the sedimented, taken-for-granted sociomaterial arrangements that produce the effects of disabling the particular human body in that particular entanglement.
>
> (p. 172, emphasis in original)

In these examples, the contingencies and consequences of particular agential cuts are highlighted. The conceptions of human bodies in Dale and Latham are not merely discursive constructions, and the entanglements of interest are not merely human. The concept of agential cuts provides a useful tool to examine how particular phenomena emerge from the complicated configurations of agencies, suggesting that the posthumanist performativity interest need not be solely with technological artifacts, but with an array of issues related to working and organizing in contemporary capitalism.

Questions of Agency and Heuristic Value

One important critique of sociomateriality and the agential realism upon which it is based is Mutch's (2013) and Leonardi's (2013) concern that this work, in its ontological commitment to the constitutive entanglement of agencies in the conduct of practices, ironically *prevents* meaningful empirical analysis. Considering studies that have attempted to transcend discursive-material (and subject-object) dualisms, Jarzabkowski and Pinch (2013) argue that "even though such studies acknowledge the complex, mutually constitutive and shifting arrangements between actor and object within the unfolding activity, they still separate material and human agency" (p. 581).

Mutch specifically suggests that studies guided by agential realism produce no novel insights, largely because the theory (a) conflates agency and structure, (b) forces analysts to make a priori distinctions between elements marking the practice—that a commitment to deferring determinations regarding identities and boundaries of participants in a practice is impossible, (c) has no theory of temporality (and thus can only *describe* change, not explain it), and (d) lacks nuance in presenting all relations between participants as *internal* relations—that connections between entities are constitutive, always making the agencies what they are— when many other forms of relation are possible. To address these problems, Mutch and Leonardi turn to critical realism, which re-introduces ontological distinctions between action and actors, including materiality: "like any structural property, materiality predates the actions to which it will be put and the perceptions it will help create" (Leonardi, 2013, p. 69). The interest for Leonardi and Mutch is the ways in which the discursive and the material, the human and nonhuman, are woven or tiled together, or *imbricated* (see Taylor, 2011), in practice.

Although a full review of this disagreement, and of critical realism as an alternative, are beyond our scope here, we see the debate as highlighting two important concerns. First is the question of novelty: The issue of whether agential realism/posthumanist performativity generates insights unique enough to warrant the exertion working from them (and entering into their often-challenging vocabulary) requires. To a large extent, this is an empirical question—one that can only be answered after a critical mass of research (research that is still in its infancy) can be scrutinized. The second issue is whether agential realism (along with the other relational ontologies described in this chapter) offers onto-epistemological positions that outpace existing methodologies. As presented in the preceding paragraph, Mutch and Leonardi suggest they do; others, such as Fox and Alldred (2015)—who, based on a review of 30 empirical studies, concluded that several principles unite new materialist research—argue that transcending dualisms is possible with existing methodologies, though not simple. The question here is what purposes we want these theories—again, as heuristic devices—to serve.

In the previous chapter, we argued that the organization studies field requires theoretical approaches that enable analysts to make sense of the complex set of characters participating in the story of working and organizing under contemporary capitalism. In the present chapter, we have argued that pursing this aim highlights the need to acknowledge multiple, hybrid, and indeterminate agencies; posthumanist performativity in particular argues for the need to defer determinations about the locations of agency until analysts have grasped the intricacies of practice. The alternative suggested by Mutch and Leonardi, where agencies are separate but imbricated together, carries with it a preference for the agency of the human over the material (Kautz & Jensen, 2013).

As Leonardi (2011) notes, "By keeping the distinction between human and material agencies, the imbrication metaphor asserts a slightly different relationship [compared to ANT]: people *have* agency and technologies *have* agency, but ultimately, people decide how they will respond to a technology" (p. 151; emphasis added). Leonardi focuses on the interdependence of agencies, but his assertion that agency is a possession of both things and persons, and that these agencies are ontologically distinct (and that boundaries can be drawn around "a" technology in a priori fashion), suggests that this critical realist alternative is likely to be of limited use for analysts seeking epistemologically novel devices in examinations of working and organizing.

Actor-Network Theory

Actor-Network Theory (ANT; see Callon, 1986; Callon & Latour, 1981; Latour, 2005; Law, 1986) has explored a relational ontology for the past 30 years or so (and, we should note, has reflected several important conceptual shifts over that period). Although it is often difficult to summarize what comprises ANT, we could define it, at least in its origins, as an attempt to acknowledge and analyze the performative dimension of so-called intermediaries, tools, or media. Less a theory than a sensibility, ANT begins with the premise that for any actor to act, it must enroll a wide array of other elements (other *actors*); ANT argues that remaining sensitive to the activation of networks in the accomplishment of activity leads analysts to produce rich case studies of working and organizing (Law & Singleton, 2013).

A Plenum of Agencies and Ontological Politics

One of the controversial ideas that ANT proposed from its outset is that *things do things*. That is, as we suggested in our first premise earlier, things—a vast category, indeed (Latour, 2005)—should be considered *actors* to the extent that they make a difference in the world in which we evolve (Bencherki, 2016). Although traditional sociology has always used the terms "action," "actors," and "agency" to talk about what human beings, and only human beings, do (e.g., Emirbayer & Mische, 1998; O'Donnell, 2010), Callon (1986) and Latour (1986, 1987; Latour & Woolgar, 1979) were among the first to notice that we could not fully understand how a project functions, how a society is structured, or how an organization operates without acknowledging the difference that technologies, devices, apparatuses, or machines make—i.e., what they do or perform (Pickering, 1995). (See also premise four.)

This explains why the term "nonhuman actor" is often associated, for better or worse, with this perspective. Although this terminology certainly has its own merits (for instance, it invites us to pay attention to what often remains invisible, such as the contributions of tools, machines, and artifacts), it is problematic to the extent that it ends up working against the symmetry it is supposed to introduce into analyses. The distinction between humans and nonhumans, in other words, creates an awful *asymmetry* as it gathers everything that is considered nonhuman into a single category, which then encompasses beings as diverse as animals, plants, minerals, technologies, buildings, tools, and the like (Cooren, 2010).

Furthermore, speaking of nonhumans becomes highly problematic when we refer to things such as ideas, passions, attitudes, discourses, texts, or drawings—that is, things that are usually associated with what humans develop, produce, or make, but that have a relative distinctiveness, individuality, and autonomy. Are ideas nonhuman? Well certainly not, if we consider that they are often associated with the humans' mind they happen to cross. Are texts nonhuman? Well, not really if we consider that they tend to be written by human beings, or, in some cases, by machines that have been designed by human beings. Are passions nonhuman? Hard to say, given that they tend to be associated with the people they animate and enthuse (Hennion, 2007).

This becomes even more problematic if we consider that human beings' bodies are themselves comprised of so-called nonhumans (genes, cells, organs, fluids, bones, etc.). As both Tarde (1895) and Whitehead (1920) pointed out, human beings can themselves be considered *societies* (this is the term they both use)—that is, collectives, assemblages, concrescences, or configurations that are literally *made of* other beings. Instead of speaking of nonhuman agency to characterize what ANT focuses on, we thus prefer to say that it highlights everything that is deemed as making a difference in a situation—while also acknowledging the specific beings that tend to be reproduced through these contributions. Everything we take to be an "entity," then, consists of networks of heterogeneous sociomaterial elements. As Callon and Law (1997) note, "the methodological lesson is this: that objects—for instance, people and texts—are processes of transformation, compromise or negotiation" (p. 167) such that our analytical techniques must be sensitive both to the constitution and to the ongoing (re)constituting.

Latour (2013) uses the expression "being-as-other" (p. 162) to both acknowledge the hybrid character of our world—the fact that it is made of beings with various ontologies—while recognizing that such hybridity, heterogeneity, or alterity cannot be identified without recognizing a form of identity, homogeneity and repetition (otherwise, there would not be, by definition, anything to make hybrid). A good example is an organization. An organization is literally made of spokespersons, organizational charts, operations, managers, employees, machines, cultures, buildings, etc. (Cooren, 2006). In other words, its mode of existence is, by definition, *hybrid*. However, in order to be *recognized* as such, an organization also has to manage, somehow, to *materialize itself* through *its* various representatives or embodiments (see, again, premise three). The spokespersons have to be *its* spokespersons, the organizational charts have to be *its* organizational charts, the cultures have to be *its* cultures, etc. (Bencherki, 2012; Nicotera, 2013; Taylor & Van Every, 2000). Latour (2013) uses the term "script" to talk about this specific way by which organizing take place—that is, specific programs of action that ultimately define organizing and organization.

For instance, spokespersons can talk on behalf of their organization because they have normally been *entitled* to do so; that is, they have been *authorized* and *accredited* to exercise this responsibility. In other words, they are under *multiple scripts* (which exist as part of the actor--network) that are supposed to define their actions: they *have* the title of spokesperson, they *have* a sort of canvas that defines how the position of their organization should be defended, they *have* the authority to talk to specific people in specific circumstances, etc. The same logic operates for other beings such as organizational cultures, for instance. In order to be recognizable, a given culture has indeed to express itself *through* specific attitudes, traditions, jargons, practices, etc. (Barker, 1993, 1999; Cooren, 2015), which also function as scripts—that is, programs of action.

Far from being reduced to reflections on, and analyses of, nonhuman agency, ANT invites us to pay attention to what happens on the *terra firma of interaction* (Cooren, 2006)—*and nowhere else* (as mentioned in our premise two). This explains why actor-network theorists tend to systematically avoid the term "structure" in their explanations and analyses, because this term ends up functioning like a hodgepodge behind which the agencies of a plethora of things are likely to hide (Ashcraft et al., 2009; Cooren & Fairhurst, 2009; Putnam & Nicotera, 2009).

If we indeed start acknowledging that we live in a *plenum of agencies* (Cooren, 2006), what traditional sociologists tend to call "structures" then become reconceptualized as various scripts whose agency can be specifically unveiled and explained. For instance, an organizational chart is a diagram that is supposed to *define (materialize)*, formally, the structure of an organization. This means that it graphically (iconically) *indicates* or *materializes* the different relations of responsibility and subordination between various departments and people. We highlighted the verbs "define," "indicate," and, especially, "materialize" to show the agency or performativity of this diagram—that is, what it literally accomplishes. Instead of reducing this chart to a simple intermediary that does not really make a difference (i.e., does not really do anything or fails to represent accurately the relations marking organizing), ANT invites us to recognize the difference this kind of document makes in practice—that is, its specific agency.

The potential (and perhaps likely) existence of the aforementioned multiplicity of programs of action circulating in a given scene suggests the beginnings of an ontological politics associated with ANT. A recognition that reality is *multiple*, and that multiplicity is dispersed—and not the constructionists' move that reality is singular but could have been otherwise—and always *performed* into existence is also a recognition of the relevance of choice (as explained in premise two). Choice, in the register of ANT, is not about human decision making, but is about the trajectory of performance, a trajectory always formed by the convergences of agencies.

Describing arguments about differing models of treating anemia, Mol (1999) presents the political question:

> What [the arguments] do, each of them, is shift the site of the decision elsewhere: to move it along. So they displace the decisive moment to places where, seen from here, it seems no decision, but a fact. These places are, respectively: the intricacies of measurement techniques, considerations about good and bad reasons for treatment, and health care budgets.
>
> (p. 80)

What Mol is signaling here is *ontological politics*: That there is never a single site of decision, and rarely straightforward conceptions of the good, operating in and through actor-networks (Law & Singleton, 2013). She also argues that conventional accounts of problems like anemia tend to single out particular elements (or tensions between them), missing the complex interconnections across and through complex actor-networks. Moreover, Mol holds that there are likely interferences between agencies comprising the network such that the very conception of the "political" problem is likely to shift over time—as well as in response to efforts to intervene. Although others fault ANT for its ability to contribute to critical theorizing (e.g., Roberts, 2012; Whittle & Spicer, 2008), ANT contends that beginning inquiry with questions and, from there, developing rich descriptions *is* a political move (Doolin & Lowe, 2002); as Law and Singleton (2013) assert, *"to the extent that ANT explores the contingencies of power it also generates tools for undoing the inevitability of that power"* (p. 500, emphasis in original).

ANT Analyses of Working and Organizing

Using ANT in studies of working and organizing requires that analysts take into consideration all the beings that make a difference in constituting (structuring and/or de-structuring) the actor-network, knowing that some of those beings will act from a distance. ANT invites us to trace these *trajectories* of agency in time and space (Vásquez, 2013), because engaging in this tracing enables a depiction of working and organizing that remains in the domain of practice. Remaining in the domain of practice, never leaving the *terra firma* of interaction (Cooren, Kuhn, Cornelissen, & Clark, 2011) means that it will always be possible to retrace various forms of agency that explain a given situation without having to resort to this *deus ex machina* sociologists call "structure."

Case studies employing ANT show that different practices generate different actor-networks, and multiple actor-networks can coexist when there are multiple practices. For example, de Laet and Mol's (2000) study of a water pump in the Zimbabwean bush showed that what might ordinarily be understood as *a* technology (in the singular) is instead many things. Because it is fluid in the sense that it is adaptable and responsive to changing needs, because it is repairable with simple materials, because it summons a community to bore holes to initiate wells, because its use requires sealing wells to keep invaders such as *E. coli* out of water supplies, and because it is not "owned" by any single human inventor, it is multiple, its identity is shaped by the actor-network in which it is embedded. As de Laet and Mol explain, the pump "is a mechanical object, it is a hydraulic system, but it is also a device installed by the community, a health promoter and a nation-building apparatus. . . . In each of its identities the bush pump contains a variant of its environment" (p. 252). It is not possible, then, to provide a single definition of what the bush pump *is*, because it cannot be detached from actor-networks. In other words, "it" is not a stable entity, but a reference to how *it* is *done*; this doing varies as the so-called object travels in/through practice. As a case of organizing a community, de Laet and Mol's case study thus disrupts conventional accounts of artifacts, actors, and organizing.

Research in the ANT tradition moreover rejects notion that structures or ideologies such as neoliberalism or financialization work in top-down fashion, imposing themselves on localized practices. Instead, "ANT tends to assume that the whole world may be discovered within any specific scene or set of practices" (Law & Singleton, 2013, p. 500). In the case of working and organizing in contemporary capitalism, analysts have examined how the user-generated content associated with social media enters a network of agencies that produces modifications in the artifacts typically identified as technologies (Siles & Boczkowski, 2012). Others have shown how agency is hybrid, determined only as a relational network is activated in practice, as in Brummans's (2007) moving depiction of the materialization of a euthanasia declaration across a complex network of agencies. If ANT is about the performativity of things as they are ensconced in hybrid networks, the questions it asks about contemporary capitalism have to do with how particular elements become materialized, and made to matter such that those elements appear (to actors and analysts) as agents authorized to participate in, and shape, working and organizing. ANT suggests that understanding how our world is organized (or, for that matter, disorganized), requires that we take into consideration all the "beings" making a difference in this structuring or de-structuring, knowing that some of them will act from a distance, but that it will be possible to retrace how they end up tele-acting.

Affect Theory

Our final approach departs from the language of science and system. It begins by staving off definition in recognition that affect itself is a tease. While we feel and respond to its pushes and pulls, it always evades grasp, even when seizing us in its possession. Perhaps conceptual dealings with affect should honor this feral quality instead of seeking to cage it.

But once again, the linguistic relations in which we (literally) find ourselves oblige us to "thing-ify" affect for sensibility. Succumbing to yet repelling this imperative, affect theorists describe "it" as "an energetics that does not necessarily emerge at the level of signification" (Rice, 2008, p. 201), or "bodily meaning that pierces social interpretation, confounding its logic, and scrambling its expectations" (Hemmings, 2005, p. 552). Although corporeal, it entails "pre-individual forces that escape and exceed the human body . . . an intensity of relations that are always in excess . . . a transpersonal capacity taking place before thought kicks in" (Beyes & Steyaert, 2012: 52). Likewise, Seigworth and Gregg (2010, p. 2) describe affect as "forces of encounter" that include "all the miniscule or molecular events of the unnoticed," "the ordinary and its extra-," offering this summary:

> Affect can be understood then as a gradient of bodily capacity—a supple incrementalism of ever-modulating force-relations—that rises and falls not only along various rhythms and modalities of encounter but also through the troughs and sieves of sensation and sensibility, an incrementalism that coincides with belonging to comportments of matter of virtually any and every sort.

As these elusive definitions assert, affect is about ineffable feeling rather than recognizable emotions (see Massumi, 1995). Affect is feel*ing* before it gets sifted into distinct feeling*s* that "one has," as if the borders afforded by self and skin are sufficient to contain emotion. Whereas emotion bears the filtering of language, cognition, and culture, affect is dubbed prepersonal because it is the transpersonal stream of sensation (i.e., sense-*ability*) on which any meaningful moment (i.e., sens*ibility*) arrives. Put another way, it is that felt energy that creates a scene, punctuating matter into what matters.

To say that affect is an energetic stream is to insist on a force in motion even while speaking of "it" as a noun. As a verb, affect moves in a few ways. First, it touches and changes bodies, stirring them to feel, become, and do. To be affected, in this sense, is to *be moved*—flung into action and rest, propelled toward and away from objects, inclined to take up relative positions. Affect thus spurs, derails, and redirects effort and volition; it motivates the postures of practice, or activates modes of being through relating. Second, affect roams across space and time, skipping from one scene to another and leaving faint ties and traces in its wake. Finally, affect mutates along the way. Its currents constantly change in character (e.g., an atmosphere heavy with apprehension morphs into relief) and intensity (e.g., ebbing and flowing), never stationary even when mired (as in depression). In short, affect moves in that it *affects*, *travels*, and *modulates*. Equipped with this triple sense of "moving," we might abridge affect as *the moving flow of sensory force that animates worlds* and mark it as necessarily agentive, even synonymous with agency (e.g., Fox & Alldred, 2015). Affect *makes* a difference.

Resonance with our earlier premises is evident.[6] Affect highlights the sociomateriality of feeling, rejecting the division of social and material, specifically by treating the social *as* (another sort of) material. In affect theory, making sense is a matter of sensation that occurs through and upon matter of all kinds. As distilled earlier, sens*ibility* requires sense-*ability*. Words are hissed and purred, imprinted on page or screen, registered in the gut and with laughter or tears, indexed in physiological surges. Signs and symbols strike us through varied forms of physical display, interjecting narrative shards from elsewhere into the felt present. Interpretation and meaning transpire through sensate contact, that is, and the energy born of such encounter precedes and exceeds linguistic and cognitive sorting. Hence, the claim that affect is pre- and extra- discursive and ideational. In sum, affect is a *materially felt social relation*, a mode of sensing connections beyond sensemaking.

In fact, the very term "sense," like "matter," bears relational fruit. Affect theorists call on its multiple denotations—as tangible sensation detected through physical receptors, intuition or vague awareness, and precise meaning—to call out the sociomaterial practice of becoming through feeling, much as other relational ontologies invoke the dual meaning of "matter" to similar effect.

Further resonance resides in the claim to affect as the force that animates worlds, which highlights the emergence, indeterminacy, and multiplicity of sociomaterial relations. Affect theorists condense this notion with the term *worlding(s)*, which refers to concrete enactments of the real carved out by affective flow, or to the ongoing affective practice of world-making. As in other relational ontologies, worlding cannot be reduced to social constructions of *the* (independently existing) world. It emphatically entails the sociomaterial becoming, or performativity, of *worlds* in the plural. Producing social (dis)orders is a material practice that enlists all manner of human and nonhuman participants in *doing* the real, not just coming to know it, along certain lines. Like other versions of performativity reviewed here, worlding invariably slips and falls off course, as affective pathways are projected from one moment to the next, thereby altering the range of possibility. Worlding, in sum, is an *ontological practice*, a phrase telling of the flat and multiple ontologies at work in this approach.

With affect as its fuel, worlding also decenters human agency and subjectivity. Humans, conceived as a particular kind of sensing body, are among its participants, but they are not necessarily the pivotal characters. Nor do they own the rights to agency. Their *sense* of self, intent, and effort comes into contact with other bodies and forces that variously help, hinder, and deplete trajectories of action. Agency is therefore "strange, twisted, caught up in things, passive, or exhausted. Not the way we like to think about it. Not usually a simple projection toward a future . . . Circuits, bodies, moves, connections. It takes unpredictable and counterintuitive forms" (Stewart, 2007, p. 86). For many affect theorists, agency is more like a drunken stagger or an intoxicated dance. Creature will meets energy and matter, and their melding stumbles in the direction of potential achievement, but also toward disturbance, seduced by other shiny suitors.

As this view of agency suggests, affect theory does not treat humans as pre-bounded individual selves. For one thing, human bodies are vulnerable to the transpersonal flow, or *transmission*, of affect, which bumps up against their "own" affective histories in unruly ways and contributes to their ongoing social *and* physiological constitution (Brennan, 2004). Moreover, a crucial part of worlding is the production of boundaries among matter of various kinds. It is not that humans arrive on scene as self-contained individuals, ready to perform the leading role in making worlds out of stuff. Rather, staging "the human" as autonomous actor at the center of the universe, and "nonhuman stuff" as inert or passive objects of human intention, is *the* constitutive performance of modern Western worlding.

Putting Affect to "Work"

Although we later distinguish among strands of affect theorizing, for now we rely on Stewart's (2007) formulation of "ordinary affects" to illustrate the profound implications for scholarly analysis. Guided by the hybrid and multidirectional conception of agency developed earlier, the central task of affect theory is to *sense* the lines of possibility already evolving. As Stewart puts it, "It is not my view that things are going well but that they *are* going." She thus calls for "a speculative and concrete attunement" that is sensitive to "moving forces immanent in scenes, subjects, and encounters" and "takes off with the potential trajectories in which it finds itself in the middle" (p. 128, original emphasis).

But what, more precisely, might *attunement* entail? To cultivate its practice, Stewart (2007) reimagines "the ordinary" as the only site for staying in the middle of things, for resisting the urge to jump ahead or outside of the present. Here, the ordinary is not diminished as mere "micro" contrasted against the "macro" of magnificent structures. Instead, the ordinary is *the* lived contact point among potentialities arriving here-and-now from elsewhere. It is worth underscoring again the flat ontology operating here. "Structure" does not impose its will from lofty heights, nor does "cause" orchestrate the surface from hidden depths. Above and below are mythic sites of explanation. Rather, structure and cause arrive as energetic figures from other scenes of practice and bump into this one—or tiptoe, glide, thud, and so forth. Indeed, the *texture* of contact is the central question of attunement, and ordinary affects are what serve it up.

In keeping with the ordinary defined as encounter, *ordinary affects* are "a surging, a rubbing, a connection of some kind that has an impact" (Stewart, 2007, p. 128). Ordinary affect is sociomaterial sensation as it moves and matters in everyday life, transcending common binaries such as public and private, living and inanimate, human and nonhuman. Ordinary affect is not about intersubjectivity, "not about one person's feelings becoming another's but about bodies literally affecting one another and generating intensities: human bodies, discursive bodies, bodies of thought, bodies of water" (p. 128). Approached as ordinary affect, capitalism is not a monster that engulfs us from the outside, but energetic currents running through mundane practices (e.g., a shameful blush or ulcer of unemployment, the fleeting high of "retail therapy," avoiding eye contact with those who reek of need, feigned deference to managerial "mansplaining"). Put another way, capitalism is thoroughly sensate, an ongoing encounter that embroils bodies and objects in chronic banal performances of market relations. It is deeply, if sometimes numbly, *felt* in intricate vibrations—of precariousness, desire, attachment, distress, excess, shame, fatigue, and boredom, to name a few. Ordinary affects are what lend capitalism "the quality of a *some*thing to inhabit and animate" (Stewart, 2007, p. 15; emphasis in original).

The first task of attunement is to tune in to these energetic reverberations of practice and ride along where they might be going, instead of addressing capitalism as an abstract system or ideology to be pinned down for critical reflection. Stewart (2007, p. 4) describes the challenge as staying with/in the stream of sensation in order to "slow the quick jump to representational thinking and evaluative critique." Just as affect displaces intersubjectivity, so this analytical task of *sensing* cannot be conflated with the interpretive impulse to understand. Sensing does not reach clear meaning, and it forfeits the stable author who grasps (at) meaning through sequential acts of immersion and distance. The practice of attunement entails the descriptive translation of sensory becoming through *continued* immersion in its palpable yet also ambiguous and ambivalent unfolding. And the attuning author is a hybrid vessel (e.g., human flesh and consciousness, fused with theoretical texts and research instrumentation, now encountering *this* scene), sensing their relational becoming, and becoming undone, along with others, all *from within* the flow of affect.

Affective Politics

This is not to say that attunement eschews political claims or interventions. On the contrary, the politics of affect, and the affective character of politics, are of utmost concern to many affect theorists (e.g., Ahmed, 2014; Clough & Halley, 2007; Gregg & Seigworth, 2010; Massumi, 2015). However, power is a different sort of beast here (or not a beast at all), one that can only be known by *inhabiting* its ordinary operations. As Stewart (2007, p. 15) explains, "Politics starts in the animated inhabitation of things, not way downstream in the various dreamboats and horror shows that get moving." Power is "a thing of the senses" that "lives as a capacity, or a yearning, or a festering resentment" (p. 84). "Ideologies happen. Power snaps into place. Structures grow entrenched," she observes (p. 15). It is precisely this eventful quality that summons analytic attention. If power exists to the extent that it inhabits or is inhabited, if it is *effective* when *affective*, then concrete inhabitations of power demand even more notice than the deposits they send downriver (e.g., institutional racism). Yet such residue commands far more critical attention.

Two additional tasks of attunement follow recognition that worlding is a political as well as ontological practice. First, attunement involves not only sensing the texture of sociomaterial relations in bloom but also *discerning* promises and threats that flower within these relations, or "what potential modes of knowing, relating, and attending to things are already somehow present in them in a state of potentiality and resonance" (Stewart, 2007, p. 3). This provisional mode of critique is how affect theorists practice what we earlier called *ontological politics*: "Not a politics of *who* (who gets to speak; act; etc.) but a politics of *what* (what is the reality that takes shape and that various people come to live with?)" (Mol, 2014, n.p.; emphasis in original). Second, attunement entails *cultivating*, or nudging along, budding promises that glimmer beyond articulation. These flashes of possible futures "do not arise in order to be deciphered or decoded or delineated but, rather, must be nurtured . . . into lived practices of the everyday as perpetually finer-grained postures for collective inhabitation" (Seigworth & Gregg, 2010, p. 21).

All three tasks of attunement—sensing, discerning, and cultivating—can *only* proceed from within ordinary inhabitations. To be clear, there *are* no other grounds for critique or emancipatory intervention. The difference between promise and threat "is only found at the level of lived experience . . . can only be sensed and felt, and it is these sensations and feelings that actually create the conditions required for the expression of experience as alienating and estranging, or else releasing and escapist" (Wood & Brown, 2011, p. 520). For affect theorists, then, doing ontological politics is an inevitably sensual enterprise. Compared with previous approaches that hold out hope for a map of relational networks and narratives, affect theory is more like a tour guide who lives on the premises, content to point out—by way of inhabiting—the recalcitrant flow of "sense," and to gesture toward potentials that glimmer from other horizons.

Conclusion

This chapter has traced the contours of four lines of thought (performativity, posthumanist performativity/sociomateriality, ANT, and affect) on relationality that hold promise for thinking against the grain of the excesses organization studies has encountered in the wake of the linguistic turn. Throughout, we have avoided asserting that the linguistic turn was (is) misguided; indeed, its radical claims on conceptual and methodological fundaments have transformed the field in ways not only fruitful but also in ways that make the encounter with relationality outlined here a possibility.

Recall that our rationale for turning to these ontologically and episte-mologically distinctive lines of thought—perspectives that exert a toll on those who endeavor to understand, and operate from within, them—was grounded in the complexity, the messiness, the multiplicity of working, and the organizing on the terrain associated with contemporary capi-talism. Instead of suggesting that these perspectives, in their complex-ity, correspond with (or are a better match for) the messy "reality" of contemporary capitalism, our turn toward relationality was driven by a desire to generate novelty in the interrogative mode by which organiza-tion studies approaches working and organizing. Our elaboration of five (non-foundational) premises undergirding relational ontologies and our depictions of the four (somewhat overlapping) approaches presented ear-lier suggest several inventive points of entry into practices of work and organization.

Yet as we draw this discussion to a close, we sense opportunity amid this array of relational possibilities. Because each conception of relation-ality builds on the legacy of the linguistic turn to reconfigure the rela-tionship between the domains of the ideational/symbolic and material while simultaneously directing attention to the (precarious and ontologi-cally multiple) conduct of practice, we turn to theorizing that provides capacities to hone in on the phenomena involved in accomplishing those practices. In the next chapter, we pick up the threads of relationality and weave them together with theorizing that foregrounds communication, producing a hybrid we shall call "communicative relationality." Our pre-sentation of communicative thinking is not an effort to highlight pur-ported deficits in these relational ontologies, but is an effort to extend their empirical and explanatory reach.

An important trigger for our efforts to extend, or augment, these per-spectives is the criticism often directed at them. As mentioned earlier, Mutch (2013) faults the Barad/Orlikowski vision of agential realism for creating epistemological confusion in its refusal to articulate ontological distinctions between agency and structure. Others express concerns that one or another of these approaches is seen as a passing intellectual fancy (see discussions in Jarzabkowski & Pinch, 2013; Kuhn, 2011). Harman (2016), for instance, dismisses "new materialism" by suggesting that premises of the sort we introduced earlier are "usually advanced with an air of gallant novelty," but that "it is striking how mainstream they have become throughout the human sciences" (pp. 14–15). Though we might argue against his contention of the normalcy of these positions (and only wish we could strike the sort of intrepid and noble pose in his accusation), the larger point—as touched upon briefly earlier—is that scholars across disciplines who examine working and organizing are not interlopers or tourists; they are attracted to, but concurrently straining to grasp the implications of, relationality. Chapter 3 offers some tractable itineraries for their travels.

Notes

1. We use the notion of the linguistic turn here to capture related "turns" as well: The semiotic, discursive, interpretive, and cultural. Although each has placed emphasis on somewhat different elements, the family resemblance is strong enough to convince us to employ the term with the longest history and broadest recognition, if for no other reason than to reduce terminological proliferation.
2. This is not, of course, an exhaustive list. Left out of our review are the speculative realism (and associated object-oriented ontology) of Harman (2016; see also Shaviro, 2014) and the assemblage thinking of DeLanda (2016), among many others. Given our aim to contribute to the study of working and organizing, our selection of these four approaches was driven by the degree to which they have been appropriated in organization studies scholarship.
3. Though Austin never used the term performativity, performativity theorizing builds on his distinction between constative and performative utterances, which he later called into question. For Austin, constative utterances are those that can be rendered true or false (e.g., "You look pale" or "It's beautiful today!"); these are contrasted with performatives, which describe utterances by which an action is performed (e.g., promising, asking, apologizing, etc.). At some point, however, Austin himself realizes that constatives are, in fact, performatives to the extent that even saying, "You look pale" or "It's beautiful today" amounts to doing something: telling someone something. Performatives can be divided further: *locution* refers to the saying, to the ostensive referent of the utterance; *illocution* is about what was done in saying something; and *perlocution* refers to what happened as a result of the saying, even if that fails to align with the illocutionary intent. Illocutionary acts are those that bring about a particular state of affairs, as when a judge renders a decision in a court of law or a referee in sports makes a call; the illocutionary force of a speech act is the force with which the speech act is performed (compare, for instance, a suggestion vs. an order). Perloctionary acts, in contrast, depend on the effects produced on others, effects that characterize the relationship between parties in the stream of practice. Perlocutionary effects persuade, intimidate, call forth, induce anxiety, encourage a realization, or conjure up images; they are about the achievement of some state of reality regarding practice. Both illocution and perlocution, however, depend upon the presence of a framework of agencies and meanings that allow such utterances to produce effects (for more details, see Cooren, 2000).
4. Callon and Law (2005), following Franck Cochoy, refer to this calculation as *qualculation*, with the neologism denoting a way to address the notion that qualities are what are being calculated. The notion of qualculation implies that there exist some combination of human and nonhuman technologies and devices (including algorithms, components, intuition, rules, etc.) that combine to produce a semblance of value. And MacKenzie (2011, p. 1780) uses the term *evaluation* rather than valuation "because I want to encompass practices such as credit rating that contribute to knowledge of economic value but do not themselves generate a monetary valuation." The interest in economic performativity, in short, is in calculative *practices*, not in numbers.
5. The lack of a hyphen between "socio" and "material" is meant by Orlikowski to imply the sort of indissolubility of human and nonhuman, discursive and material, that we (via Barad) addressed earlier.
6. For a streamlined conception of affect theory and economic performativity, comparisons between them, and applications of both perspectives to social and organizational problems, see Ashcraft and Kuhn (in press). Our discussion of both perspectives in this chapter, as well as their relation to communication developed in Chapter 3, draws on this earlier work to reconceive agency through relationality.

3 Communicative Relationality

In Chapter 2, we presented four approaches to relationality, each of which bears implications for rethinking the character of working and organizing in contemporary capitalism. Each body of thought has generated its own brand of novel insights on organizational practice, and each has challenged orthodoxies marking organization studies scholarship. This chapter, in contrast, is less exhibition than contemplation. We explore here the possibility that paying extended attention to a process implicated in, but rarely explicated by, those relational ontologies can pay an empirical dividend. In other words, we are interested not in filling some onto-epistemological gap in those theories, but in extending, expanding, and augmenting those views' conceptual reach. We shall refer to the set of possibilities developed here as *communicative relationality*.

To do so, we first consider conceptions of communication in the field devoted to theorizing it. Like any vibrant discipline, communication studies evinces varied, and often conflicting, conceptions of its central figure (Shepherd, St. John, & Striphas, 2006), in no small part because "communication" has been marshaled to meet numerous disparate social aims over time (Peters, 1999). This chapter outlines three versions of communication and explores the capacity of each to contribute to, or refine, the relational ontologies introduced in the preceding chapter—and, in so doing, to generate insight into working and organizing. Before that, however, we provide a brief overview of the typical enactments of communication in studies of work and organization.

Transcending Traditional Conceptions of Meaning and Communication

Communication scholars are fond of posing two contrasting visions of their object of interest. They typically start with a version of communication intended as a foil against which they present an alternative—and, typically, they contrast a *transmission* view with a *dialogic* approach (e.g., McDaniel, Kuhn, & Deetz, 2008). A transmission view, first, is historically associated with Shannon and Weaver's (1949) mathematical theory of communication.

DOI: 10.4324/9781315680705-3

Their model sought to increase both the expeditious throughput of signals through a system and the accurate duplication of messages. Shannon and Weaver's vision of communication was a manifestation of information theory, which concerns how information—understood as the elimination of uncertainty—is transmitted, received, and processed.

Information theory portrays communication as the act of conveying messages between interactants (individuals or collectives), assuming that the symbols they choose are straightforward representations of these actors' intentions. Meanings reside in the messages exchanged by persons, and communication can be said to occur when message-sending and -receiving behavior occurs. Communication, in this perspective, becomes a metaphorical *conduit* through which runs messages and influence (Reddy, 1979). When communication is seen as a conduit, important concerns become the channel and the code selected for transmission, the presence of noise affecting message exchange, and whether message redundancy is needed for successful transmission (Schramm, 1954).

Some version of this has long been the most common conception of communication in both organization studies theorizing and the popular consciousness (Axley, 1984, 1996). Although it can serve many ends, contemporary communication scholars tend to highlight the transmission approach's limited ability to address the generation of meaning in interaction, its assertion that persons are the fount of meaning (and that they *insert* their meanings into symbols that *represent* their intentions), for its simplistic conception of agency, and its disregard for ambiguity.

The alternate path typically presented by communication scholars is some version of a dialogic model of communication, where communication is the symbolic *process* (rather than an *act*) in and through which meaning emerges. Rooted in the linguistic turn presented in the preceding chapter, a dialogic view sees communication as the co-construction and negotiation of meanings and subjectivities. Neither symbols nor persons possess meanings; meanings are emergent (and ongoing) products of sociohistorical-situated interactions that link to one another across space and time.

Where the transmission view sees persons as unproblematic sources of communication who encode pre-existing meanings into symbols, a dialogic view tends to examine how social subjects interpret, produce, and participate in a meaningful world. Communication, then, is not merely about interpersonal interactions; it is just as much a social institution that carries with it "historically developed dimensions of interests, the lines along which things will be distinguished" (Deetz, 1992, p. 130). The subjectivities that appear independent are, rather, yoked to social domain because all communication, all participation in practice, is shaped by a system of linguistic distinctions that precedes, and is activated by, language use.

Such a vision of communication has, especially among scholars of communication, led to increased claims about the centrality of communication for studying organizations and organizing. This line of thought uses, as its point of departure, the claim that communication is *constitutive of* social realities. In an earlier piece, we suggested that this view defines communication as *"the ongoing, dynamic, interactive process of manipulating symbols toward the creation, maintenance, destruction, and/or transformation of meanings, which are axial—not peripheral—to organizational existence and organizing phenomena"* (Ashcraft et al., 2009, p. 22; emphasis in original). Yet, as we argued then, the assertion of meaning's centrality, and the focus on symbolism, has the potential to render the material and ideational character of communication ontologically distinct—the remediation of which is the project of the relational ontologies presented in the preceding chapter.

Accordingly, in that earlier article we nominated an alternative conception of communication: "the ongoing, situated, and embodied process whereby human and non-human agencies interpenetrate ideation and materiality toward meanings that are tangible and axial to organizational existence and organizing phenomena" (Ashcraft et al., 2009, p. 34; emphasis in original.) This definition has the advantage of signaling the irreducible and simultaneous symbolic/material character of communication. It suggests that communication constitutes working and organizing by bringing together a multiplicity of agencies in the production of meanings that generate and sustain processes of coordination and control.

This second definition is clearly more compatible with the relational ontologies from the previous chapter. Yet, in its abstractness, this definition leaves open important questions about how, specifically, communication can be understood to be the constitutive force for which that definition argues. Just *how* communication theory can extend the reach of relationality, therefore, requires attention; that is the task of this chapter.

Version 1: Communication as Relating/Linking/Connecting

The first conception of communication we propose amounts to going beyond the classical opposition between the transmission view, traditionally represented by media, management, and information theorists, and the dialogical view of communication, advocated by interpretivists, conversation analysts, and social constructionists (Peters, 1999). From the transmission view, we retain the notion that communication *always* has a material dimension, which means that it can refer not only to people conversing with each other but also to machines interacting through a network, or forces being transferred from one body to another. From interpretivists, conversation analysts, and social constructionists, we retain the notion that communication is, however, also a matter of *co-construction* where the identity of who or what communicates to (or with) whom or what can be constantly problematized, not only by the analysts but also by the interactants themselves.

Communication as Materializing Relations/Links/Connections

According to this first version we propose, communication thus refers to any phenomenon by which a first entity gets *related/linked/connected* to a second entity through a third entity that will produce, perform and "materialize" this relation/link/connection (Cooren, Bencherki, Chaput, & Vasquez, 2015). This also means that the notion of communication is, as we will see, intimately associated with the notions of relation, link, or connection. When two rooms communicate, it means that a *connection* is established/materialized between them through the existence of a doorway, for instance. The doorway is therefore the way by which this link is made possible, a link that, for instance, allows people to walk from one room to another.

Similarly, when two people—let us call them Kathy and Paul—communicate, it means that they exchange, for instance, looks and words that will define, materialize, establish, for another next first time (Garfinkel, 2002), the relation they find themselves in (Heritage, 1984; Watzlawick, Bavelas, & Jackson, 1967). For instance, Kathy, who happens to be Paul's boss, can ask the latter to retrieve information she needs, a request to which Paul can respond favorably by saying, "Yes, no problem" and fetching the piece of information Kathy asked for. In this example, we see that Paul is *linked* or *related* to Kathy not only through the *request* she made *to* him but also through the *acceptance* voiced by Paul, an acceptance that marks his intention to do what she requested him to do.

If Paul manages to retrieve the information requested and gives it to Kathy, she might thank him, which, among other things, functions as a way to close this episode. Although Paul is still connected/linked/related to Kathy through his task description—a task description that specifies, for instance, that he is expected to respond to his boss, who happens to be Kathy in this case—the closing of this episode also shows that links can not only be communicatively *established* but also communicatively *concluded* (Schegloff & Sacks, 1973). Regarding this specific task, which consisted of fetching information for Kathy, he is not interactively linked to her anymore, except of course if Kathy realizes that this is not the information she actually asked for.

As we see through these illustrations, some links, relations, or connections can be relatively episodic and evanescent—this is, for instance, what happens in the fetching information episode between Kathy and Paul—while others appear more long lasting and enduring. This is not only the case of the supervisor/subordinate relationship that at least partly defines/materializes how Kathy and Paul are linked or related to each other but also the case of the doorway that allows the two rooms to communicate with each other. One thing is, however, crucial to understand these links/relations/connections, whatever their level of duration or evanescence: *they (the links/relations/connections) have to materialize themselves somewhere somehow* in various acts of communication (Ashcraft et al., 2009).

This material dimension will be essential in our demonstration as it allows us to depart from traditional views of communication. Communication, in order to take place, has, by definition, to be embodied in something or someone: *through* the request that Kathy made to Paul, *through* the acknowledgment of this request by Paul, *through* the information Paul consequently communicated to Kathy, *through* the thanks Kathy expressed to Paul at the end of this episode. A request, an acknowledgment, a piece of information and marks of appreciation have to be voiced and expressed, which means that they have to somehow *materialize themselves*, in order for communication to take place.

However, this logic also works for more durable forms of link or relation. If Paul feels that he has to do what Kathy is asking him to do—i.e., fetching the information she needs—it is, among other things, because he signed a contract with the company they are both working for. This contract (and the act of affixing a signature) is understood to *stipulate*, for instance, that he has to comply with his task description, a task description that *indicates* that one of his responsibilities is precisely to *respond to* his supervisor, who happens to be Kathy in this case. This might feel like a long analytical detour to talk about something that looks, at first sight, relatively straightforward: Paul simply doing his job. However, behind this straightforwardness lies another key aspect of our position The fact that what more durably relates/ links/connects Paul to Kathy is another (past) act of communication—the signing of a contract—that appears to be still *effective* in this situation (simply because both Paul and Kathy *know* this is the case).

But of course, some element of Paul's relationship with Kathy could supersede the contract that was signed. For instance, his loyalty to Kathy or his fear to displease her or the company he is working for could lead him to do things exceeding what the contract stipulates. In this new economy, we know all too well how high expectations can be subtly or not-so-subtly cultivated in a company to enjoin employees—gig workers, especially, but not only—to go beyond what they are legally required to do: working extra hours, responding to emails from home, doing work that does not correspond with their task description, etc. From a relational viewpoint, this means that things such as *expectations* can be said to also *matter* to the extent that they lead employees such as Paul to normalize a work situation that could legally be considered unacceptable.

From a relational perspective, things as seemingly abstract as expectations can thus *make a difference* to the extent that they *materialize themselves* in how Kathy never hesitates to ask Paul to work extra hours, but also in how Paul himself decides, consciously or not, to play this game. Expectations thus matter or count precisely because they *materialize* in people's practice—that is, they express themselves in what they do or do not do. If Paul can be said to be linked to the company by a contract, he is also linked to it by specific expectations that can be consequential in the way he works and conceive of his work.

By insisting on the *materiality of communication*, we also realize that *what* links, connects, or relates beings—here, Kathy and Paul—always demonstrates a form of *performativity*—that is, *it is doing something* (Cooren, 2004, 2008, 2009). The contract, which has been signed some time ago by Paul and a representative of the company, technically *compels* or *enjoins* Paul to do what Kathy is asking him to do, as long as it appears to fit with his task description. Of course, what this document enjoins Paul to do is always open to interpretation (legal or otherwise), but interpreting would then consist, by definition, of *stating what this document stipulates.*

In other words, even if there could be some disagreement about what a contract or task description stipulates, the core of this dispute will always be about *what the document says, dictates or stipulates* (Ashcraft et al., 2009). As we see in this illustration, another interesting thing happens when we study communication: we realize that *people are not the only ones doing things when they communicate with each other* (Cooren, 2010; Kuhn, 2008). They also talk on behalf of/in the name/for other beings that can also make a difference—i.e., display a form of *agency*—in a given situation (Latour, 2005). For instance, talking about what a contract or task description says or stipulates amounts to implicitly positioning oneself as the *medium/intermediary/voice* by which this contract might make a difference in a given situation.

The same logic applies, of course, for expectations. Employees and managers are going to implicitly or explicitly express or convey expectations in their requests, actions, and evaluations, which means that these members can then be considered the media/intermediaries/voices by which these expectations might make a difference in the way things work in this company. Studying the materiality of communication thus enjoins us to acknowledge that human beings should also be considered *media* or *phonation devices* (Latour, 2004) through which other beings express themselves in a given situation (Cooren, 2015).

These beings—whether they are contracts, policies, statuses, protocols, groups, organizations, ideologies, preoccupations, expectations, interests, emotions, facts, etc.—can participate in the definition of the situation precisely because they can make a difference in the way communication unfolds. Communication, as we alluded to at the beginning of this chapter, is therefore not *only* about people talking or writing to each other, it is *also*, more generally, about links/connections/relations being established between various beings, whatever their ontological status might look like.

Communication, Mattering, and Possession

Communication should therefore be conceived as a *relational practice*—that is, a *practice by which various beings relate to each other through other beings* that or who act as their intermediaries/voices/media/ representatives. In keeping with the sociomaterial turn advocated by Orlikowski

(2007) and Orlikowski and Scott (2008, 2014), we thus see that what *relates* various being to each other—which is what we usually mean by *sociality* (Martine & Cooren, 2016)—always has to *materialize* itself in something or someone. Conversely, what *materializes* itself in a given interaction always is what *relates* various beings to each other (Barad, 2007).

When a preoccupation *speaks to* another preoccupation, it is, for instance, because two people are not only voicing them at a specific point in a given discussion but also managing to find ways to articulate, link, or relate them with each other. In this specific case, these two preoccupations not only *materialize* themselves in a given discussion but also appear to find ways to *relate to, connect to,* or *meet* each other.

Studying the detail of conversations thus often amounts to identifying how these links/relations/connections manage to establish themselves or not. A dialogue of the deaf will consist of two or more parties incapable of finding a passage point (Callon, 1986) through which their respective preoccupations will meet, connect, or respond to each other, which is another way to say that the parts of the world to which they are attached will not manage to articulate themselves. As we see, communication is a lot more than people simply talking to each other; it is also the way by which matters of concerns, expectations, or interests will or will not manage to relate to each other.

If, let's say, environmentalists are talking to oil company representatives, chances are that both parties will talk *on behalf of/in the name/for* their respective interests or preoccupations. For environmentalists, these preoccupations or concerns will likely be the state of ecosystems, while for oil company representatives, it will likely be their capacity to drill wherever they deem profitable to do so. This means that something such as the interest of an ecosystem can thus manage to *materialize* itself in this discussion through what the environmentalists will say on its behalf. Conversely, something such as an oil exploration project will also manage to *materialize itself* through what the company representatives will say on its behalf.

In related fashion, something or someone has to be connected, related, or linked to other beings in order to exist and be what it/she/he *is*. A person, for instance, exists because she *has* a body, organs, genes, attitudes, fears, desires, emotions, but also identities, reputations, and statuses that all materialize her existence. All these attributes, traits, or properties that she is said to have are, by definition, the expression of *relations* that connect this person to what is supposed to materialize what she is or looks like (DeLanda, 2011). This is what Latour (2013) calls "being-as-other," that is, what *someone or something is has to be connected to other beings in order to be what it/she/he is.* Being, in other words, is always already relational.

Any quality/trait/feature/characteristic should, therefore, be understood as the expression of a relation. This is why any relation always expresses itself through a form of *possession, ownership,* or *attribution.* For instance, we *have* enemies, friends, colleagues, parents, readers, and we also *have* genes, organs, attitudes, passions, identities, statuses and reputations (Bencherki, 2012; Bencherki & Cooren, 2011; Tarde, 1895/2012). This point is crucial in this argument as we see that what appears to be *proper* (as in "property") to someone or something is, to some extent, also always already *improper* (Derrida, 1993), precisely because the property always expresses/materializes itself through a relation, a link or a connection with something or someone else.

Something such as a reputation, for instance, can be considered proper to a specific person, but this reputation is, by definition, also the product of attributions cultivated by others based on past experiences/relationships/encounters they possibly had with this person. In other words, if this reputation was absolutely proper to this person (i.e., solely the person's possession), it could not, by definition, exist, as even the words to speak about it could not be used to talk about other people, which cannot be the case. Similarly, an attitude, preoccupation, or passion is, by definition, always *related* to what constitutes the object of this attitude, preoccupation, or passion, which means that the latter, in order to exist and be identified, has to be connected to something or someone else.

Similarly, what is considered proper or appropriate to specific situations, contexts, or environments will always express itself *through* specific media or intermediaries, whether the latter are people or other means of communication (codes of conduct, signs, etc.). From a normative viewpoint, what is considered appropriate or proper to specific situations—expectations, for instance—thus also follows the same logic of inappropriateness or improperness: it will always be relative to *what* or *who* expresses it, which means that it will, from its outset, be never *absolutely* proper or appropriate.

The world in which we evolve is therefore a world made of relations, links, or connections, which is why communication is so central to understand how it works. As we know, even someone who does not want to communicate paradoxically signals that he or she does not want to interact with others (Watzlawick et al., 1967), an attitude that might participate in the establishment of his or her reputation, a reputation that might precede him or her wherever he or she happens to go. Thinking the world relationally and communicatively, which is something we are not used to, thus forces us, as we see, to rethink how we conceive of the world we live in.

Pragmatism and Semiotics in Materialization

William James (1912/1976), the famous pragmatist, had perfectly understood this when he noticed that "the relations that connect experiences must themselves be experienced relations, and any kind of relation experienced must be accounted as 'real' as anything else in the system" (p. 22). In other words, a relation always is *something* or *someone*; that is, it has, by definition, to be embodied or materialized in something that or someone who establishes that relation. We never leave the *terra firma* of interaction (Cooren, 2006)—that is, *any connection, in order to be what it is, has to be performed and materialized in one way or another.*

It is not by chance that Charles Sanders Peirce (1991) is considered both the founder of semiotics and pragmatism, as both approaches precisely insist on the relational nature of our world (Misak, 2013). A sign, which is what semiotics is supposed to study, always is an entity—let us call it C— by which an entity A makes itself *present* to another entity B—that is, how it communicates its existence (past or present). For instance, a photograph (C) will allow people (B) to see what someone (A) looks or looked like, a relation that Peirce identifies as *iconicity*—that is, a connection based on a relation of *resemblance* (which is precisely what photography is supposed to express, even if, of course, manipulations can be made, as we all know too well). This photograph therefore is the being through which this person will be made present, make herself present, or be *presentified* (Benoit-Barné & Cooren, 2009; Cooren, 2006, 2015; Cooren, Brummans, & Charrieras, 2008; Nicotera, 2013) to whoever happens to look at it.

Similarly, a footprint (C) will allow people (B) to notice that someone (A) passed by, a relation that Peirce (1991) identifies as *indexicality*—that is, a connection based on a relation of *causality*, as it is possibly the passage of a person in a specific trail that causally left this footprint where it happens to be now (it could be a lure, as signs can, of course, be deceiving). This footprint is therefore the sign by which someone's passage is made present, makes itself present, or is being *presentified* to observers. By leaving a footprint behind her, this person thus unwillingly *communicates* her past presence along a specific trail. This footprint thus constitutes the relation by which this person's passage and past presence is communicated to others.

Finally, a word such as "contracts" (C) for instance, will allow beings called as such (A) to *make themselves present* to people (B) who speak or read English and know/learned what the term "contract" means, whether these people are hearing it in a conversation or reading a fiction or organizational document where this term appears. Peirce calls this type of relation *symbolic*, as it is based on a *conventional* relationship between A and B (only people who happen to speak English can indeed know and recognize what this specific word is supposed to refer to). By saying, "Could you give me the contracts please?" someone is indexically referring to something called "the contracts" that symbolically *make themselves present* to her interlocutor through this specific request.

Here, we allude to something absolutely essential to semiotics, but that is often not even problematized even by semioticians themselves (Nöth, 1995), which is that signs—whether they are iconic, indexical, or symbolic—are, by definition, *media, means,* or *intermediaries* through which various aspects of the world communicate, make themselves present, or relate to us. For instance, having pictures of our loved ones on our desk is a way by which these people *make themselves present to us*—that is, the way they presentify themselves to us at work. In other words, pictures are supposed to *make a difference*—i.e., they do something—to the extent that, among other things, they literally transport our loved ones to our office, possibly enlightening the routines of our daily work.

Similarly, stock market indexes such as the Dow Jones or the NASDAQ composite, for instance, are the *media, means* or *intermediaries* through which values of sections of given stock markets will express/materialize themselves to potential investors and observers. If these indexes are supposed to give, more generally, a *picture* of the stock market in its globality at a given point in time (which means that there is an iconic component), they are also the expression of a form of indexicality—that is, a type of *causality* between the data collected and the result of the calculations that are made to come up with these indexes (usually weighted averages). Indexes are therefore *telling us things* about other beings they are supposed to represent or presentify—i.e., make present.

Finally, the words that we pronounce, the utterances we produce, the conversations in which we engage can all be considered media, means, or intermediaries through which various aspects of the world conventionally express/materialize/embody themselves (Cooren, 2010). As already pointed out, when environmentalists are talking about ecosystems in a meeting, they are not only referring to their matters of concern but also *making them and the latter's interests present* to their interlocutors (Fairhurst & Cooren, 2009; Perelman, 1982, Perelman & Olbrechts-Tyteca, 1969). The conversational world should therefore not be considered separate from the world in which it emerges. *It is part of this world—that is, it allows this world to express/materialize/embody itself in a specific way.*

Concretely speaking, and this is something that Peirce's (1991) semiotics helps us understand, the world that we are part of should not be considered mute or voiceless, as it literally and figuratively expresses itself iconically, indexically, and symbolically through various phonation devices (Latour, 2004), whether we are speaking of figures, indexes, graphs, numbers, testimonies, reports, conversations, photographs, etc. As mentioned earlier, the relational ontology we propose thus invites us to acknowledge that human beings are not the only ones who say things, but that other beings say things too in various situations (Cooren, 2008).

Invoking a protocol in a meeting is, for instance, a way to *make it say something*, a move that might sometimes be quite consequential in the way a discussion evolves (Cooren, 2010). As we also know, *making numbers speak* is, often times, a very powerful way to convince people about the financial state of a project or organization (Fauré, Brummans, Giroux, & Taylor, 2010). Finally, showing pictures to an audience can be extremely effective to suggest how a situation should be read and understood—i.e., what the situation *dictates* (just think of Colin Powell's 2003 United Nations speech and his PowerPoint presentation showing photographs of sites of weapons of mass destruction).

But what is crucial in this semiotic explanation is to realize that *media never are media in and by themselves*, a position that we also find in media studies, especially Kittler's (1999, 2010) work (see also Griffin, 1996; Winthrop Young, 2011). In other words, the terms "media" and "medium" should themselves always be understood *relationally*. For instance, if someone starts to position herself or is positioned as speaking *in the name of* an organization, she will be, by definition, the medium through which this organization will supposedly express itself at this point in time and space. In other words, she will be the intermediary C through which an A (the organization) will manage to communicate with a B (whoever is listening to this person; a whoever who could also represent a whatever), knowing that this activity of mediation could be, of course, momentary and contested.

At another point, she could start speaking as a friend, a mother, an American, a professional, a member of a specific community—that is, she could position herself, or be positioned as, speaking or acting as someone other than the mouthpiece of her organization. Although our position of medium, intermediary, or even sign constitutes an *intractable* aspect of our existence, we see that this work of positioning can vary depending on the interactions we engage in. In other words, communication is consequential (Sigman, 1995) precisely because *it is always eventful*.

What semiotics finally teaches us is that being positioned or positioning oneself as a medium, intermediary, or sign does not mean that one is not doing anything. In other words, *expressing/materializing/conveying the existence of something or someone else is a contribution/action/performance in itself*. This first conception, then, presents communication as a relation/link/connection between A and B, which always has to be *performed* by a third party, C. Whether we are talking about a channel through which information will be transmitted from one point to another (Shannon & Weaver, 1949), a picture that will tell us how a person used to look 30 years ago (Barthes, 1981), a stock exchange index that warns us about the current state of the market (Latour, 2005), or a press release that shows us how an organization will position itself within the next few years (Cooren, 2010), we see that all these so-called intermediaries are, in fact, consequential and *doing something*.

Studying working and organizing from this relational perspective thus invites us to acknowledge both their eventful and iterative aspects. Eventful because any relation has to be performed for another next first time, as Garfinkel (1967, 2002) would say. Iterative because this performance, in order to be recognized (by the analysts or the participants), has, by definition, also to be envisaged as an iteration, reproduction, or repetition. This also means that we can then follow not only how organizational members implicitly or explicitly stage, invoke, or enact various things or beings—predispositions, documents, principles, absent persons, etc.—in their interaction or work but also how these very beings and things manage to *represent themselves* in interaction.

A relational ontology augmented by communication (as relating/linking/connecting) thus allows us to follow, longitudinally, the evolution of various beings and things throughout interactions (an illustration will be given in

Chapter 4). Since everything or everyone is potentially a medium—an inter-mediary by which or whom other beings or things express themselves—it becomes possible to empirically identify how the latter make themselves present in various situations. Studying working and organizing from this perspective therefore amounts to not only analyzing the details of local interactions but also acknowledging what constantly dislocates them, con-necting them with other interactions throughout space and time.

Version 2: Communication as Writing the Trajectory of Practice

A second conception of communication builds on the picture painted by the-orists of economic performativity (e.g., Callon) presented in the preceding chapter in which an *agencement*—as both verb and noun simultaneously—is the site from and through which conjunctions of agencies become config-ured into (what is considered to be) *an* agent. The economic performativity literature pays scant attention, however, to the processes by which agen-cies are configured, or brought together, to produce the conditions by which action unfolds. Moreover, as Ingold (2008) argues, network-based relational ontologies such as economic performativity direct attention to relations between entities/participants, but those relations are rendered transparent, never recognized as having a material presence. We suggest that communication offers not merely a route to address these omissions, but holds the potential to expand performativity theorizing.

To begin this expansion, recall Butler's (2010) argument about Callon's portrayal of performativity described in the preceding chapter. She charged that Callon's theory papers over messy contingencies, like those we suggested are endemic to working and organizing under con-temporary capitalism. She charged that Callon and his fellow travelers work with a limiting conception of performativity, one that is interested in the bringing together of elements into an assemblage (or *agencement*), but one which renders conflicts and contradictions *outside* performative acts. Butler argued, in contrast, that the site of the political, and of the possibility of change, must be located *inside* the performative act itself.

We turn to a conception of communication that, we argue, can (a) address the configuration of *agencements* with an attention to the formation of links and connections between agencies, and (b) enables an analysis of the "seams and fissures" (Butler, 2010, p. 149) characterizing performativity. A conception of communication capable of contributing to performativity would also (c) recognize that communication generates *both* similarities and differences among the agencies participating in a practice; it would thus lend itself to accounts of both configurations and disjunctures in an *agencement*. Moreover, if communication can be said to constitute reali-ties that influence practices in other spaces and times, its contribution to economic performativity theorizing must also (d) connect the practice with the broader matrix of practices associated with contemporary capitalism.

Infusing Economic Performativity With Articulation Theorizing

We start this exploration by drawing on articulation theorizing, a body of work typically associated with Ernesto Laclau (as well as Stuart Hall). This might seem an odd move, or at least a detour from the relational line of argument in the preceding chapter, given articulation theory's frequent association with discourse theorizing and cultural studies. If this seems a violation of the foundational assumptions of performativity theorizing, recall that Callon himself effected a similar tension in borrowing the concept of *agencement* from Deleuze and Guattari and then developing it in an ANT frame (see Cochoy, 2014). Nevertheless, our aim here is neither to resolve conceptual tensions nor to engage in arguments regarding conceptual purity, rather it is to present a communicative stance on how elements in a socioeconomic scene become configured—a stance that can expand economic performativity's analytical purchase on working and organizing.

Because we are interested in the multiple and shifting contingencies marking contemporary capitalism, and because we seek a perspective that can explain the (temporary and contested) emergence of meaning from a given practice, seeing communication as articulation is a useful supplement to performativity thinking. Specifically, we see two contributions offered by this line of thought. First, Laclau encourages a careful consideration of the character of the links among elements marking a social practice. His term for this process is *articulation*, which is the fixing of signs' meanings by placing them in (contingent and non-predetermined) relation to one another. Slack (1989) describes the propositions of articulation:

> (a) Connections among the elements are specific, particular, and nonnecessary—they are forged and broken in particular concrete circumstances; (b) articulations vary in their tenacity; (c) articulations vary in their relative power within different social configurations; and (d) different articulations empower different possibilities and practices.
> (p. 331)

Articulations, then, are connections that capitalize on the multiplicity of signs' potential meanings (their polysemy). They temporarily and partially fix meaning around *nodal points*, privileged signs in relation to which other signs derive meaning (Laclau & Mouffe, 1985). Theorists of performativity recognize that any given element is connected to other elements in intimate, complex, contingent, and constitutive ways (e.g., Cochoy, 2014); articulation theorizing additionally recommends that these connections be understood as sites of simultaneous contradiction and possibility.

A second contribution comes from Laclau's argument that those articulations both create, and are influenced by, a *totality* that fixes, stabilizes, and guides meaning (again, only temporarily and partially). However, the totality is not an overarching structure imposing itself on practice, but a relational complex, a conjuncture of agencies, through which practice is generated. Although some critics insist that positing totality necessitates "structural integration as the precondition of signification" (Kaplan, 2010, p. 255), Laclau denies the existence, or conceptual necessity, of any pre-existing (or external) foundation driving communication (Cederström & Spicer, 2014). Indeed, articulation theory operates in an *anti-foundational* manner: There are no ontologically prior structures or mechanisms directing practice: "Elements do not pre-exist the relational complex but are constituted through it" (Laclau, 2005, p. 68).

The relational complex, the totality, is not totalizing. For Laclau (who draws upon Althusser's notion of *overdetermination* in this regard), the relational complex is rife with contestation, contingency, and contradiction. Every nodal point, every agency participating in a practice, is the site of multiple and conflicting relations—relations that are always contingent and antagonistic, and which respond to something rendered "outside" the practice. These contradictory relations are not merely present for a given element, however; they are characteristic of the larger relational complex in which those elements participate.

Performativity-based analyses of working and organizing, then, would be unsatisfactory if they restricted themselves to examining how particular elements (e.g., subjects, artifacts, discursive resources) are positioned by discourses; the articulation theory claim is that it is also necessary to chart how a depiction of, or narrative about, the practice emerges and how that narrative itself is shot through with contradictions and contestations. This conception of narrative is not about human sensemaking through story-telling, but is instead a logic regarding, or account of, the practice and its trajectory that is useful in stitching together the relational complex.

Communication, then, is the process of bringing *agencement* into being by articulating meaningful relationships between elements that realize a practice and guide its trajectory. The logic of practice developed and deployed in communication is a site of agency, because agency is always "bound up with the idea of a trajectory, a directionality or movement away from somewhere, even if the toward-which it moves is obscure or even absent" (Bennett, 2010, p. 32; emphasis in original). Yet, as articulation theorizing instructs, the trajectory of practice is also the site of contestation and contradiction; it must not be assumed to be unitary or monolithic.

Contributions of a Communicative Extension

Considered as an extension of Callon's version of economic performativity, this (rather partial and selective) appropriation of two components of Laclau's thinking is useful in terms of how we might theorize the assemblage of elements configured together in a practice. Accepting the tenets of articulation requires descriptions of *how* relations are made and, in so doing, it encourages analysts to highlight meaning not as the contents of individual minds, but as the logics characterizing the always-shifting relational complex.

Our extension suggests that analyses of *agencement* should acknowledge that the conjuncture of elements "is never 'sewn up,' or an absolutely fixed unity, but a web of articulating, dynamic movements among variously homogeneous and heterogeneous forces and relations. . . . articulation is an ongoing process of disconnecting, reconnecting, and contradicting movements" (Slack, 2006, p. 226). In this sense, the meeting of articulation and *agencement* might be better understood as *reticulation*, the constitution of a network of agencies; questions can thus be posed about the proximity or distance between nodes, the strength and density or weakness and sparsity of connections, and the accentuation or interference engendered by relations. Key analytical aims, therefore, are to display the communicative work required to materialize the nodal points in that network, and to sustain any semblance of coherence, or stability, in a practice.

Drawing upon articulation theorizing enables economic performativity to respond to Butler's (2010) claim that the theory, as presently formulated, pays scant attention to the complexity, messiness, and contingency marking performances. For Butler, performativity is about both organization and *dis*organization, about doing and undoing simultaneously (Riach, Rumens, & Tyler, 2016), about the continual production of possibilities for dislocations in which new relational arrangements are possible (Holmer Nadesan, 1996). Additionally, the attention to conflict and contradiction would complicate analyses of authority in organizing, showing that the influence of elements such as persons or economic theories need to be understood as bound up in struggles for control over the narrative characterizing a complex set of relations. If economic performativity theorizing aims to "trace relationships of domination as they are dynamically established" (Çalişkan & Callon, 2010, p. 9), then both the identification of a logic of a practice and the analysis of the activity required to maintain its articulations are necessary.

Communication, then, refers to the creation of meanings that configure a temporary and contingent arrangement of agencies in the pursuit of materially embedded practices. Although articulation theory is not typically associated with the drive to transcend discursive-material divides in the terms described in the preceding chapter, the perspective provides a platform from which to grasp *mattering* in economic performativity. We come to see that human and nonhuman elements come to matter in the production of a practice not independently but because they are connected with other elements at nodal points, where they (temporarily and partially) fix meanings. Meaning is the mattering of the manifold articulated agencies comprising an *agencement*, always located within practice. And, perhaps more to the point, each node in the *agencement* is always already relational in that it materializes a conjunction between a host of participants, each of which is also hybrid, that are made to matter in articulating the node as meaningful in conduct of the practice.

To reiterate, in this version of communication we are not proposing a theoretical melding of articulation theory with Callon's thinking on performativity. We see the former as providing two inspirations for the latter, and we offered those to expand economic performativity's analytical reach. A communicatively reformed economic performativity would, accordingly, insist upon analyses of the struggles over meaning's emergence at particular nodal points—a struggle summoning discursive and nondiscursive agencies alike. In doing so, it would acknowledge conflicts and contradictions marking an *agencement's* logic of practice. It would urge analysts to ask how conjunctions of participants—each of which can be understood as a sociomaterial hybrid—establish particular relations and sketch the contours of an agentic network, and how overdetermination provides the potential for revised relations. It would call for analyses of how a given logic of practice emerges from a network and, at the same time, infuses (and potentially disrupts) other seemingly distant and disparate practices.

Illustrating the Extension

To demonstrate the novelty-generating potential of this communicative amendment to economic performativity theorizing in the context of working and organizing, we return to the issue of flexible employee scheduling (also known as "just-in-time" or algorithmic scheduling) in the retail and service sector presented in Chapter 1. We presented the putative flexibility as a social problem in that the practice highlights the unequal control over relations of employment between managers and staff, as well as between service and professional workers. This practice heightens precarity, strengthens surveillance, and inhibits employees' collective voice (Lambert, Haley-Lock, & Henly, 2012; Sewell & Wilkinson, 1992; Wood, 2016). Our communicative extension to performativity theorizing would begin by enumerating the elements participating in the practice (acknowledging that the identification of distinct elements is a contestable choice, as in Barad's conception of ontological cuts), along with discussing the connections between elements.

How, then, does such an analysis proceed? A first step is to understand the array of agencies, or elements, comprising the *agencement*. A useful question to guide this step is about the multiple and heterogeneous elements that enable a focal agency to materialize, to matter. In the case we are considering here, the practice of flexible employee scheduling can be understood as enabled not only by technological advancements but also by existing relations of authority and obligation marking retail organizing, by labor laws, by a widespread valorization of "just-in-time" techniques in manufacturing and operations management, by a system where frontline shift workers are remunerated with hourly wages rather than salaries (workers who contrast with the salaried managers and executives of these enterprises), by a belief in the interchangeability of workers, by the unpredictability of workers' responsibilities beyond the workplace (e.g., child care, which falls primarily on the shoulders of women), by the absence of health insurance provided through retail work (at least in a U.S. context), and by an extensive acceptance of a precarious and contingent workforce.

In this workforce, unionization is rare, and when employees are scheduled at the last minute or when a shift is cut short, there often is little recourse for contesting the decision (Kantor, 2014). The practice has been made to appear necessary because of an "objective" feature of these settings: Razor-thin profit margins that are associated with retail and service work in competitive sectors, such as fast food—which, incidentally, also is used to justify low hourly wages. Many have noted, too, that the practice could not have attained the prevalence it has without the pervasive quantification and computerization of work practices, materials, and customer demand—along with the development of algorithms to predict needed staffing (which often takes decisional power away from supervisors on site).

Practices of quantification and the use of algorithms are, of course, supported by discourses of precision, accuracy, and standardization as desirable elements of retail work, elements that produce the sort of efficiency seemingly required to meet the challenges of these low-margin settings. As we noted in Chapter 1, creative and professional work has thus far been immune to flexible scheduling, perhaps because retail and service work is more frequently embodied at the point of customer contact, workers need to transport their bodies to and from work; when understanding the practice from the perspective of those workers and their bodies, it is also possible to see that the temporal unpredictability associated with flexible scheduling threatens desires for consistent pay as well as for those employees' efforts to arrange for childcare and eldercare (Cauthen, 2011).

By mirroring the discussion in Chapter 1 on working and organizing under contemporary capitalism, it is clear that flexible scheduling is materialized by a multifarious and intricate array of elements. From the perspective of economic performativity, the preceding paragraphs would be an attempt to sketch the components of the *agencement*, the acting assemblage. And, as suggested earlier, messiness reigns. Although it might be tempting to map all the elements mentioned in the preceding paragraph in an effort to grasp the shape of the complex configuration, such a move is unlikely to tell us much about the *practice*. A second analytical step, therefore, is to examine a particular practice—not the abstract proliferation of flexible scheduling, but a practice that could be observed *in situ*. Thus, examining "the practice of flexible scheduling" is likely to be unmanageable; instead, one might focus on routines, performances, or patterns (Leonardi, 2012), such as managers' interactions with frontline workers when shifts change unexpectedly, or the sequences of activities in which workers engage to mitigate the effects of inconsistent work schedules.

A communicative vision of performativity would highlight particular nodal points in terms of the relations they exhibit through the practice. For instance, the meaning of the algorithm—with meaning defined here not as the signification of the sign, but *how the element engages in the practice*— might be understood as materialized by (i.e., articulated through) relations with an array of human and nonhuman participants. The element, of course, is not ontologically independent; what we take to be "the algorithm" is understood as an ongoing (and malleable) accomplishment of the configuration of agencies around it—the identification of which is always an empirical question. And, as suggested earlier, the multiplicity of relationships overdetermining the nodal point is likely to generate conflicts and contradictions such that one might observe labor-management exchanges that draw on alternative enactments of the relations surrounding the algorithm, or actions that appropriate the scheduling software in ways not written into its code.

Overdetermination also suggests the possibility of using the machinery of efficiency in alternate ways—for altering the relations materializing and articulating a given element. For instance, the belief in the interchangeability of workers in these positions could be used to provide greater freedom from the schedule for the worker if a practice were developed in which a free- -floating set of "gig" workers were available in an ad hoc manner to cover shifts regular workers needed to relinquish to address sporadic demands. Regardless of the particular possibilities for capitalizing on overdetermination, analysts should be attentive to the ways in which *matter* enters practices at these nodal points: How space is made present, how money (e.g., wages and sales) infuses practice, which bodies are made (ir)relevant to the practice, and how data and its sources stimulate alternative forms of action. Perhaps unsurprisingly, being attentive to each of these requires a recognition that each of these matterings occurs only in and through communication.

The third step is to describe the logic of practice guiding the trajectory of the *agencement*. The importance of stipulating the boundaries of the practice in question, as described in the second step, becomes even clearer here. In the case of the aforementioned interactions occasioned when managers and frontline workers interact because the algorithm instructs the manager to terminate a worker's shift early, analyses could highlight the meaningful relations among elements that make particular interactional moves (un) reasonable and (in)appropriate. The question to be answered here is about *why* the particular elements generating this practice hang together as they do—and, in turn, what this is likely to imply for subsequent action and the possibility of movement. Recalling that Callon's version of performativity is interested in how economic models performatively create economic realities, the identification of a logic is a device useful for examining how such models stitch together the agencies participating in a practice.

Earlier, we quoted Jane Bennett's (2010) suggestion that understanding practice requires attending to what agency is avoiding, as well as to what attracts it. She advances a key issue for understanding a logic of practice: What the practice fears can be as relevant as what it desires; what it seeks to *avoid* is important as its productive aims. To think in the register of a *practice* "fearing" and "desiring" here is not an unjustified anthropomorphism; it is, instead, a route for investigators to attend to the struggles regarding control over the trajectory of the practice. In the case of flexible scheduling, one would first begin by stipulating and describing the practice, and then posit that a logic of practice (such as efficiency, or technological domination, or quality, or integration, or something else altogether) drives the connections comprising the relational complex. (Though it is perhaps obvious, specifying the logic of the practice also enables a connection with the broader matrix of practices we call contemporary capitalism, since any such logic would be responsive to a constitutive outside.) Yet the identification of a logic is clearly not the aim or end of analysis; it is only a component of an examination of *agencement* that informs understandings of the trajectory of the practice.

Summarizing the Extension

The important question is whether, and how, novel insights are likely to be generated from analyses guided by this communicatively expanded conception of economic performativity. One insight, to be explored in Chapter 5, is that the logic of practice is also a site for investigating *authority* in organizing. If the logic of practice provides a rationale for the configurations of elements, then the capacity to shape that logic is crucial in authoring the trajectory of the practice. And because the logic is a site of conflict and contradiction, analyses employing this notion would be able to see authority as a process of human and nonhuman agencies vying to "author" the *agencement's* trajectory.

Another contribution of this communicative extension is the ability to attend to the sort of misfires suggested by Butler. As described in Chapter 2, Butler would urge analysts to ask how it could be that the introduction of flexible scheduling in retail work could possibly *fail*, and to look *inside* performative acts for evidence of failure. Using Laclau's thinking on articulation means that performativity theorizing would see the sources of failure in, rather than as external to, the conjunctions between elements comprising the practice. Investigations would then examine not how particular persons or objects interrupt flexible scheduling, but how the conjoint agency comprising nodal points encode politics and can challenge an existing logic of practice. An important task, then, is to consider how the meanings emerging from a nodal point have the potential to alter the trajectory of practice. An outgrowth of this line of questioning is that analyses interrogate the contingencies that create (in) stabilities in practices such as those associated with flexible scheduling.

If performativity is about the production of meaning in the present that endures beyond the moment (La Berge, 2015), communication theory—particularly a vision of communication influenced by articulation theorizing—is a useful extension. Communicative insights associated with articulation theorizing provide a vehicle to understand both the production of meaning in the moment and in the relations between elements that have a longer-lasting existence. Communication, then, is the process by which both those connections and an encompassing logic of practice are created, recognized, analyzed, and altered. Similar themes, though with a rather different assumptive ground, characterize our third extension.

Version 3: Communication as Constitutive Transmission

At a glance, affect theory is at significant odds with the conception of communication outlined at the start of this chapter. In fact, a closer look at affect as rendered in Chapter 2 suggests that it is defined *against* communication as we know it. Recall, for instance, that affect precedes and exceeds subjectivity as well as the discursive and ideational, that it is distinguished from emotion on the grounds of the latter's symbolic capture, and that it meets intersubjectivity and interpretation with indifference. Affect prioritizes relational intensities which unaccountably permeate and (dis)organize sociomaterial worlds, and especially corporeal experience, precisely *because* they evade articulation and representation.

On the one hand, affect swirls all around communication, as that ineffable "stuff that goes on beneath, beyond, even parallel to signification" (O'Sullivan, 2001, p. 126), or "the capacity of interaction that is akin to a natural force of emergence" (Beyes & Steyaert, 2012, p. 46). Yet it can hardly be said to cooperate, operating on its own register distinct from linguistic processes and powerfully "unassimilable" for just that reason (Massumi, 1995, p. 88). Defiantly beating to its own elusive drummer, affect flouts constructions of meaning and somehow orchestrates worldings anyway. Affect appears not only to surround but also to overpower, communication. The linguistic turn shudders.

How, then, could affect ever ally with communicative theories of working and organizing, bent as they are on demonstrating the efficacy of human discourse? Certainly, many constitutive, dialogic accounts of communication have acknowledged its embodied and emotional character but, just as surely, affect theory is a leap too far. What is *inter*action without the individuals, those precious speaking and feeling subjects, who engage in intersubjectivity? Is it not the human struggle over meaning, above all, that makes things *matter*?

Against such antagonistic readings, we argue that affect and communication need one another to facilitate lively engagement with the late-capitalist landscape portrayed in Chapter 1. Affect theory calls into question long and deeply held, yet constricting, notions about what communication must be in order to qualify as a robust process. Specifically, much communication theory continues to celebrate the hard-won battle whereby communication ascended to its rightful constitutive pedestal against the foil of "mere" transmission. Affect theory resoundingly validates transmission as a constitutive process, whereas communication can help affect theory address something of a black box: the *how* of affective transfer. We begin by examining more closely what happens to communication, as we now know it, through an affective lens.

What Becomes of Communication Defined as Human Interaction That Makes Meaning of the World?

As sketched earlier, most contemporary accounts designate communication as the realm of (a) language, understood as a human system of signs and symbols put to use in verbal and non-verbal (i.e., embodied but unstated) ways; (b) discourse, loosely defined as narrative formations, and their everyday practice; (c) intersubjectivity, pursued and achieved in and through interaction; and/or (d) the contestation and negotiation of meaning, which crafts the world by collaboratively making sense of it, through ongoing interpretation. Of course, these renditions overlap and offer only a distilled sampling, but they illustrate the tie that binds—namely, a view of communication wherein signification and subjectivity are of utmost concern. Put crudely, signification reigns as the central activity of social construction, and the status of the human subject engaging in and with signification is a pivotal problematic.

These issues are not discarded by affect theory, but they do assume a more modest place. The linguistic turn is not so much repudiated or undermined as it is called to humility. Symbols retain ontological force, tangled up with other kinds of participants, but their use is not *the* ontological force.

So what, more precisely, becomes of subjectivity? It is certainly not irrelevant, but it is also not the main show, and it is decidedly vulnerable. However, affect theory generally means this in a different way than familiar poststructuralist claims to the fragmentation and fragility of identities as discursively constituted. For affect theory, subjectivity is vulnerable in that it is *hybrid*—plural and precarious, colliding at various discursive intersections, yes, and constantly interrupted, disjointed, dispersed, and crossbred because it is "caught up in things" (Stewart, 2007, p. 86). Subjectivity is not simply relational in that it is constituted within discourse; it is relational in its dependence on the sociomaterial matrix that gives it life and form to wriggle within and against that enabling matrix, with which it constantly breeds (Butler, 2015; Roberts, 2005). Subjectivity becomes post-human, in short.

As the *trans*personal flow of sensory force that animates worlds by traversing bodies, affect enlivens but also disrupts the subject, enticing "it" into other arrangements or leaving it crumpled on the floor like last night's attire. This is how affect is *pre*personal: it is "prior" to, or necessary for, the constitution of subjectivities as well as "the individual" who comes to inhabit them. It is *extra*personal in that it transcends the emotional borders of skin, capable of rendering selves irrelevant, inept, or entirely undone.

Notice the contrast with a typical communicative focus on the *inter*personal, which presumes pre-bounded people who enter into and leave interaction, even if the particulars of their selves are made and unraveled within that or successive exchanges. Here, the sensory force that awakens and deadens scenes takes center stage, even as "the human" players are not taken for granted.

In this spirit, Stewart (2007) offers a post-human translation of the ethnographic eye/I, which becomes object-ified and thrown toward "she." However, she is not a stable third-person, and certainly not an objective observer with a god's eye or a bird's view. She is a feeling, knowing, becoming, and constantly disrupted body-vessel, a self only known—and a thousand times lost—in and through affective flow:

> "She" is not so much a subject position or an agent in hot pursuit of something definitive as a point of contact; instead, she gazes, imagines, senses, takes on, performs, and asserts not a flat and finished truth but some possibilities (and threats) that have come into view in the effort to become attuned to what a particular scene might offer.
>
> (p. 5)

This move provides a glimpse of how reflexivity unfurls in affect theory, less concerned with the researcher's subject positionality and curious instead about the ontological politics evolving as a body of research mingles with other (not necessarily human) bodies in practice.

As with subjectivity, affect theory does not disregard signification either, but its ontological mattering gets a serious makeover. Stewart (2007, p. 3) explains that ordinary affect

> works not through "meanings" per se, but rather in the way that they pick up density and texture as they move through bodies, dreams, dramas, and social worldings of all kinds. The question they beg is not what they might mean in an order of representations, or whether they are good or bad in an overarching scheme of things, but where they might go and what potential modes of knowing, relating, and attending to things are already somehow present in them in a state of potentiality and resonance.

MacLure (2013) clarifies that this shift in focus is not a rejection of signification but, rather, a reworking of its significance: "The critique of representation does not deny that it does indeed happen" (p. 559) or that representational logic is useful as it allows us to navigate a steady sea of meaning with other durable interlocutors. But it is crucial to acknowledge that "words collide and connect with things *on the same ontological level*, and therefore language cannot achieve the distance and externality that would allow it to represent—i.e., to stand over, stand for and stand in for—the world" (p. 660, emphasis added).

This is exactly why affect theory, like other relational ontologies, emphasizes sociomaterial production (i.e., doing worlds, or the enactment of hybrid agencies) instead of social construction (i.e., knowing the world through language). Approaches based on social construction empower language *over* matter, holding that language matters more because it makes things matter. However, such a claim can only stand if we ignore that language *is* (also) matter. Words too must materialize on page, screen, or embodied voice, for example, to matter at all. Talking and listening are material as well as social practices that enlist human and nonhuman participants. It is therefore not entirely in "our" power to speak, or silence, the world into being. This is the move toward humility: signification, still potentially powerful, becomes another mode of *mattering*. We might say—with less arrogance and tongue in cheek—that "words *matter*," and "language is still *a thing*."

This demotion of the ontological status of language explains why intersubjectivity, as the negotiation of shared meaning through language between already established subject-entities, is beside (literally, alongside) the point. It may help to recall here affect theory's claim that sens*ibility* arrives on sense-*ability*. The point is that meaning moves among us *materially*, for instance, through physical senses and objects. Meaning is spat, thrown, whispered, torn up, and poured. It slaps me in the face, averts your eyes, quivers in his throat, and takes wing as a butterfly in her stomach.

Massumi (1995) refers to this ubiquitous capacity of communication as the expression *event* (see also Grossberg, 1982)—that dynamic flow of transitory intensities which constitutes relations as always indeterminate, and which is drained of blood, or erased altogether, when semantics or semiotics are privileged. Reviving this eventfulness, Riley (2005, p. 3) situates language as an agentive conduit for affective flow that "exerts a torsion on its users." She observes that "there is a forcible affect of language which courses like blood through its speakers" (p. 1) and "stands somewhat apart from the expressive intentions of an individual speaker" (p. 5)—"an affect which seeps from the very form of the words" (p. 2) and from "common twists of speech which themselves enact feeling, rather than simply and obediently conveying it as we elect" (p. 3). Here the question is not so much "How to Do Things with Words, as Austin's title had it, but how words do things with us. And that 'with us'—as distinct from 'to us'—is pivotal" (p. 3).

The sociomateriality of language itself, and the hybrid agencies entailed in its use, begin to come into relief. For example, during the 2016 U.S. presidential elections, the word "tweet" was lingered upon like a tasty treat, stretched out and flung on various tongues across various scenes, a missile of trivialization and emasculation that could never be caught red-handed, exceeding its designated meaning with the feeling texture of the word itself, and flooding campaign venues with irrepressible if fleeting delight (e.g., "a man you can bait with a *tweet* . . ."). John Oliver's viral takedown of the potent name "Trump" (as opposed to the original "Drumpf"), as it materializes capitalist dreams with brassy public flexes of success, emblazoned in outsized gold and block lettering across one phallic object after another, and blurted from the mouth like a belligerent triumph, lends another unforgettable example.[1]

When it comes to matters of meaning, then, affect theory highlights its material transfer, and it is in this charged transmission that meaning comes to *matter*. As with the first two revisions of communication proposed in this chapter, language is still about forging connections, but the links of most interest are not emerging maps of signification but, rather, relational intensities born of contact.

A novel vision of communication begins to emerge through affect theory: as transmissive *and* constitutive, or constitutive *because* transmissive. As outlined earlier, transmission models of communication are generally cast in opposition to constitutive models. Transmission is dismissed as the antiquated notion that interaction is simply a passive channel through which humans relay information and express an already formed world. Hence, communication becomes constitutive—the interactive production of meanings with tangible consequence—on the back of transmission, or through its denigration. Affect theory unsettles this binary with a robust reading of transmission, which highlights, among other things, how language exerts powerful relational pulls beyond meaning effects. It thereby calls us to reconsider the vitality of a *trans*personal, rather than *inter*personal or intersubjective, model of communication, which would prioritize how signs, symbols, and meanings are felt, unleashing and accumulating intensities, as they pass through and connect bodies of all kinds, skipping from one scene of encounter to the next. Transmission, in this *sense*, "makes a difference." It galvanizes those distinctions and relations that offer up inhabitable worlds, and it makes those worlds mobile and contagious—in a word, "communicable." Communication as the transmission of affect is a constitutive process, albeit even more transient and unruly than communication as we have known it until now.

A Slippery Slope: What Else Then Becomes of Communication?

Thus far, we have seen how affect theory treats communication as currently defined: ongoing human interaction that gives meaning to the world. Guided by the linguistic turn and numerous strands of social constructionism, this definition grants top ontological billing to the signifying operations of language such that discursive activity becomes the primary constitutive force, and communication as transmission appears outmoded and impotent. Without rejecting the efficacy of language, affect theory calls it to ontological modesty while expanding appreciation of the ways in which it is efficacious. Specifically, affect theory reframes signification as one mode of mattering, on ontological par and colliding with others, and it points curiosity toward relational effects of language and interaction that go missing amid preoccupation with meaning effects, particularly the generation and travel of sensory intensities. In sum, affect theory retains interest in discursive activity, but it redirects attention from the construction of coherent meanings to their erratic material circulation. It asks how signification moves around like other matter and becomes sensed and impactful. Ahmed's (2014) work on affective economies of hate that trade in "metonymic slides"—gatherings of signs, discourses, and objects that become stuck together and garner communities of investment through circulation—provides an excellent example of one such approach.

Affect theory thus prompts us to double back toward transmission and challenge feeble accounts thereof. It hints at a productive redefinition of communication as *the constitutive process of affective contact and transmission*, or elaborated, as *the encounter, conduction, and transduction of energetic intensities that move worlding*, in the multiple senses of movement developed in Chapter 2. "Conduction" and "transduction" are two key traveling potentials of encounter, as currently understood in affect theory. By conduction, we refer to the transfer of sensation and feeling among proximate bodies (again, human and nonhuman) acting as fertile if unwitting producers and carriers. Transduction refers to the transfer of felt forces of potential, or the imminent virtual, from one relational actualization (i.e., tangible bodies or scenes) to another, enabling emergence and transformation into something else as yet unknown (Massumi, 1995).

Caution is in order, for this shift opens a proverbial can of worms that may prove more "productive" than anticipated. Presuming that the circulation of language and meaning is not the only means of affective contact and transmission, what then? Do other modes of transfer also entail communication such that the very term no longer belongs to the realm of human discourse? Are we equipped for the ramifications of this? Scholars studying quantum physics (Barad, 2003, 2007, 2014), bio-semiotics (see Kohn, 2013), and material semiotics (see Law, 2009), for example, have long pursued affiliate questions. But the potential dividends of studying other material "languages," or sign systems, for organization and communication studies remains to be seen. A foray into what is arguably the most expansive treatment of affect transmission to date can help to clarify the daunting proposition at hand.

In a provocative case for heightened attention to the transfer of affect, Brennan (2004) hosts an often dizzying encounter among demarcated fields, such as psychoanalytic theory and practice, social theory and philosophy, neuro and biological sciences, and theology. Her goal with this wide arc is to theorize the sociomateriality of affect transmission, or in her words, the fact that "the social or psychosocial actually gets into the flesh" (p. 25):

> What is overlooked, in the rearguard actions of those who defend the social construction of persons, is the way that certain biological and physical phenomena themselves require a social explanation. While its wellsprings are social, the transmission of affect is deeply physical in its effects.
>
> (p. 23)

While controversial (see Forum, 2006), Brennan's account raises several prospects pertinent to the redefinition of communication earlier. First, she demonstrates that the claim to affect transmission is all but incontrovertible; available evidence in multiple fields confirms that feeling which courses through one body can most certainly enter another. Second, such energetic transfer can take multiple forms (e.g., alignment through contagion or complementary opposition through projection) that move through several channels. Chief among the avenues of contagion is what she calls "olfactory communication," also known as chemical entrainment, wherein pheromones emitted into the atmosphere by one or more bodies elicit consequential physiological responses (e.g., hormonal fluctuations) in others. Palpable physiological changes are also induced through "nervous communication," or electrical entrainment, such as that entailed in touch, sound, and sight, especially through varying intensities of rhythm and vibration.

Lest such pathways be hastily dismissed as biologically determined matters, predictable mechanisms of stimulus and response that belong to the physical sciences and hardly count as "communication," Brennan builds a compelling case for the complicated interpretive labor required and its sociomaterial indeterminacy. In a nutshell, in any encounter, a "horizontal or heartfelt axis of communication that imbibes molecular information directly from the other" collides with "the vertical or historical line of personal affective history," or tailored accumulations from previous interactions that bodies bring—and, often, drag like baggage—to a scene (p. 86). Complex, volatile, and customized processing akin to linguistic communication is therefore always involved.

The simultaneous operation of multiple modes of communication suggests "that we regard the human being as a receiver and interpreter of feelings, affects, attentive energy" (p. 87) in far more complex ways than presently recognized. Brennan specifies the human body as a particular kind of vessel for affective flow by revealing its engagement in constant, plural, and parallel communication activities. "Parallel" is an important term here. She argues that language, interpretation, and meaning are not the sole province of conscious social interaction and sensemaking, practices that are of course also physical, as argued earlier. Rather, human bodies alone practice several forms of knowing through doing, which can all be usefully regarded as interpretive practices that make meaning out of sensory information. Brennan goes so far as to call for "understanding fleshly languages as languages" (p. 141), as *homologous* modes of communicating: "Such knowledge is a chain of communication and association in the flesh (with its own anchors in the brain) that is also structured like language and functions in a parallel way (p. 23)."

Stepping further, Brennan argues that natural affinities among these concurrent modes of communication are severed in Western societies by the demand for a self-contained subject, which serves to "split the order of signification from the orders of the flesh," dubbing the former refined and reflexive against the allegedly primitive reflexes of the latter (p. 147). The irony is that fleshly languages appear to process complex cues more quickly and reliably than discursive activity precisely *because* they are not also performing endless upkeep on a fragile subject. Less burdened by rigid boundaries of the self, they do not have to pause to dress up, trip

over, or tiptoe around them. Poststructuralist thinking is thus on a productive track in contesting abiding faith in this subject, but much of it hits
a snag in preserving the distinctiveness and primacy of discursive activity as *the* epistemological practice. Brennan's ultimate quest is to recon-
nect linguistic, fleshly, and even environmental modes of communication
through the cultivation of *discernment*, the bodily practice of bringing
multiple sensory languages into awareness—a notion that resonates well
with Stewart's (2007) discussion of attunement, reviewed in Chapter 2.

Regardless of how this brief review of one sweeping analysis may strike
you, it joins with allied efforts across fields of inquiry to throw down
a gauntlet of sorts, or at least a formidable invitation, for communication theorizing. Namely, it suggests that the time has come to contribute
to the development of a post-human conception of communication in
which neither human discourse nor human bodies enjoy a monopoly on
the term. To be sure, the first shift in focus proposed here—from the
social construction of meaning to the material circulation and transfer of
meaning as affective flow—serves up plenty to do on its own. However,
the redefinition to which that shift in attention leads—communication as
the constitutive process of affective contact and transmission—opens the
door to momentous and, we think, exciting challenges and collaborations.

In the model proposed here, communication remains constitutive,
not because it crafts solid worlds out of symbols, but because it makes
the becoming of worlds *communicable*—felt in material symptoms and
infectious. This model facilitates a "fuller-bodied" conception of communication, first, by foregrounding corporeal encounters with language and
meaning and, second, by insisting that multiple human and nonhuman
bodies and modes of communication participate in sensory transmission.

How affect travels is a particularly pressing question for working and
organizing in these times. Now more than ever, it is affect that performs
the heavy lifting for that behemoth known as advanced capitalism, whose
vigor persists only as its countless currents are carried into the ordinary:

> Affect is itself a real condition, an intrinsic variable of the late-
> capitalist system, as infrastructural as a factory. Actually, it is beyond
> infrastructural, it is everywhere, in effect. Its ability to come second-
> hand, to switch domains and produce effects across them all, gives it a
> meta-factorial ubiquity. It is beyond infrastructural. It is transversal.
> (Massumi, 1995, pp. 106–107)

Conclusion

This chapter's aim has been to suggest three routes by which relational
analyses of working and organizing under late capitalism might be
extended by taking communication seriously. Just what it means to take
communication seriously, however, varies dramatically across the three
versions depicted here. Yet in each, the aim has been to eschew the notion

that communication provides a "perspective" or "take" on working and organizing distinct from other fields (see the third path presented at the end of Chapter 1); instead, we have asserted that there are novel insights to be gained by conceiving of working and organizing *as* communication phenomena. The three versions we advanced portray communication as either (a) the site and surface of the semiotic materializing of relations/ links/connections, (b) the articulation of agencies constituting *agencement* and, thus, writing of the trajectory of practice, or (c) constitutive transmission in which language is the sociomaterial stuff that engages and transfers energies.

We term this set of potentialities *communicative relationality*. Mindful of the irksome academic penchant for neologisms and catchphrases, our coining of this term is an attempt to encapsulate the contributions offered in this chapter. We think of these not as *sui generis* onto-epistemological positions, but as conceptual tools that, in conjunction with the relational ontologies presented in Chapter 2, foster analysts' capacity to trace modes of mattering in working and organizing. The "work of communication," then, is not merely that communication has become a key feature of work in contemporary capitalism; it is also a stance that advances communication, in its various relational guises, as the principal explanatory apparatus in investigations of working and organizing.

The three chapters to follow take up these communicative extensions in the order presented in this chapter, displaying the generativity of each vision of communicative relationality for instances of working and organizing particularly pertinent in contemporary capitalism. Each case explicitly foregrounds working and organizing, but the three differ markedly—as do the visions of communicative relationality described in this chapter. An important axis of difference is that the discursive manifestations of those working and organizing practices become less central through the progression of the chapters. Specifically, in Chapter 4 we provide a detailed analysis of how action that is typically relegated to the domain of the symbolic and ideational can be fruitfully understood relationally by shifting our conception of mattering and, in turn, considering how solidification occurs. Chapters 5 and 6 start with problems of working and organizing associated specifically with contemporary capitalism, deploying conceptions of communicative relationality that decenter talk in the attempt to understand the conjoint accomplishment of agency. Across these three chapters, we show how modes of mattering are deeply sociomaterial, post-human, and performative; yet each case approaches this analytical task with contrasting inflections, allowing us to demonstrate a range of possibilities for pursuing communicative relationality.

Note

1   www.youtube.com/watch?v=DnpO_RTSNmQ.

4 Creativity and Relationality

Following the Becoming of an Idea

While contemporary capitalism has often been associated with the ideas of a creative economy (Carayannis, Dubina, & Campbell, 2011) or creative classes (Florida, 2003), research on creativity—usually defined as the capacity to generate novel and appropriate ideas, processes, products or solutions (Amabile, 1996; Ford, 1996; Shalley, 1991)—tends to focus primarily on the individual (Hargadon & Bechky, 2006). This is all the more surprising given that creative achievements in organizational settings often rely as much on collaborative efforts as on individuals' contributions (Engeström, 1999). Mensch (1993) argues, for instance, that "Teamwork is an essential ingredient for successful innovation and transformation. Studies of successful innovation have repeatedly emphasized the need for, and importance of, close cooperation among members of multifunctional groups" (p. 262; see also Perry-Smith & Shalley, 2003).

Most researchers, however, restrict their inquiries on collaboration to the implementation phase of a creative idea and leave out the detailed analysis of social processes of ideation as such (Sonnenburg, 2007). Although this body of research reaffirms the relevance of approaching creativity and innovation from a collaborative viewpoint, the investigation of how interactions and communication might play a key role in creative processes still trails behind. In keeping with our relational ontology, this chapter thus proposes to follow the becoming of an idea by showing how its materialization is collaboratively negotiated and established during a creative event called Museomix.

Instead of conceiving of creativity just as an individual phenomenon, we will show that different elements (technologies, texts, drawings, etc.) can contribute to its emergence. Although individual creativity is not denied, a relational approach thus insists, as we will show, on the various contributions (human, technological, artifactual, etc.) that make innovation possible. With a relational approach, we can therefore track how an idea not only emerges but also evolves, articulates itself, gets tested, fades away, etc. We can thus literally *follow it* and see all the relations and materializations that contribute to its trajectories. Far from being a disembodied phenomenon, creativity thus *materializes* through the multiple ways an idea resists to objections, produces various forms of alignment,

DOI: 10.4324/9781315680705-4

as well as through its capacity to reconfigure situations. If we seem to be in the immaterial world of ideation and inventiveness, we are always, in fact, in the concrete world of relations, a world where texts or drawings trigger collective thought processes, where technological devices ignite imagination, or where turn takings provoke free associations.

In this chapter, we thus propose to do something apparently very strange. Although we will certainly observe and analyze what participants do and how they do what they do throughout a creative process, we will keep focusing on something that appears to *drive* or *animate* their conversations and activities, meaning the very idea they decided to work on collaboratively. As analysts, our job will therefore be to *detect the multiple forms this idea takes on,* whether that formation occurs through how someone presents it for the first time, through the way it is understood and translated by other people, or through a specific drawing or prototype where it is supposed to materialize itself, to just take a few examples.

As pointed out in Chapter 3, defending a relational ontology thus consists of acknowledging that *materialization is constitutive of everything that exists.* In other words, even the most abstract idea has, by definition, to embody itself in someone's mind, in its expression in an utterance, in the reaction this expression produces in an audience, or in the fabrication of a prototype (and these, again, are just a few examples). This is, as we will see, why materiality and relationality are so intractably linked to each other. Whenever something like an idea materializes itself, a relation is ipso facto created with another materialization that preceded or sometimes anticipated it.

Peirce's semiotics does not say anything else when it claims that any sign always implies both a relation and materialization—a *relation* because something or someone always signals itself/himself/herself to someone or something else *through* another being, which precisely constitutes the relation itself and *materialization* because this relation precisely has to materialize itself in this third being, which Peirce called a sign (but that should not ever be *reduced* to a sign). The relational ontology we put forward in this chapter thus leads us to reconsider what *being something* or even *being someone* means. For instance, if an idea is deemed interesting, it is because it appears to *interest* people, which means that it is supposed to catch their attention. As we see in this (apparently) simple example, what an idea *is*—for instance, interesting—is the product of a relation: it caught people's attention or sparked their interest. It is this interest that signals what this idea is supposed to be to us as observers or participants.

This idea can thus signal itself through the effect it produces in an audience (e.g., by catching its attention). The interest it produces can thus be considered a part of its being, which is why we can speak about this effect as a *characteristic, property* or *feature* of what this idea consists of. The advantage of this relational approach is that we can then follow how a given being—an idea, for instance—evolves throughout space and time: its properties can evolve precisely because *its constitutive relations can evolve too*: its formulations, its representations, its capacity to interest people, its embodiment in a prototype, etc. Note that all these relations always *materialize* somewhere, somehow: an idea *is* a flash in someone's mind; it *is* its formulation on a piece of paper; it *is* its translation into a prototype. Its trajectory is therefore always *made of* these relations/materializations.

At no point do we leave the *terra firma* of interaction (Cooren, 2006), as an idea can be recognized—by the participants and the analysts—only through its multiple materializations, which always *relate* to each other. In other words, *an idea always evolves from one materialization to another*, as *even its very name is still a way for this idea to materialize itself in the realm of discourse*. The mistake that we need to avoid systematically is to reproduce, wrongly, the bifurcation of nature, already denounced by Whitehead (1920). Embodiment, incarnation, or materialization does not consist of embodying, incarnating, or materializing something supposedly immaterial into something material. It consists of offering to something *that already has a material dimension* another way to materialize, embody or incarnate itself *for another next first time*, as Garfinkel (2002) would say.

So how do we follow the becoming of an idea? A way to do this consists of shadowing, armed with a video camera, a team working on it. This is what we did during a creative event called Museomix, which gathers participants every year around one project: reinventing the way visitors experience museums. Founded in 2011, this event, whose slogan is "people make museums," simultaneously takes place in several museums around the world and proposes to participants of various backgrounds (graphic designers, software developers, entrepreneurs, art historians, etc.) to create, in only three days, prototypes designed to change the way people experience their visit. Our study focused on the part of the event that took place in November 2014 at one of these museums, located in a major North American city.

In its website, Museomix specifies that its vision is to create "an open museum with a place for everyone; a living-lab museum that evolves with its users; a networked museum in touch with its communities" (www.museomix.org/en/about/#vision). As for its five missions, they are (1) to "foster collaboration," (2) to "test and lead by example," (3) to "bring new ideas to light," (4) to "share freely," and (5) to "build a community that takes care of itself and its members." Although Museomix is meant to be playful and entertaining, we believe it can also be considered representative of how collaboration and even work tend to be conceived in contemporary capitalism.

If the guiding question of our book is *What have work and organization become under contemporary capitalism and how should organization studies approach them?*, we believe that the Museomix creative sessions we studied qualify as the playful version of what work has indeed become, knowing that playfulness has itself, in the so-called new economy, become part of what work sometimes (not always, of course) consists of. If *gamification* is a way to translate game-design characteristics into working contexts, Museomix could be understood as an illustration of what *workification* (Fuchs & Trottier, 2013) could look like—that is, a way to translate work-design characteristics into playful contexts. When people get together in a Museomix event, they are indeed supposed to *work* as teams, even if they are not, strictly speaking, working, but playing.

It is in this gray area between seriousness and lightheartedness that we think Museomix qualifies as a representation of what work might have, *in some contexts*, become, the difference being that at the end of this three-day event, participants can, if they want, just forget about what just happened and go back to their "normal" work life, so to speak. Having observed and studied retreats of "real" companies confronted with "real" problems in the context of creativity incubators such as the Banff Centre, Alberta, Canada, we believe that the frontiers between the playful dimensions of work and the serious dimensions of play sometimes tend, in fact, to vanish.

So what does it mean to follow the becoming of an idea? In the case of the Museomix event we studied, it meant that we had, as observers, to throw ourselves in the context of these three days during which the event took place. Armed with video cameras, the research team recorded the event from its official beginning to its end, knowing that choices would have to be made regarding which teams of creators would have to be followed at some point.[1] Given that all the Museomix teams could not be followed once created (they were a total of twelve of them), decisions had to be made on the spot. Two teams were finally followed, each by two researchers who tried to capture all the key moments that constituted the trajectory of their respective projects. It is the story of one of these two teams that we will now reconstruct for the purpose of this chapter. More precisely, it is *the story of their idea* that we will now follow and analyze.

Methodologically speaking, it is noteworthy that we proceeded *backward* to select the sequences that will be analyzed in this chapter. As we were allowed to shadow and video record the becoming of an idea from its inception to its concretization under the form of a prototype, this enabled us to select excerpts where the participants appeared to identify and define key properties of the final product. In other words, we started from the end result to reconstruct key moments of this trajectory. It is the result of this reconstruction that we now present.

The Museomix Device

However, before focusing on the becoming of an idea throughout these three days, we need to backtrack a little. From a relational perspective, it is indeed imperative not to determine a point in time as being the absolute beginning of anything, including the Museomix event. In many respects, this event had already started to exist a long time before it actually took place, especially in its planning and preparation. In other words, defending a relational perspective also consists of showing how the organization of this event participated in its being and becoming, and consequently in the being and becoming of all the ideas that emerged during these three days.

Although we will not focus in this chapter on how the idea of organizing this specific event emerged or even on how the three days were concretely organized, it is noteworthy that before their actual *formulations*, all the ideas that emerged from the event were, in fact, anticipated under the form of a series of *requirements* they were supposed to meet (for more details, see also Martine & Cooren, 2016). As the participants learned when the organizers explained the program during the first plenary session of Museomix (see Figure 4.1), ideas would have to be first written down on various post-it notes, which each participant would have to stick on large flip charts during a general brainstorming session.

Participants would then be invited to walk from one flip chart to another and talk to each other about what they considered to be the most interesting ideas. This series of dialogues were supposed to lead to the creation of "team nuclei," that is, sorts of proto-teams gathering at least two participants around a specific idea that happened to interest them the most. Each proto team would then be invited to pitch its own idea to all the participants during a second plenary session, a pitch that was essentially meant to attract more people interested in working on each specific project. Once these pitches would have been presented, all the participants would then have 20 minutes to create 12 teams of 6 people each, each team being dedicated to the concretization of a specific idea.

From a relational perspective, it is key to note that *speaking about ideas*, while not knowing yet what they actually consist of, *already is a way to give them a mode of existence*. A little bit like a house that begins to exist in its design specs or in an architect's plans, ideas started to exist as the organizers presented their requirements during the first plenary session. The ideas had to be (1) *written down* on post-it notes displayed on flip charts, (2) *discussed* by the participants, (3) *pitched* during a plenary session by at least two persons, (4) *supported/represented*

Figure 4.1 The first plenary session

by at least six participants, and (5) finally *validated* by the organizers once this magic number would have been reached. Any idea not fulfilling this selection process would then be de facto discarded—a fate that most ideas generated during this whole process ended up sharing.

These five requirements, presented by the organizers at the beginning of this event, can thus be considered *ways by which ideas started to material- ize themselves before their actual formulation.* At this point, it is impor- tant not to bifurcate: their actual formulation on a post-it certainly was an important way by which ideas materialized later on, but the formulation, by the organizers, of their requirements—and this is a key aspect of our analysis—*was also already a form of materialization.* How do ideas mate- rialize at this point? Through what is presented as *expected* or *required* of them and their creators/supporters—that is, through the presentation of their expected features during the first plenary session. The expression "have to" conveys very well what expectations and requirements consist of: they are features, properties, or characteristics that something or some- one does not have yet, but that it/he/she *has* to have (which means that a requirement already is, by definition, a property).

In other words, ideas (started to) exist *through* their requirements—that is, through the features, properties, or characteristics they *had* to have: being written down, discussed, pitched, and represented/supported by enough supporters and validated by the organizers. These requirements thus materi- alized not only *through* their presentation and expression by the organizers but also *through* their comprehension, discussion, and application by the participants. This point is crucial, as these ideas, which have not yet been formulated per se, can be said to *already have a mode of being,* even if this mode of being depends on the formulation of these requirements, which define what features they will have to have in order to be selected.

The Birth of the Idea

As expected, most participants played the game and started to stick close to a hundred post-its on six flip charts, each panel being dedicated to one "grand challenge" that had also been identified and presented by the organizers during the first plenary session ((1) renewing the visitor's expe- rience, (2) show the unshowable, (3) being at the museum, (4) museum and senses, (5) museum business development, and (6) copyrights at the museum). Armed with their video cameras, the members of the research team wandered throughout the crowd, desperately trying to capture moments of ideation and discussion, without really knowing who or what to focus on. While some participants were sticking post-its on flip charts (Figure 4.2), others were reading them, trying to find out whether one of the ideas would spark their interest. This is during this brainstorming ses- sion that team nuclei progressively formed, as people started to discuss the merits of some of the ideas they had produced or read.

Figure 4.2 Participants sticking and reading ideas on flipcharts

If we focus on the ideas themselves, we thus realize how they pass, during this brainstorming session, from the status of having *to be* written down on post-its to having *been* actually written down on these supports. This new type of materialization is, of course, crucial as it allows them to be formulated, discussed, and evaluated as such. While they already existed under the form of requirements (and mental representations), they now acquire another form of existence: they have a specific formulation and they are displayed on post-its, which have all been stuck by participants on six flip charts. Relationally speaking, we also see how their being evolved: some of them will be the object of discussion, while others will be completely ignored, depending on the interest they are able to raise in participants. In other words, some ideas will start to exist *more*, while others will unfortunately end up existing less, as they will be ultimately discarded and forgotten.

Existing more, for an idea, consists here of passing several tests of selection. If it manages to raise the interest of at least two participants, an idea is authorized, according to the requirements previously presented by the organizers, to be pitched during a second plenary session. It means, for all practical purpose, that this idea exists not only *as* formulated on a post-it but also *as* discussed, *as* possibly supported by at least two participants, and *as* pitched in front of an audience. Existing less, on the contrary, means that it will not materialize in discussions, evaluations, and/ or reinterpretations, which means that ultimately it will not materialize under the form of a pitch. For all practical purposes, all these unsuccessful ideas will disappear and cease to exist, except maybe if they happen to survive in the head of the persons who initially formulated them.

Following the becoming of an idea thus consists here of following the various beings *through which* it materializes/signals/embodies itself during these first moments: *as* requirements formulated by the organizers, *as* a "flash" in someone's mind (this is how the actual birth of the idea that ended up being followed was described by its initiator), *as* formulated on a post-it, *as* supported by participants, and *as* pitched in front of an audience. Each time, we observe that a given idea literally *acquires* various properties, features, or characteristics, which participate in its identity and evolution, *making it exist more*. Interestingly, we also note how each of these features always is the product of a performance: presenting its requirement, flashing in someone's mind, being written down on a post-it, sparking interest, and being pitched to an audience.

Each property, feature or characteristic can thus be identified with what Karen Barad (2003, 2007) calls an *agential cut* or *phenomenon*. For instance, an idea can be deemed interesting because it manages to *raise interests* in some participants who are then ready to defend and pitch it. Of course, other factors might play a role in the fact that some people will end up getting together to work on a specific project (maybe they already knew each other, maybe they ended up having no choice, etc.), but what matters is that, *ceteris paribus*, any property that an idea will end up having will always be the product of a specific *relation* that has to be established/performed. Some ideas will *make the (agential) cut*, so to speak, while others will not, and this precisely what we observe here.

Making the cut here means, relationally speaking, that through a certain configuration of beings—a certain formulation, an audience made of participants with specific interests, their reactions, etc.—certain singularities will emerge and become identifiable—that is, acquire a distinct form, separable and identifiable from the rest. In this case, these singularities will be called "interesting ideas." As you can imagine, the researchers were like the participants, and they were also looking for an idea that would also catch their attention. This is what happened during the second plenary session when the team nuclei had to present their respective pitches. One of these pitches generated much applause and excitement in the audience, which led one of the researchers to select it as the team he would shadow for the remaining two days.

Although this specific pitch was already analyzed in previous articles (Cooren, 2015; Martine & Cooren, 2016), we will reproduce it here, because it is a vivid example that demonstrates lucidly the process of relating/linking/connecting (the passage in italics were translated from French to English):

Excerpt #1

1		((Eva, Pierre, and Bruno step onto the stage. Eva grabs
2		the microphone.))
3	EVA:	Hi
4		(1.0)
5	EVA:	Just before, when you were in the tour through the
6		Museum, did you notice the monkeys?
7		(0.3)

8	AUDIENCE:	um::: ((approvingly))
9	EVA:	((nodding)) The funny sculpture. And did you happen
10		to notice that the painting, just behind, of the woman
11		(.) it was like the portrait of a woman and she kind of
12		has her face averted like this ((imitating the woman by
13		turning her face)) as if she was kind of like (.) tired of
14		having to look at the monkeys all [day long
15	AUDIENCE:	[((laughs))
16	EVA:	((nods and smiles)) So we want to kind of like give
17		those portraits and the artworks a <u>voice</u>. Kind of like (.)
18		[lay open, reveal
19	SOMEONE:	[Oh:: ((admiring))
20	EVA:	kind of the relationships that they have to establish just
21		by hanging out all day long=
22	AUDIENCE:	=((laughs))=
23	EVA:	=It's like- ((looking at the wooden sign where the name
24		of the project is written)) The project is called ((Pierre
25		lifts up the sign to show it to the audience)) "The secret
26		life- The secret <u>social</u> life of artworks"
27	AUDIENCE:	Ohhh ahhh ((appreciating, laughing and clapping))
28		((Eva gives the microphone to Pierre))
29		[((The camera lingers on the sign (5.0). It is divided in
30		four parts by four titles printed in black. Under each title
31		some text is handwritten in pink. Under "**title**" is written:
32		"the secret social life of artworks." Under "**description**"
33		is written: "performance," "after- hours," "spotlights,"
34		"conversation," "gossip," "(social) networks," and
35		"personalities." Under "**challenge**" is written: "renewing
36		the visitor's experience." The text written under "**team**"
37		is not readable. See also Figure 4.2))
38	PIERRE:	[((From this point on, the interaction is in French)) *Um*
39		*yes so "the secret life of artworks" uh:: in French. And*
40		*we would like to lay open a little this <u>secret</u> life that is*
41		*happening, these secret exchanges that may happen be-*
42		*tween a painting, a sculpture, a sculpture that is outside,*
43		*and so on (.) try to lay open this a little. Uh::*
44	ÉLODIE:	*Which profiles do you need? [°to complete°*
45	PIERRE:	*[At the moment we have a*
46		*developer ((turning slightly toward Eva)), me I am more*
47		*in UX, [user] experience, and Bruno who is a graphic*
48		*designer. We are looking for someone in communication*
49		*and mostly in content, very much, I think we are going to*
50		*need it ((Bruno nods yes)) and making too (.) makers of all*
51		*stripes, join us ((Bruno nods yes, smiling)) and we're also*
52		*looking for someone who is not necessarily a participant*

53		*but someone from the museum who could give- make ref-*
54		*erences, well* [*who has knowledge of the content*
55	ÉLODIE:	[*This, they're going to go around, yes. No*
56		*need to put it in your team, it's all right. Thank you*
57	PIERRE:	[*Thank you*
58	ÉLODIE:	[*Great* ((she starts clapping while Eva, Pierre, and Bruno
59		step down from the stage))
60	AUDIENCE:	((Clapping))

What is happening in this sequence? A lot of things for sure, but let's focus first on Eva as she is presenting, for the first time, the idea of her team. We note that she is doing something very clever, as she decides not to spell out the idea right away (this only happens on lines 16–17). Instead of this, she begins her speech by asking the audience a question: "Just before, when you were in the tour through the museum, did you notice the monkeys?" (lines 5–6), a question that has the merit of catching the audience's attention. The participants are indeed expecting the pitch of an idea and instead of that, they are asked if they remembered "the monkeys," as Eva calls one of the sculptures presented in the museum where the event is taking place.

Having secured that at least some members of the audience do appear to remember this sculpture (we hear members responding approvingly to her question on line 8), she then asks if they remember another artwork, which she presents as the portrait of a woman, whose face she mimics, "as if she was kind of like (.) tired of having to look at the monkeys all day long" (lines 13–14), a move that, as we see, manages to create a lot of laughs in the audience (line 15). Although the idea per se has not been revealed yet, Eva's pitch seems up to this point treated as being *related* to what her team has in mind. A certain suspense or expectation has now been created around the idea they are supposed to present, as the audience seems already enraptured, given its positive reactions so far.

After nodding and smiling, Eva then ends the suspense by saying, "So we want to kind of like give those portraits and the artworks a <u>voice</u>. Kind of like (.) lay open . . . reveal kind of the relationships that they have to establish just by hanging out all day long" (lines 16–21). This revelation draws, this time, gasps of admiration (line 19) and laughs (line 22); it enacts an agential cut that defines the obvious success of this idea, at least for this specific audience. At this point, we can therefore note that this idea manages to pass another test successfully: After attracting three people (Eva, Pierre, and Bruno) around its destiny, it seems good enough to draw gasps of admiration, confirming the interest it appears to trigger around itself.

Note the relational character of the idea we are now focusing on. After being *written down* on a post-it by one of the participants (we later learned that it is Pierre who initially got this idea and posted it on the panel titled "Renewing the visitor's experience"), this idea was *discussed* by Pierre and Eva (a colleague Pierre happened to know), who both decided that it was worth being pitched in front of the other participants.

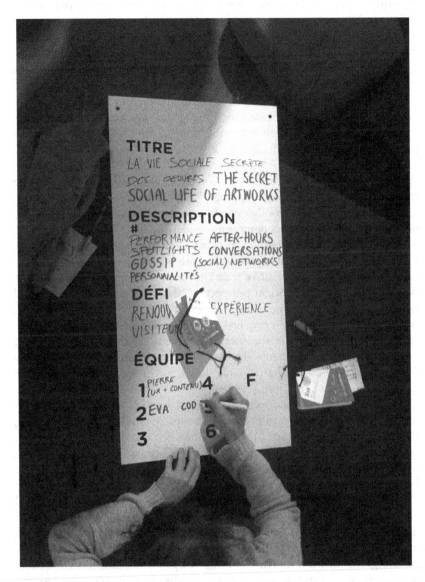

Figure 4.3 Eva writing on the wooden sign where the idea/project is described

In preparation for their pitch, Pierre and Eva were then given, as all team nuclei born from this brainstorming process, a wooden sign on which four sections would have to be filled in: title (*titre*), description, challenge (*défi*) and team (*équipe*) (see Figure 4.3).

Under the section called *title*, Pierre and Eva wrote "the secret social life of artworks"; under the section called *description*, they wrote seven keywords ("performance," "after hours," "spotlights," "conversation," "gossip," "(social) networks," and "personalities"); under the section called *challenge*, they wrote, "renewing the visitor's experience"; and under the section called *team*, which could include up to six members, they wrote "1. Pierre (UX and content)," "2. Eva (developer)," later adding "3. Bruno (graphic designer)" after meeting him as they were waiting in line to pitch their idea. It is therefore armed with this wooden sign that Eva, Pierre, and Bruno went up on the stage and this is this sign that Eva was reading to the audience as she finally revealed the official name of their idea: "It's like-((looking at the wooden sign where the name of the project is written)) The project is called ((Pierre lifts up the sign to show it to the audience)) 'The secret life- The secret *social* life of artworks'" (lines 23–26), a revelation that again triggers very positive reactions from the audience ("Ohhh ahhh ((appreciating, laughing and clapping))" (line 27)).

In part thanks to this wooden sign filled out by Eva, the idea officially *has* not only a name but also a description under the form of seven keywords, a challenge that it is supposed to meet, and a team nucleus made of Bruno, Pierre, and Eva. Its level of existence thus can be said to *increase* again, especially if we consider the positive reactions from the audience when the title is revealed. From a relational perspective, these positive reactions indeed *enact* and *confirm* its interesting/exciting/attractive character. This idea, whose name has now been revealed, literally *made an impression*—that is, impressed members of the audience, which a priori increases its chance of attracting enough participants around its destiny. Chances are that this idea now *also* exists in some participants' heads as the latter reflect on which team they might want to join.

Having taken the microphone that Eva handed to him, Pierre then repeats the title, this time in French, and explains the idea one more time, in French too (lines 38–43). As the organizers try to expedite the pitches, he is then interrupted by Élodie, the master of ceremonies, who asks him what type of profile they need in order to complete their team (line 44). Pierre responds by first mentioning what expertise they already have ("At the moment we have a developer ((turning slightly toward Eva)), me I am more in UX, [user] experience, and Bruno who is a graphic designer" (lines 45–48)) and then specifies the expertise they need: "We are looking for someone in communication and mostly in content, very much, I think we are going to need it ((Bruno nods yes)) and making too (.) makers of all stripes, join us ((Bruno nods yes, smiling)) and we're also looking for someone who is not necessarily a participant but someone from the museum who could give- make references, well who has knowledge of the content" (lines 48–54).

Although their team needs this expertise, it is also, and by proxy, *their idea that needs it*. In other words, we see how this idea, once formulated, can again be defined by what it *requires* or *has* to have. A certain *tension* is therefore enacted around its existence: it now needs various fields of expertise that Pierre, Eva and Bruno hope to find among the participants:

an expert in communication, an expert in content (meaning someone who is an art expert or historian), a maker, and someone from the museum. All these people that Pierre says the team is looking for could indeed contribute to the becoming of this idea within the next two days.

A few minutes later, three additional participants—France, a historian; Mai Anh, a communication specialist; and Julia, an advertising expert—join the team. Having six team members to support it, the idea has now reached the official threshold and can then be validated by the organizers, which is what happens. This means that the six team members can start working on it.

Concretizing the Idea

We could have titled this section "Materializing the idea," but this title would have then be a little misleading. We now understand that the materialization of the idea already took place from the very beginning of the creative process, and even before, as we saw with the requirements formulated by the organizers. So far, this idea has indeed materialized under the form of (1) the specific requirements spelled out by the master of ceremonies at the beginning of the event; (2) the flash in Pierre's mind; (3) the post-it note he wrote down; (4) the discussion he had with Eva; (5) the wooden sign where its official title was mentioned; (6) the pitch Pierre, Eva, and Bruno made in front of the audience; (7) the (positive) reaction this idea produced in the participants; and (8) the official validation the idea benefited from once the team was completed.

All these features compose as many ways by which this idea has materialized so far, meaning that its existence already appears sustained or supported by these other beings. Instead of speaking of materialization, which is accurate, but somehow misleading, we could then speak of *concretization*. Why concretization? Because this idea, despite its multiple materializations, remains a little abstract so far: it has certainly been spelled out, written down, discussed, pitched, admired, and validated, but its mode of existence is essentially textual and iconic, even if it is also made of affects (as people seem to love it). Concretizing the idea thus means that it will start to literally *solidify* or *harden*.

Concretizing comes indeed from the Latin *concrescere*, which literally means to grow (*crescere*) together (*con*). Beyond its formulation under the form of texts (e.g., its title "the secret social life of artworks") and visual representations (e.g., when Eva gives the example of the woman in the portrait being tired of looking at the monkeys sculpture all day long), and beyond its attractive character, this idea now has to grow and evolve into something that will possibly take other forms, hoping that at one point *all these forms will grow together*—i.e., coagulate into something that could, somehow, *stand on its own*. This is this process of concretization/coagulation that we will now observe and analyze.

Two Versions of the Idea

So let's see what is happening during the first brainstorming session that follows the official formation of the team. In this excerpt, we find Bruno talking about two versions of the idea that he thinks he recognized so far (given that Bruno is not a native speaker of English, we took the liberty of correcting some aspects of his interventions to facilitate comprehension).

Excerpt #2

457	BRUNO:	I want I want to uh- It's an open question for everyone. I
458		want to know uh uh (0.5) what kind of uh things we want
459		them to talk *about*. Like the (.) content like art- is art. Uh
460		when you- when you guys ((pointing to Eva)) pitched me
461		the (.) project I could feel a bit of humor in that
462	EVA:	Yeah
463	BRUNO:	And when you- when you arrived at the project ((looking at
464		France)) you were looking for more uh, maybe uh not seri-
465		ous but like more=
466	FRANCE:	=Social issues [xxx art
467	BRUNO:	[Social yeah issue, like what represents deeply
468		this- this art. So I want to know if we- we want to, like (.)
469		*keep* our mind open, to maybe having more like uh uh deep
470		and interesting uh thought about what the- the what the
471		art *thinks* or- and we want to explore sometimes funny and
472		like just uh in terms of relationships in this one room like
473		(.) maybe like uh there is uh I don't know a communist art
474		and uh uh uh uh how can I say uh a capitalist one so maybe
475		it's like they don't have the same points of view on on that
476		point. I don't know if we want to.
477	PIERRE:	uhu
478	BRUNO:	I want to know (.)
479	FRANCE:	But [does funny uh exclude serious?
480	BRUNO:	[what you guys feel- Sorry?
481	FRANCE:	((In French)) *Does something funny exclude [uh uh*
482	BRUNO:	[No, that's
483		*why. I don't think so. I think indeed*
484		[*that*
485	FRANCE:	[*content, in fact.*
486	BRUNO:	I think it can be both, totally=
487	PIERRE:	=And there is two things right. There is the topic of the dis-
488		cussion, like what they are talking about and there is the
489		tone of the discussion, what- are they using humor, poetry=
490	EVA:	=Yeah=
491	FRANCE:	=*Yeah*

As we see, Bruno invites his teammates to try to figure out what the art-works will talk about. Having presented what he is about to say as an open question (line 457), he indeed says, "I want to know uh uh (0.5) what kind of uh things we want them to talk about" (lines 457–459). Through this question, he is presenting to everyone around the table, we can identify an attempt to *concretize* what the dialogue between the selected artworks will be made of. Concretizing here means that even if the team members know that the project consists of making artworks speak, they still have to think about what will be assembled to materialize this dialogue.

Having asked this open question, we see him starting to respond to it by himself when he says, "Like the (.) content like art- is art" (line 459). In other words, a way to concretize the dialogue to come consists for him to announce that it will be about art, a position that will not be openly called into question later on by the other participants. He then goes on by looking at Eva while saying, "when you—when you guys ((pointing to Eva)) pitched me the (.) project I could feel a bit of humor in that" (lines 460–461), an interpretation that Eva confirms by responding "Yeah" on line 462. These two turns of talk are interesting as they show the *effect* the idea pitched by Eva apparently produced on Bruno: he could, as he says, feel a bit of humor, a feeling that is indeed confirmed by Eva: the humor was indeed there, according to her, so it is sort of normal that he also felt it.

Following the idea thus consists here of noticing what it appears to be/ become *for* Bruno: a project with a certain dose of humor, something that Eva confirms, which is important for its identity and degree of existence. But we then see Bruno turning his head to France, as he says, "And when you—when you arrived at the project ((looking at France)) you were look-ing for more uh, maybe uh not serious but like more" (lines 463–465), a turn of talk that France completes by saying "social issues" (line 466), which is then confirmed by Bruno ("Social yeah issue" (line 467)). One way to interpret what Bruno is doing at this point is to note that he appears to be translating what the idea/project could become with France: a project that talks about social issues, as this is what she is apparently looking for.

Although he specifies he is not necessarily claiming that France's ver-sion of the idea is more serious (he explicitly says, "you were looking for more uh, maybe uh not serious but like more" (lines 463–465)), a sort of *contrast* is marked by Bruno: on one side, a project with a certain touch of humor, a version represented, according to him, by Pierre and Eva; on the other side, a project speaking about social issues, a version represented for him by France. This contrast is reinforced as Bruno adds, talking about France's version: "like what represents deeply this- this art" (lines 467–468), where the *depth* of France's social issues seems to contrast with the *lightness* of humor proposed by Pierre and Eva.

Having marked this contrast, Bruno then tells his teammates that he wants to know whether they (a "they" in which he includes himself, as he says "we") want to "keep their mind open" (line 469) regarding these two options, two options that he defines as "having more like uh uh deep and interesting uh thought about what the- the what the art thinks" (lines 469–471) and/or "explor[ing] sometimes funny and like just uh in terms of relationships in this one room" (lines 471–472), two options that he also illustrates with an example featuring a communist artwork and a capitalist artwork talking to each other (lines 473–474). Asking this question can thus be interpreted as a way to explore the possibility of maintaining (or not) a tension between these two versions of the project. In other words, *these two ways of concretizing/materializing the project could be managed and reconciled by the participants as they move forward in its completion.*

As we see, France reacts by saying, "But does funny uh exclude serious?" (line 479), which means that she apparently heard Bruno presenting these two options as being mutually exclusive, something she is implicitly calling into question through this turn of talk. Bruno then responds that he does not precisely think that they are incompatible and that this is the reason why he is asking them this question ("*No, that's why. I don't think so. I think indeed that . . .* I think they can be both totally" (lines 483 and 486), to which Pierre adds, "And there is two things right. There is the topic of the discussion, like what they are talking about and there is the tone of the discussion, what- are they using humor, poetry" (lines 487–489), which is approved by both Eva ("Yeah" (line 490)) and France ("Yeah" (line 491)).

A sort of compromise seems to come out of these discussion, as Pierre implicitly proposes that the content/topic of the discussion could be about social issues (France's version of the idea), while the way this content/topic is delivered—what Pierre calls the tone—could be humoristic (Pierre and Eva's version), a solution that seems to please both Eva and France. In terms of becoming, we thus see how the idea/project progresses through these turns of talk, a progression that consists here of defining what the main ingredients of the dialogue to come should look like, a dialogue that should be made of social issues and humor.

Throughout this brainstorming session, we also observe the teammates drawing or writing their ideas on a big roll of paper that they have installed on their working table (Figure 4.4). In many ways, this is also a way by which their project materializes, as this roll will sometimes be used to remind them what they agreed on or what their challenges are supposed to be. Later on— and in a way that resonates with a practice described in Chapter 5—this piece of paper will be hung on a wall so that they all can see it easily while working on the project. Their ideas exist not only *through* the way they are discussed and remembered by the teammates but also *through* this roll of paper, *standing on their own,* so to speak. For instance, Pierre will, at some point, write the word "*historytelling*" on the roll, a portmanteau word that is supposed to synthesize their desire to both address questions of history (France and Mai Anh's concerns) and storytelling (Pierre and Eva's concerns).

This roll of paper is important, as it allows the teammates to give their ideas a mode of existence that exceeds their formulations in a discussion

Figure 4.4 The working table with the roll of paper. The word "historytelling"
appears at the bottom of the roll in the middle

or as memory traces. These ideas have now what Derrida (1988) would
call a certain *restance*—that is, a staying capacity (Cooren, 2000). They
not only exist *through* the discussions and mental representations of the
six participants, they also exist *through* this roll of paper, which participates in their solidification/concretization.

How the Monkeys and the Woman Deconcretized

The teammates still have, however, to figure out what artworks will be
selected for their project. As we saw earlier, Eva and Pierre had in mind
the idea of a dialogue between a monkey sculpture and a woman in a
portrait—an idea that happened to be extremely successful with the audience to which they pitched it. Unfortunately for them, this idea proved to
be difficult to concretize, as shown in the following excerpt:

Excerpt #3

670	FRANCE:	*Then the monkeys also are in contemporary art?=*
671	JULIA:	*=Yes the monkeys yes the monkey sculpture yes*
672	BRUNO:	*Yes this:: is really great this room- the room is really uh*
673		*special [I find*
674	PIERRE:	*[Uhu*
675	JULIA:	*Yes*

676		(3.0)
677	MELANIE:	*Be [careful with the copyrights, however, with contempo-*
678		*rary art, it's gonna be difficult*
679	EVA:	[*Ah yes*
680	BRUNO:	Yeah?
681	MELANIE:	[*to use the artwork*
682	FRANCE:	[*Well Were there a lot of tapes in this room?* ((tapes
683		mean there are copyrights issues))
684	BRUNO:	*But we can not take them in picture*
685		(0.5)
686	MELANIE:	*Yes*
687	BRUNO:	However, we can make install- well we can manage to cre-
688		ate sort of installations?
689	MELANIE:	*Absolutely, it's just if you want to show the- the- the- force*
690		*of the narrative that is going to be woven [between the*
691		*artworks*
692	BRUNO:	[*Yeah yeah yeah*
693	MELANIE:	*It would be nice to have them (.) And there, the example*
694		*that you-* ((switching to English)) *like the example you*
695		gave in your pitch with the- the- the- woman and uh
696	FRANCE:	The monkeys=
697	MELANIE:	=The monkeys. The monkeys are allowed, but we can't see
698		the- the woman, so::: like (0.5) It might be easier to go uh::
699		in an exhibition room where you have uh no problem with
700		the art
701	MAI ANH:	But it means that we have=
702	BRUNO:	=Or we can- we can check it out like lately with the per-
703		sonnel of the museum and altogether we can like-
704	MELANIE:	Like the old masters it's like it's (.) could be interesting
705		[cause
706	JULIA:	[Yeah
707	MELANIE:	Like everything like is free to use ((Eva nods)) and some-
708		times it's more like maybe (.) boring and to create things
709		could be an interesting=
710	PIERRE:	=Um=
711	MELANIE:	=idea. Or not ((smiling))

What we indeed observe here is (the beginning of) the death of the initial version of the idea, as initially presented by Eva and Pierre during their pitch. While France, Julia, and Bruno are talking about the monkey sculpture, we see Melanie, a person who works for the museum and has the responsibility of helping the team during the creative process, warning them about the difficulty of using the contemporary art room because of copyright issues (lines 677 and 681). Although Bruno responds with solutions that could be worked out to overcome this obstacle—not taking pictures (line 684) and just making installations (lines 687–688)—Melanie puts forward the importance of showing what she calls "the force of the narrative that is going to be woven between the artworks" (lines 689–691). In other words, not being able to take pictures amounts to being unable to show the project outside of the museum once completed.

Melanie goes on by using the example of the two artworks pitched by Eva—the monkey sculpture and the woman in the portrait—to demonstrate that they would not be allowed to show the woman (lines 697–698) and invite the team members to check out other rooms that would not be as problematical (lines 698–700), an alternative that Bruno appears to consider (lines 702–703). As an illustration, Melanie mentions the idea of using the old masters' room, which has, according to her, no copyright issues (lines 704–708), an idea that Julia seems to like (line 706). As she points out, this old masters' room tends to be considered boring and could therefore benefit from the project the team has in mind (lines 707–709).

Concretizing, as we already know, also means solidifying, and it is precisely the *solidity* of their initial idea that is being tested at this point (Martine & Cooren, 2016). Through Melanie's remarks, we realize how some key aspects of the project are now being threatened. As is the case with almost all the participants in the Museomix event, Eva and her teammates are indeed interested in publicizing the result of their project, a possibility that Melanie calls into question through her intervention. The copyright laws that she implicitly invokes thus appear to disassemble what this idea/project is supposed to become once completed: an installation that would be publicized on the web and even possibly mentioned in the media.

What we also observe through this episode can thus be considered a change of trajectory for this idea. Instead of materializing in the contemporary room, as initially planned, the project will probably have to find its way in another one, hoping that it will manage to solidify/concretize/materialize through other artworks. This episode can thus also be identified as participating in a process of *deconcretization*. In other words, a big part of what had been assembled so far—the funny and serious sides of the project, the audience's enthusiasm, as well as the teammates' interests—was lying on the relation between the monkey sculpture and the woman in the portrait. *All this assemblage is now threatened to vanish* because of copyright issues.

Between Continuity and Discontinuity: The Solidification of the Idea

Let's see how the brainstorming goes on, as participants are now talking about how the artworks—whatever they would end up becoming—could *communicate* with each other. Just before this excerpt, the six teammates have been talking about the possibility of having the artworks whisper to the visitors of the museum.

Excerpt #4

1320	EVA	Yeah (0.5) I can of feel with the whispering or when you do
1321		this ((pretending she is listening closely to what a portrait is
1322		saying)), it is almost you xxx a monologue right? Like it's
1323		gonna be. How do we make it like an actual conversation?
1324		I mean the monologue would be interesting as well, some-
1325		one who would just maybe <u>bitch</u> about all the other=
1326	JULIA	=uhum= (approving))
1327	EVA	=paintings or something (.) But they said uh=
1328	JULIA	=it humanizes the character (.) because the bad human side
1329		(.) You it's humanization of the-
1330	BRUNO	Interesting so you- you think- Yeah maybe it's a dialogue
1331		or maybe it's a monologue=
1332	EVA	=Yeah yeah maybe it's like during the day there's some
1333		monologues and then=
1334	JULIA	=Yeah=
1335	EVA	=At night [they become alive and then actually talk to each
1336		other↑=
1337	PIERRE	[Yeah ((clearing his throat))
1338	EVA	=And then it's more like (.) we kind of thought about it
1339		at the beginning (.) it's right after hours, night time and
1340		then there's spotlights on the paintings [that are just talk-
1341		ing right?=
1342	PIERRE	[Yeah
1343	EVA	=And then they actually- it's a performance ((touching her
1344		ear)) so they talk loud enough ((looking at Bruno)), you
1345		know ((looking at Pierre)) (0.7)
1346	BRUNO	So=
1347	EVA	[=But you kind it's like uh ((turning her body to her right
1348		as if she was hearing something there))
1349	PIERRE	[So you put a flashlight=
1350	EVA	=Yeah=
1351	BRUNO	=and highlight the painting who is [speaking?=
1352	PIERRE	=Yeah=
1353	EVA	=Or a phase yeah
1354	PIERRE	And I-
1355	EVA	It's like theater play more=
1356	BRUNO	=Yes it's [yeah=
1357	EVA	[Yeah ((nodding))
1358	PIERRE	As a visitor you kind of (.) enter this like secret (.) life of the
1359		paintings, like you: ((raising his eyes to the ceiling, express-
1360		ing that he is thinking of something)) They are not really
1361		here for you, they are living their own life and it's you like
1362		just like peep ((closing his fist in front of his right eye, as to
1363		pretend he is looking through a little hole)) into- into their
1364		life to see how they behave when (.) nobody is around

1365		(2.0)
1366	BRUNO	Imagine you- you're visiting the museum and at one point
1367		((snapping his finger)) boo everything becomes black and
1368		you have the spotlight and they are just starting the- the
1369		conversation for two minutes and after that ((opening his
1370		hands to express that the light is coming back))
1371	JULIA	Yes
1372	BRUNO	Come back to normal
1373	JULIA	Yeah absolutely
1374	BRUNO	((pretending he is the visitor who looks surprised)) Oh
1375		[what just happened? Don't know
1376	JULIA	[it's like create some incident in the- in the visit for like tak-
1377		ing hostage like of the
1378	BRUNO	Ahhh: ((exhales loudly))
1379	JULIA	Because-
1380	BRUNO	That would be uh
1381	JULIA	((laughter))
1382	BRUNO	Hysteric ((laughter)) I don't know but if you take them by
1383		surprise
1384	JULIA	Uhu
1385	FRANCE	Uhu
1386		(1.0)
1387	PIERRE	Or you hear just one word that is "Atcha" ((pretending he
1388		is a person sneezing)) ((laughter))
1389		((all the group members laugh))
1390	( )	Atcha
1391	( )	Oh yeah!
1392	PIERRE	((pretending he is a visitor looking around where the
1393		sneeze is coming from)) It's cold in here

As we see, Eva takes up this idea of having the artworks whispering to the museum visitors but then translates it into the idea of a monologue (lines 1320–1322), something that has not been mentioned so far, as participants were initially talking about a dialogue/discussion between the artworks. While we see her wondering how they should make this monologue an actual conversation (line 1323), she then mentions that "the monologue would be interesting as well, someone would just maybe *bitch* about all the other paintings or something" (lines 1324–1327), an idea that is met with approval by Julia (line 1326), as she says that it humanizes the artworks, showing "the bad human sides" (line 1328).

We then see Bruno also marking his interest as he proposes his own interpretation/ translation of what Eva just said, "Interesting so you- you think- Yeah maybe it's a dialogue or maybe it's a monologue" (lines 1330–1331). This interpretation/translation is then immediately confirmed by Eva, but also expanded, as she proposes that "during the day there's some monologues and then at night they become alive and then actually talk to each other" (lines 1332–1336), an idea to which both Julia and Pierre react positively by expressing their approval (lines 1334 and 1337).

The initial idea thus progresses and expands as we see it opening itself to the possibility of combining monologues and dialogues, a possibility that is initially and implicitly proposed by Eva, but that is then explicitly spelled out by Bruno. The content of the monologues is also addressed as Eva mentions the possibility of having the artworks bitching about each other, which is approved by Julia as a way to humanize them. In relational terms, we can thus observe how the idea both *translates and solidifies* each time it is taken up by someone or met with approval, which happens a lot in this excerpt.

As in any trajectory, the idea also navigates between *sameness* and *otherness*. Sameness because Bruno, Julia, and Pierre all appear to *approve* the idea Eva initially presented, creating an effect of *continuity*. Otherness because we see Bruno and Eva also *building* on it, which means that they somehow *alter* or *modify* it, making it something else and creating an effect of *discontinuity*. It is precisely in this tension between sameness/iteration/continuity and otherness/alteration/discontinuity that the becoming of the idea will lie on throughout the three days.

Interestingly, its *solidification* also ends up lying on these effects of both continuity and discontinuity. Continuity because approving an idea is a way to solidify it (it is not only supported by one person, but by others too). Discontinuity because building on it is a way to *concretize* it—that is, to assemble other aspects that will possibly *make it more solid*, but also *different* from its previous state. It is this protean/metamorphic aspect of the idea/project that the following of its trajectories reveal: its completion depends, by definition, on additions/alterations/discontinuities that have to be paradoxically identified as participating in the continuity of its expressions.

The same logic operates later in the excerpt, as we see Eva reinforcing her initial idea by mentioning another thought she said both Pierre and her initially had ("And then it's more like (.) we kind of thought about it at the beginning (.) it's right after hours, night time and then there's spotlights on the paintings that are just talking right" (lines 1338–1341)). As we remember, the idea of having spotlights had indeed been written down on the wooden sign they used to pitch their initial idea (see Figure 4.3). As Pierre and Bruno again approve the idea of the spotlight, we then see Bruno building on it ("So you put a flashlight and highlight the painting who is speaking?" (lines 1349–1351)).

Just a few lines later, we see him elaborating on this idea: "Imagine you- you're visiting the museum and at one point ((snapping his finger)) boo everything becomes black and you have the spotlight and they are just starting the the conversation for two minutes and after that ((opening his hands to express that the light is coming back)) come back to normal" (lines 1366–1372). Transporting his teammates into this fictional situation can then be seen as a way to concretize what he seems to identify as a key aspect of Eva's idea. The spotlight/flashlight in the context of a museum room that suddenly becomes black would allow them to invite the visitors to pay attention to the discussions taking place between the artworks.

This idea is immediately met with a certain enthusiasm by Julia ("Yes" (line 1371): "Yeah absolutely" (line 1373)), who compares it to a situation where the visitors would be "taken hostage" (lines 1376–1377). As for Bruno, he starts imitating a visitor surprised by the blackout ("Oh what just happened? Don't know ahhh:" (lines 1374–1375)), mentioning that it would be "hysteric" (line 1382). As a certain enthusiasm is building up around the table, Pierre also imitates an artwork sneezing and a visitor turning his head toward the sound he just heard (lines 1387–1388), which triggers a lot of laughs in the team.

Interestingly, these imitations could be interpreted as a way, again, to *expand* and *concretize* the idea they are working on. The fact that they laugh at these imitations also marks the *passing of an important test*. It is a *good* idea because it is funny, at least to them, an idea that might be then worth pursuing, which is exactly what they will try to do for the rest of the process.

Passing or Not Passing the Tests of Solidity

As the brainstorming session goes on, we observe them wondering whether there is a room where they could play on the lights or the sounds, noting that some rooms of the museum already have speakers. While Melanie, the museum representative, quickly terminates the idea of playing with the lights in the rooms, the teammates pursue and examine the idea of using spotlights. It will, however, also be killed at some point by the museum management: they will not allow it, for security reasons, as the spotlights could damage the paintings. Even the idea of using the speakers of the room will have to be abandoned, which, as we will see, will lead them to build their own sound device.

What do these failures mean, relationally speaking? Precisely that, as anything, the becoming of an idea—that is, the evolution of its properties— highly depends on its capacity to *overcome obstacles* that can hinder its progression. While the team appears extremely *attached* to the idea of having spotlights in the context of a blackout orchestrated in one of the museum rooms, its concretization/translation/materialization proves to be impossible, as the management of the museum *objects* to this technical aspect of the idea (Martine & Cooren, 2016). Objecting here means that the idea cannot acquire the property/trait/characteristic that the teammates want it to have at this point. The device they have in mind should consist of two artworks not only speaking to each other (a property/trait/characteristic that still holds firmly) but also being illuminated by spotlights in a dark room (a property/trait/characteristic that proves to be impossible).

While relating always consists of acquiring new properties, we thus see how some relations can precisely prove not solid enough. Not being solid enough here means that they do not withstand a specific test, a test that consists of overcoming or circumventing an obstacle in its trajectory. The idea could have taken the form of spotlights in a dark museum room, but spotlights are forbidden as they could alter the paintings, while playing with the lights of the room is judged too disruptive to the visitors. As always, a trajectory is stopped by others, which are deemed more important: it is indeed in the name of both the visitors' tranquility and the artworks' integrity that these ideas have to be abandoned. Their respective trajectories cannot be threatened or altered.

The Selection of the Two Artworks

Despite this drawback, our teammates do not lose hope as they now decide to look for artworks that could be dialoguing with each other. As they understood that the contemporary room was a no-no, we find them in one of the other rooms of the museum, a room where Eva suddenly notices a statue of a 17th century man who appears to be staring at the portrait of an 18th century woman.

Excerpt #5

3205	EVA	That's a Medici
3206		(1.0)
3207	EVA	That would be kind of <u>funny</u> (.) because he is like the art
3208		lover right↑
3209		(1.0)
3210	MELANIE	Yeah
3211		(10.0) ((everybody gets closer to the two artworks))
3212	JULIA	((laughs))
3213	MAI ANH	It's like (whoo) ((laughs))
3214		(2.0)
3215	PIERRE	((laughs)) Oh look he's c- [he's cruising her
3216	MAI ANH	[Oh yeah yeah yeah=
3217	EVA	=Ah:::
3218	PIERRE	He is [totally cruising her
3219	EVA	[She's looking ba::ck
3220	JULIA	((laughs))
3221	MAI ANH	"I want you to be mine↑"
3222	PIERRE	Yeah
3223	MAI ANH	It's happening on
3224		(1.0)
3225	PIERRE	"I just want to:: add her on Facebook"
3226	MAI ANH	She kind like feels like she's like (.) into it too
3227	EVA	Oh yeah:: she likes it
3228	PIERRE	Yeah

3229	FRANÇOIS	But the- the dog is a symbol of faithfulness, fidelity so
3230		((camera looking at the caption next to the painting of
3231		the young lady)) so she is uh
3232	MAI ANH	She is like "Oh I like his hair (.) it kind [of look like my
3233		dog's (1.0) fur"
3234	PIERRE	[Yeah (1.5) He
3235		wants to talk to her but (.) because she has a dog and he
3236		is afraid of dogs and he can't really [approach her
3237	JULIA	[(((gasps))
3238		(4.0)
3239	BRUNO	Well another story of this one (.) the girl to- this morning
3240		said that- that was uh (.) for becom(ing) the fiancée of
3241		someone so just because (.) <u>before</u> uh (0.5) actually meet-
3242		ing her (1.0) he gets this portrait [(.) of your next woman
3243	MAI ANH	[Oh yeah
3244	EVA	Oh:[::
3245	BRUNO	[So the guy gets the portrait (.) and it takes like six or
3246		eight months to do that kind of things (.) after that you
3247		need to travel it so anyway [(((laughs)) you get it super late
3248	FRANCE	[It's not speed dating
3249	BRUNO	No, no [it's not speed dating at all
3250	EVA	[uh uh (.) yeah ((laughs))
3251	MAI ANH	[Oh I *love* it!
3252	FRANCE	[(((Laughs))
3253	EVA	[(((Laughs))
3254	BRUNO	[And you get the portrait and ah OK so this is my wife
3255		°OK°
3256		(0.5)
3257	BRUNO	And after that you see the real [wife
3258	EVA	[Yeah
3259	FRANCE	And it
3260	EVA	But ( ) (.) it's also interesting because [that's <u>probably</u> it's
3261		that person was a bit of mystery may be (.) [around it
3262	FRANCE	[I am sure she didn't
3263		have the choice of who (0.5) she was getting married to
3264		((camera turns toward the sculpture))
3265	MAI ANH	[*I like this comment of (.) this is not speed dating because*
3266		*here they really have a::* ((making a gesture with her hand
3267		back and forth between the sculpture and the painting))
3268	PIERRE	*This is slow dating*
3269	BRUNO	Slow (.) [really slow dating
3270	MAI ANH	[*Your reaction uh* ((laughs))
3271	FRANCE	Well uh it's no it's [<u>no</u> dating actually
3272	BRUNO	((speaking in French) [*Then the dog (0.5) the dog would*
3273		*be a symbol of- of- (0.5) [how do you call that=*

3274	FRANÇOIS	[*Fidelity*
3275	BRUNO	*Fidelity yeah this then of::* [*yeah that exactly*
3276	MAI ANH	[*Yeah*
3277		(2.0)
3278	BRUNO	*Which is very bizar=*
3279	FRANCE	*=Submission* ((laughs))
3280	BRUNO	*Submission a little yes °pfff absolutely°*
3281	MELANIE	*But it's* [*especially fidelity still this dog here, this period*
3282		[*here it's-*
3283	FRANCE	[*But they*
3284	MAI ANH	[*Yeah*
3285	MELANIE	*Putting a dog then* [*This means that I will be faithful::*
3286	FRANCE	[*Yeah right it (.) that's no dating at*
3287		*all (.) because she has no choice of whom she is getting*
3288		[*married to*
3289	BRUNO	[*She has no choice at all*
3290	FRANCE	[*She has no choice*
3291	BRUNO	[*Yeah yeah yeah*
3292	PIERRE	*Maybe she has feminist aspirations*
3293		(0.5)
3294	FRANCE	*She has no choice*
3295	BRUNO	*I hope she has some:: (.) I don't know (2.5) maybe hidden*
3296		[*a symbol*
3297	FRANCE	((turning to the sculpture))
3298		[*As for him, he has more choices still*
3299	FRANCE	((laughs))
3300		(4.0)
3301	BRUNO	*I like the size of this room (.)* [*and the fact that xxxx*
3302	FRANCE	[*Renaissance- yeah xxx::*
3303		(2.0)
3304	FRANCE	*Chastity at that time* ((laughs)) *for the- for- for the*
3305		*clergymen*

So what is happening in this interaction? First, we note how Eva's comments ("That would be kind of <u>funny</u> (.) because he is like the art lover right↑" (lines 3207–3208)) are, of course, immediately linked/related to the idea/project they have been working on. Choosing this sculpture would be "kind of funny," which has been, from the beginning, a trait/property/feature Eva and Pierre have been particularly interested in. In relational terms, choosing this sculpture would then be a way to *progress* toward the acquisition of this key property: being humorous. As the other teammates get closer to the two artworks, we see them reacting favorably to what Eva just noticed, especially Julia and Mai Anh. Pierre also says, talking of the Medici, "Oh look he's c- he's cruising her" (line 3215), "He is totally cruising her" (line 3218), to which Eva reacts by mentioning that "She's looking ba::ck" (line 3219), speaking of the woman in the portrait (Figure 4.5).

Figure 4.5 The two artworks noticed by Eva during their visit: on the left, the 18th-century woman, on the right, the 17th-century man

A (visual) connection/relation/link is therefore established between these two portraits (they appear to be looking at each other, at least according to Pierre and Eva), which leads Mai Anh and Pierre to imagine what the man might be thinking about while watching the woman ("I want you to be mine↑" (Mai Anh, line 3221), "I just want to:: add her on Facebook" (Pierre, line 3225)). Mai Anh then notices that the woman "kind like feels like she's like (.) into it too" (line 3226) an interpretation that Eva immediately confirms ("Oh yeah:: she likes it" (line 3227)). Through these comments, it is therefore the concretization of the initial idea that seems to be taking place—that is, an *assemblage of properties*: the project titled "the secret social life of artworks" could materialize through these two characters, who could also be seen as sustaining a loving relationship, concretized through the improvised thoughts that these two persons might have.

Let's not forget that the teammates also agreed that there would need to be a serious/historical component in their project. As France told them, these artworks should also talk about *social issues*, a theme that has been identified as not being incompatible with humor. This is what François, the ethnographer with the camera, seems to have in mind when he (clumsily?) intervenes in the scene, noting that the dog portrayed at the woman's feet is supposed to symbolize faithfulness/fidelity (lines 3229–3231), something he learned during the guided tour organized at the beginning of the Museomix event. Although this remark about the dog and its meaning could have immediately triggered a reflection on the social dimension of the painting, we see Mai Anh and then Pierre translating this reference to the dog into a funny situation ("She is like 'Oh I like his hair (.) it kind of look like my dog's (1.0) fur'" (Mai Anh, lines 3232–3233); "Yeah (1.5). He wants to talk to her but (.) because she has a dog and he is afraid of dogs and he can't really approach her" (Pierre, lines 3234–3236).

Bruno finally seems to echo François's remark when he informs the other participants that this portrait is supposed to be what the fiancé receives before getting married to the woman who has been painted here (lines 3239–3242), something he said he also learned during the guided tour. He then mentions that this process was taking a lot of time (six to eight months, according to him), which leads France to humorously note, "It's not speed dating" (line 3248), something that Bruno confirms ("No, no it's not speed dating at all" (line 3249)), a comparison that Eva, but especially Mai Anh seem to like a lot ("Oh I *love* it!" (line 3251)), possibly because of its funny character. While Bruno builds on the awkwardness of the situation (a man who only knows a woman through the portrait he receives about her, before getting married to her), Eva prefers to speak of the mystery that surrounds it (lines 3260–3261), two traits that make this painting potentially interesting.

In keeping with her strong interest in social issues, France then adds, "I am sure she didn't have the choice of who (0.5) she was getting married to" (lines 3262–3263)—a comment Mai Anh says she likes a lot (line 3265) while taking up what France was saying earlier ("this is not speed dating because here they really have a::" (lines 3265–3266). Pierre then adds, "This is slow dating" (line 3268), an appellation that is corroborated by Bruno ("Slow (.) really slow dating" (line 3269)), but that is finally called into question by France when she points out that "Well uh it's no it's <u>no</u> dating actually" (line 3271).

Later on, the discussion turns around questions of fidelity that Bruno raises up again (lines 3272–3275), a fidelity that France translates as a form of submission (line 3279), but that Melanie redefines as fidelity, invoking what a dog in a painting often meant at that time. France then builds on this remark to conclude that that this woman indeed is not dating because she has no choice in this situation (lines 3286–3288). Pierre, however, points out that she might have feminist aspirations (line 3292), but France reiterates that this woman has no choice (line 3294) and then turns to the Medici who she says has more choices (line 3298), as clergymen were not that constrained by their vows of chastity (lines 3304–3305).

As we see through this discussion, the social aspect of the project progressively builds itself and progresses/expands through François, Bruno, and especially France's interventions. France speaks of the woman's submissive condition, as well as the fact that she has no choice regarding the situation in which she finds herself. France also contrasts her condition as an 18th century woman with the 17th century man represented in the statue, a man who has more freedom, she says, despite his condition as a clergyman. All this historical development could thus be interpreted as a way to show the social relevance of this artwork. In other words, it appears to *materialize* France's requirements to the extent that it could also *concretize* what she is looking for in this project.

A certain tension can, however, be felt between Pierre and France, even if it is hardly perceptible at this point. As we saw, when Pierre speaks of "slow dating" (line 3268), France later reacts by saying that "it's no dating actually" (line 3271), something that she reiterates once again later (lines 3286–3287). In contrast, when France says that the woman in the portrait "has no choice" (line 3290), we hear Pierre pointing out that this woman might have "feminist inspirations" (line 3292), to which France reacts by reiterating, "She has no choice" (line 3294). In other words, even if the team members identified humor and social issues as compatible, we start to feel that these two traits might sometimes be difficult to reconcile, something that, as we will see, will be confirmed later on, at least in the case of this project.

However, what matters at this point is that the team appears to have found what they have been looking for: two artworks that can fictitiously be described as sustaining a relationship. Furthermore, this relationship could allow them to be both humoristic (flirting always seems to be an infinite source of humor) and informative (in reference to the social conditions of the woman and the man represented). The project could thus *materialize/concretize/progress/expand* through these two figures, which is what ultimately happens.

Imagining a Technical Device to Circumvent Obstacles

Having selected the two artworks, the team can then start working on the device they have to install to create the illusion of a dialogue. In a way, this work has already started, as they had already discussed some technical aspects of the project before actually selecting the two pieces. For instance, as they are walking through the museum rooms, Bruno comes up with the idea of having two mini-speakers hidden close to each artwork. Here is what happens:

Excerpt #6

2357	BRUNO	But you see look (1.0) I would find it still interesting that
2358		(.) when I passed by him ((speaking of an artwork he is
2359		point at)), I hear his viewpoint.
2360	PIERRE	hmm
2361	BRUNO	And I don't hear right away his ((pointing at another
2362		artwork))
2363	MAI ANH	hmm
2364	BRUNO	And then when I get close to him, I hear his viewpoint

2365	MAI ANH	hmm
2366	BRUNO	But [you know, in terms of technological simplification, if
2367		it's each time just a mini-
2368	FRANCE	[But they are you know-
2369	BRUNO	speaker that is hidden on the side of- of the artworks,
2370		just- just the simple proximity with=
2371	PIERRE	=mm=
2372	BRUNO	=makes me hear that
2373	FRANCE	But [aren't they a little far in space?
2374	PIERRE	[( ) not hyper loud
2375	BRUNO	But precisely do I want that (.) hear the two of them at the
2376		same time? Maybe there is one who 'hmmmmmmm,' he
2377		looks at me ((showing the second artwork)), he mumbles,
2378		you see, and then he is like "scissors" ((showing the first
2379		artwork))
2380	PIERRE	((laughs))
2381	BRUNO	It's anyway, it's like just an example, because it's super=
2382	MAI ANH	=Yeah=
2383	BRUNO	=It's super stupid what I am telling you, but that I don't
2384		necessarily hear them at the same time, but that I hear
2385		first him and then him=
2386	PIERRE	=Yeah and then maybe the speaker [it is there xxx here
2387		((pointing at the second artwork))
2388	BRUNO	[Yeah right, it's eas-
2389		ier to hide it here or like find zones that can-
2390		(2.0)
2391	BRUNO	Because if we cannot operate the flashlights then-
2392	JULIA	hmm
2393		(1.0)
2394	PIERRE	But we could even hang a speaker like here ((showing a
2395		place in the ceiling)) have an iPhone with some tape.
2396	BRUNO	Yeah right and at what level cannot we precisely hide-
2397		(2.0)
2398	BRUNO	It's a little low technology but hey ((laughs))
2399	PIERRE	No but it's a prototype
2400	EVA	it's a perfect like that
2401	PIERRE	Yeah
2402	EVA	it's about getting the effect across, not the
2403	BRUNO	Yeah, yeah, no it's clear
2404	EVA	Not hiding it

As we see in this interaction, Bruno's idea would consist of installing two mini-speakers close to each artwork, which would then allow visitors to hear their viewpoint as they pass close to them (lines 2357–2362). While the team initially had the idea of using big speakers already installed in the room's ceiling (an idea that would anyway prove later to be impossible to implement), Bruno proposes another solution that could create a better illusion. The artworks would indeed really look like they are speaking, given that the sound would appear to come from each of them, which is what Bruno alludes to as he describes the situation. Furthermore, this device would then have the advantage, according to him, to be simpler, technologically speaking (lines 2366–2367).

As it often happens with new ideas, we see, however, someone—here, France—testing it by asking whether the two artworks Bruno is using as an example would not be too far from each other (line 2373). In other words, visitors could not hear them at the same time, as Bruno is speaking of mini-speakers with less sound power. Interestingly, Bruno responds "But precisely do I want that (.) hear the two of them at the same time?" (lines 2375–2376), which could be heard as an invitation to redefine the way they have been thinking about the whole project so far. Instead of a dialogue, Bruno then invites them to also think about two artworks that do not really speak to each other, but that express themselves anyway. This is what he alludes to when he recreates a situation where the two artworks are each engaged in a monologue that has nothing to do with the other: "Maybe there is one who 'hmmmmmmm,' he looks at me ((showing the second artwork)), he mumbles, you see, and then he is like 'scissors' ((showing the first artwork))" (lines 2376–2379).

Bruno thus invites his teammates to question how the project has been imagined so far, an invitation that Pierre seems to accept as he says, "Yeah and then maybe the speaker it is there xxx here" (line 2386) while pointing to an area where one of the two mini-speakers could be installed (Figure 4.6).

A few seconds later, Bruno will even add another argument in favor of his idea, invoking the spotlights that they are not apparently allowed to install (line 2391). In other words, Bruno also presents his technical solution as a way to *circumvent the obstacles* that have been erected by the

Figure 4.6 Pierre showing Bruno where a speaker could be located

museum management so far. With mini-speakers installed close to each artwork, they do not need spotlights anymore, as visitors will, by definition, know which artwork is supposed to be speaking, since the sound will be coming from them. This also means that the team does not need big speakers anymore—big speakers that they are not allowed to use anyway.

As we see at the end of this conversation, Eva, Pierre, and Bruno seem quite happy with this solution. Even if Bruno describes it as "low technology" (line 3298), Pierre implicitly defends it by invoking the prototypical character of the project (line 3299) while Eva adds, "it's a perfect like that" (line 2400), insisting that what they are looking for is the effect (line 2402) and not hiding the speakers (line 2404). The idea, as concretized/ translated here through Bruno's proposal, seems to pass another important test, as it appears to please at least Pierre and Eva, who happen to be its two originators.

Relationally speaking, we thus see how the technical solution imagined by Bruno allows the idea to progress by overcoming most of the obstacles that have been raised so far in its trajectory. This solution can thus be seen as a concretization in both senses of the word: its solidity is reinforced, but this solidity comes from its capacity to *reassemble what had been disassembled*. While the absence of speakers and spotlights could have made the project unfeasible, the introduction of mini-speakers makes this absence potentially irrelevant.

Completing the Project/Idea

Having decided that they would use their own speakers, Eva, Pierre, and Bruno then start working on the technical facets of the device, while France, Mai Anh and Julia decide to work on the historical dimension of the project, trying to find any information they can get about the woman in the portrait—described as probably being Countess Mary Josephine Drummond, painted by Nicolas de Largillierre around 1710–1712—and the man represented by the sculpture—Cardinal Leopoldo de' Medici, 1617–1675, fabricated in Giovanni Battista Foggini's workshop, around 1690. From this historical work, they will also be in charge of building a first draft of the dialogue.

While we observe France, Mai Anh and Julia surfing on the web to cumulate as much information as possible about these two historical characters, Eva, Pierre, and Bruno begin to test two mini-speakers they managed to get from the Museomix organizers. After speaking with a technician, they come to the conclusion that they will have to use two boxes in which the mini-speakers will be installed. That way, the sound will be sufficiently amplified and therefore hearable by the visitors. Having designed them on their computer, they build, not without difficulty, the boxes, which are now planned to be placed in front of the two artworks (Figure 4.7a). Each box will also contain a touchpad in which the dialogues will be recorded. We thus observe the idea progressively taking shape: from a flash in Pierre's

(a)

(b)

Figure 4.7 Pierre and Eva working on the sound box and the final result

mind, to discussions, to images on a computer screen, and to the actual device itself (Figure 4.7b).

Relationally speaking, we thus see the idea solidifying, a solidification that can also be understood as a form of *completion*. Completion here means that from its materialization *as* a project (which etymologically means "something thrown forth"), the idea is supposed to be *recognizable* in the materialization *of* the project itself. We thus pass, as mentioned earlier, from one materialization to another, as if each materialization were creating the conditions for the next ones. Here also, effects of discontinuity and continuity are visible, as each materialization can be seen as a *discontinuity creating effects of continuity*—discontinuity because we saw that the trajectory of the idea always evolves through the production of multiple beings with variable ontologies. Continuity because these beings—whatever or whoever they are—have to be precisely *recognized* as expressing/translating/ materializing the very idea, especially in its formulation. Completing the idea therefore means that it is supposed to be *completely* materialized.

What thus characterizes this process of completion is the *accumulation/ articulation of matters*, as we observe the idea progressively taking multiple forms: a flash in someone's mind; a pitch to an audience; a brainstorming session; drawings and words on a roll of paper; a web page where each teammate uploads reflections, pictures, and videos; images on a computer screen; two sound boxes, each containing a mini-speaker and a touchpad, etc. It is through this accumulation of matters that we can indeed speak of a passage from something (relatively—that is, never totally) abstract (the flash in Pierre's mind) to something (relatively—that is, never totally) concrete (the device), which is supposed to *complete* the process.

But what about the dialogue itself? We just observed Eva, Pierre, and Bruno working on the sound box, speakers, and touchpads, but we left aside France, Mai Anh, and Julia who have been working on the historical aspect of the project, collecting as much information as possible on the two persons represented in the artworks. It is thanks to this material that the team is supposed to be able to do some *historytelling*, as Pierre calls the type of story they should enact through this dialogue, a story made of humor and lightness (social life) but also of history and seriousness (social issues).

This is where things get a little complicated. After reading the first draft Mai Anh and France wrote for the dialogue, Pierre decides to rewrite it, probably thinking that it is too heavy in terms of history and information and too light in terms of lightness and humor. Having completed his rewriting, he (playing the role of Leopoldo de' Medici) and France (playing the role of Mary Josephine Drummond) then test the new version of the dialogue in front of their teammates. While they all agree that the length of the dialogue seems perfect (2 min. 15 s, as they initially planned), Mai Anh points out that the historical content is now too weak, a viewpoint that France appears to share when she says, "Yes, this has become, you know, small talk very quickly" (line 8657) and then, "I find it depressing that we've done all this work, in fact, for that" (line 8659). Both of them appear quite disappointed as they feel that all their historical work has now been reduced to a few allusions in the final product.

Pierre then responds that France and Mai Anh's work will not be lost as it will still appear on the web version of the project, but they retort that what matters is the dialogue that the visitors will hear and listen to, as nobody will go to the web version. Speaking of the new version Pierre just wrote, France says, "This is chitchat, there is no personality" (line 8675), "there is no content" (line 8679). At some point, we see the conversation evolving as follows:

Excerpt #7

8691	PIERRE	But (.) After (.) I don't know how you- you see this proj-
8692		ect but (.) it's (.) not necessarily its function to convey
8693		historical content, I think that it was clear from the begin-
8694		ning in our intentions.
8695	FRANCE	Well ((pointing to the roll of paper stuck on the wall)) I
8696		think that one of the objectives, it's written "learning his-
8697		tory" [it's:::: one of the first thing
8698	PIERRE	[Yeah, but uh- Yeah, but uh this does not
8699		mean that it must be only about that. For me, it's a ques-
8700		tion of proportion also in there, and the proportion of
8701		history (1.0) in there is not necessarily as important as:::
8702	FRANCE	As what?
8703		(0.5)
8704	PIERRE	Well that it be a fluid conversation between two people
8705		((France shrugs her shoulders, looking disappointed))

Two versions of the idea thus appear to clash with each other here. On one side, the idea as it had materialized the first day through Eva, Pierre, and Bruno's pitch, but also through the new version of the dialogue that Pierre just rewrote: a way to speak about the *social life* of artworks. On the other side, the idea as it had materialized through the way France initially made sense of their pitch: a way to speak about *social issues*. Speaking about the project, Pierre indeed says, "it's (.) not necessarily its function to convey historical content, I think that it was clear from the beginning in our intentions" (lines 8692–8694), to which France quickly reacts by pointing toward the roll of paper where "learning history" has been written down.

While we saw that the team originally agreed to work on *history-telling*, we realize here that two trajectories of what is supposed to be the same idea have some difficulty to merge. Where Pierre sees the glass half full, France and Mai Anh see it half empty. After some negotiations between the two parties, with Bruno playing the mediator, a final version of the dialogue will be agreed on and recorded. The whole device is now ready and can be installed. The visitors can now arrive. The artworks are speaking (Figure 4.8).

Conclusion

So what did we learn from this exercise? Maybe the most important aspect is that any materialization always is *relative/relational*. By choosing the becoming of an idea as what would be observed throughout these three days, we selected what can be considered the most abstract being that can be imagined. But even an idea always has, *even before its inception*, a material component—be it only, as we saw, through a series of

Figure 4.8 Visitors experiencing the final device

requirements that are supposed to define what it should look like. This is the paradox of materiality: if something is deemed *completely* immaterial, it cannot, by definition, exist, as there is absolutely nothing to sustain/support/withstand its existence.

This does not mean, however, that we cannot speak about immateriality anymore. It just means that immateriality becomes the equivalent of *inexistence* or *nonexistence*. Furthermore, this inexistence/nonexistence is paradoxically threatened as soon as we come to speak about it, as speaking about something that supposedly does not exist immediately amounts to giving it a level of existence, at least discursively speaking (this is, for instance, how even atheists could attribute a level of existence to God, saying that it indeed exists but only through the way it is talked about and iconically depicted by believers). Immateriality therefore becomes a *relative/pragmatist/relational notion*, as it describes the state of something whose existence is only sustained by a few other beings, and that therefore appears as (relatively) immaterial.

This is, for instance, what happened at the beginning of the ideation process when the idea virtually existed only through its *requirements* (as even virtuality always has, by definition, a material dimension) or when it started to actually exist in the *flash* Pierre said he had while looking for ideas during the first brainstorming process. The idea could then be said to be *relatively* immaterial, as the materials that sustained its existence were precisely scarce. What we observed during this three-day process was, however, an accumulation of matters that supported its existence, making it exist more and more. From its status of a relatively abstract and immaterial being, the idea became more and more concrete and material, cumulating embodiments under the form of discussions, drawings, texts, documents, technologies, artworks, etc.

The becoming of an idea thus depends on this accumulation of matters, but it also depends, as we saw, on its capacity to be *recognizable/identifiable/detectable* throughout these materializations. In other words, if we were able to highlight the protean/ metamorphic/mutable aspects of the materialization process, we also witnessed a lot of discussion regarding its recognizability. Materialization indeed involves effects of *discontinuity* and *alterity*, but we also saw that it also involves effects of *continuity* and *identity*. This is precisely what happened when Mai Anh and France could not recognize the/their idea anymore, as they considered it had *dematerialized* in Pierre's dialogue. Nothing appeared to indeed sustain/support the existence of a key aspect of the idea/project they thought they were working on—i.e., its historical dimension.

Finally, what this analysis also shows us is how the properties of an idea can, by definition, never be absolutely *proper* to it—a paradox that Derrida (1988) already identified under the term *exappropriation*. As we saw, the becoming of an idea was longitudinally identified through all the *properties* that it progressively acquired, from its requirements, to its formulation, to its prototypification. However, these properties were, as we saw, the result of *appropriations*—that is, relations that were literally *performed* throughout these three days. If these properties were absolutely proper to the idea, these processes of appropriation would not need to take place, as appropriating precisely consists of acquiring what was not initially proper.

It might be in the management of this paradox that the becoming of any project/idea lays: appropriating always consists of acquiring something that will always somehow remain improper. However, this appropriation has to be performed in such a way that it still appears sufficiently proper to what was projected, something that has, as we saw, to be often negotiated. What is supposed to complete the project/idea is also what, by definition, somehow alters it, which means that one needs to find alterations that create the conditions of their own effacement, as if altering was becoming a way to get to what the project always had to be. Any completion, which always is an alteration, therefore has to create, paradoxically, the gap it is supposed to fill. This might also be where the secret of creativity lies.

Let's hope at least that this chapter itself will be seen, reflexively, as the materialization of an idea, an idea according to which any idea always has to materialize itself in order to exist. If it is, indeed, in the accumulation of what constitutes it that an idea manages to concretize itself, I hope that all the empirical materials analyzed in this chapter will have contributed to its solidification.

Note

1. We would like to thank, in alphabetic order, Gerald Bartels, Juliette de Maeyer, and Thomas Martine for participating in the recording of this event. Special thanks to Thomas Martine, who first contacted the Museomix organizers and gave us access to this event.

5 Speculative Value

Articulating and Materializing the "Product" in High-Tech Startup Entrepreneurship

Entrepreneurship has emerged over the last two decades as arguably the most potent economic force the world has ever experienced.

(Kuratko, 2005, p. 577)

Every age gets the entrepreneur it deserves.

(Jones & Spicer, 2009, p. 86)

Introduction: Unpacking "Value" in Digital Technology Startup Entrepreneurship

Among economists and politicians, entrepreneurship is heralded as a key source of job creation and economic development. Particularly in the digital technology sector, entrepreneurship is seen as the very epitome of contemporary capitalism because it leverages new media and new forms of working to disrupt entrenched modes of operation, generate jobs, and create personal wealth (e.g., Audretsch, 2002; Lazear, 2005; Valliere & Peterson, 2009). Entrepreneurship, moreover, caters to common dreams about work, at least in the West: independence, self-determination, lasting impact, and financial affluence. As a consequence, entrepreneurs have become heroes in contemporary narratives of business and society (Anderson & Warren, 2011; Sørensen, 2008), and several institutions, including universities and governments, now actively encourage individuals to create startup businesses, despite the high failure rate—a rate estimated to range between 75% and 90% in the first four years (Dalkian, 2013; Gage, 2012).

Recently, entrepreneurship "accelerators" have sprung up around the world to nurture startup ventures (Hoffman & Radojevich-Kelley, 2012; Kempner, 2013; Miller & Bound, 2011). Accelerators are

> programs of limited duration—lasting about three months—that help cohorts of startups with the new venture process. They usually provide a small amount of seed capital, plus working space. They also offer a plethora of networking opportunities, with both peer ventures

DOI: 10.4324/9781315680705-5

and mentors, who might be successful entrepreneurs, program gradu-
ates, venture capitalists, angel investors, or even corporate executives.
Finally, most programs end with a grand event, a "demo day" where
ventures pitch to a large audience of qualified investors.

(Cohen, 2013, p. 19)

And the notion that accelerators have "sprung up" is apt: Bernthal (in
press) notes that there were roughly 5,500 accelerators worldwide in
2015, a more than twofold increase from the year before—with the trend
showing no signs of abating. These accelerators tend to be businesses
themselves: The economic capital they invest in their startups is provided
by a set of outside investors who seek sizable financial returns. An accelerator takes a stake (usually less than 10%) in the companies it accepts
into its program, aiming to recoup its investment when these companies
either are sold to other companies (i.e., "exit") or when they "go public"
through an IPO, an initial public offering of stock. Accelerators, then, are
clearly sites where the accomplishment of organization and the production of a precarious financialized economy occur.

Early stage startups encounter tremendous ambiguity. This is true
both for the conduct of their work and for the trajectory of the nascent
organization, especially given unknowable competition, unclear technologies, unproven ideas, and untested entrepreneurs. Entrepreneurs know
is that if their startup is to grow past its early days, infusions of cash
from investors like venture capitalists (VCs)—firms that provide funds
in exchange for ownership stakes in startups that they see as having high
growth potential—are often essential. These investors, too, inhabit a
world fraught with ambiguity: Because there exist no straightforward
and foolproof indicators of a startup's quality, they tend to rely on intuition as the basis of their speculative activity (Huang & Pearce, 2015).
For both entrepreneurs and investors, predicting startups' success or failure is much more art than science.

Assessments of (i.e., speculations about) *value* are thus obviously at
issue. How to attach value to a startup is, however, often deeply ambiguous to all concerned. The issue we pursue in this chapter engages with
the ambiguity around value; it addresses how startups, particularly those
groomed through an accelerator, cultivate a valuable "product." This
product, as we shall show, is both shifting and rarely tangible in a conventional sense—and, therefore, must be *materialized*, made to matter, to
attract investors' interest.

The next section examines conceptions of value, based on insights
from the developing field of valuation studies. Following that, we draw
upon one form of communicative relationality presented in Chapter 3 to
frame the practices by which startups materialize a valuable product. We
end the chapter with a consideration of the benefits this line of thinking
offers for analyses of working and organizing.

Communicative Relationality and the Emergence of a Valuable Product

The notions of value and value creation are at the core of understanding capitalism. Typically, value is rendered as the outcome of the machinations of a market, where the buying and selling of commodities occurs. This version of value is *capitalization*, where action transforms things into assets, into *capital* (Muniesa, 2014). This is typically what analysts generally mean when they talk about the *value of a business*: the composite of its potential streams of capital (its earning power, as in discounted cash flows) over some span of time—in other words, its ability to *capitalize* on its assets. In the developing and interdisciplinary field of valuation studies, however, value is understood in more expansive terms. They begin by asserting—as have accounting scholars such as Power (1997)—that ascertaining value-as-capitalization is far from a straightforward conclusion to be drawn from "objective" data. Value is always about prediction and relative confidence; it is about human judgment and guesswork. And because, in the world of startup entrepreneurship, valuation is a competitive game for investors who seek to make a profit, understanding the cues they employ is important for understanding the array of "calculations" they make.

What valuation studies scholars recognize is that when valuation is framed as capitalization, we are led to *what* and *which* questions, such as *what* can be identified as the "correct" capitalization and *which* assets are key in generating streams of revenues. A broadening out of the concept of valuation— carrying with it the desire to ask *how* questions—began with John Dewey. Dewey (1939) rejected the notion that value was an inherent characteristic of an object or idea and, instead, framed valuation as an *activity*. He suggested investigating the practices through which value is claimed and attached to elements of the social world. The inheritors of Dewey's position argue that valuation depends upon practices that create both similarities and distinctions between things, followed by practices that compare those things and valorize one set of characteristics over another (Fligstein & Calder, 2015; Kornberger, Justesen, Madsen, & Mouritsen, 2015; Lamont, 2012).

Value, note Boltanski and Esquerre (2015), is a device for the justification of prices. Neither an "objective" feature of economic transactions nor a calculation about the potential for capitalization, value is a claim deployed to attract resources (financial or otherwise) from a network of participants configured together in the conduct of practice. In the domain of startup practice, entrepreneurs generally operate in preparation for or in anticipation of generating resources, often—but, as we shall show next, not exclusively—in the form of financial capital, for their fledgling businesses. (These funds are most commonly of the venture capital variety, but could also be the price paid by a corporate acquirer or the investors in an IPO.) The question, then, is not *what* the correct prices are, nor is it the presence of (dis)agreements on valuations between various parties. The interesting question is how startups, influenced by accelerators, organize such that they can advance *claims to value*. Valuation, from this perspective, is the attraction, accumulation, and accentuation of resources via claims to value.

Understanding valuation *as an organizing practice* encourages us to see how claims to value invoke a set of sociomaterial relations (Vatin, 2013). Foregrounding practice rejects the notion that value and valuation are pre-given and objectified phenomena and insists that these elements emerge in situated practice (Gehman, Treviño, & Garud, 2013). In Chapter 2, we mentioned that Callon's version of performativity has been employed to examine valuation, particularly by seeing *agencement* as a calculative agency. The *creation* of value, in turn, is a practical accomplishment that requires the configuration of a heterogeneous set of agencies arrayed over time and space to generate evaluations of worth. Interrogating "the product" can underwrite an examination of value that builds on these commitments.

Seeing communication in terms of its capacity to write the trajectory of practice (the second version of communication introduced in Chapter 3) draws attention to the configuration and action of an *agencement*. As suggested in that chapter, analyses building on this conception of communication start with an effort to trace the array of agencies comprising the *agencement*, examine practices in which the *agencement* is implicated, and then highlight particular nodal points to examine potential conflicts and contradictions marking the *agencement's* articulations. Analyses must also describe the logic of the practice in an effort to explain why the participants in the *agencement* are stitched together in the observed configuration (in other words, how performativity is accomplished), as well as to explore potentials for alteration. This section pursues such an analysis in an effort to display what can be gained by using a communicative extension to economic performativity theorizing.

Methodological Commitments

What, then, are the methodological commitments, and challenges, of studying claims to value in the emergence of "the product" in startup entrepreneurship? First is that the nodal points must be understood as always already hybrid: No element is either human or nonhuman, either material or discursive, but both simultaneously. An entrepreneur, for instance, is not merely a human; she can only be taken to be a "real" entrepreneur, can only substantiate claims to an entrepreneurial identity, when reticulated with (i.e., embedded in a set of networked relations to) "things" such as business plans, financial capital, technology, other persons, appropriate garb, and a set of activities an audience would associate with entrepreneurship. The meaning and significance of "the" entrepreneur, then, is (over) determined by the amalgamated relations invoking the position.

A second methodological commitment involves a recognition that nodal points rarely present themselves to analysts in a simple or straightforward way; their "voices" can be heard only through doings and sayings through which they materialize, or come to matter (Cooren, 2015; Mazzei, 2010). It is not uncommon, then, for investigators to draw upon instances of talk and text to understand complex relational practices, including *agencement*—in ways that, at first blush, appear similar to conventional discursively focused work. For instance, Bruni's (2005) ethnography of practices surrounding digital clinical records in a hospital was an explicit (and in many ways, novel) attempt to shadow nonhumans in the sense of "following the object" sense (e.g., Engeström, Engeström, & Kerosuo, 2003; Latour, 2005); his data, however, consisted of cases in which employees talked about or interacted with the records. This is the same for a host of other similar studies employing some version of a relational ontology (e.g., Knorr-Cetina, 1999; Rennstam, 2012; Suchman, 2000), because the voice of an object very frequently materializes in the practices, actions, and reflections accessible to the ethnographer—and these typically hinge upon human actors.

Avoiding the hazard of overemphasizing the social/discursive/human requires the researcher's effort in both data collection and analysis to access what the *agencement* and its nodal points, as the loci of agency, *summon*: What they demand from the practice in question (Suchman, 2000), and, in the context of this chapter, what claims to value they demand and allow with respect to the *product*). The notion of summoning implies that analyses of *agencement* do not merely highlight nodal points' articulations as sense and reference (Frege, 1948), but that analyses attend to what those nodal points *call forth from the practice*—their prospective implications. This requires that the analyst grasp both the overarching logic of practice and the modes of mattering by which the nodal points make their "voices" heard; doing so entails an understanding of the practice detailed enough to address how the articulations at the nodes imply the need for, and responsibilities of, other elements of the *agencement*.

The analyst must, additionally, be able to describe the correspondences and contradictions between nodes, and delineate how those relations develop over time. If, for instance, a particular electronic device emerged as a participant in a given practice, the notion of summoning would enjoin a researcher to address how the activities in which the device participates stitch together segments of the *agencement*—an aim that would necessitate not only grasping the technological features of the device or its use (or its discursive representation) by humans but also how the logic of practice is performatively reconstituted through the *agencement*. As a part of our extension of economic performativity theorizing, summoning resists the reduction of any participant to either its putatively discursive or material facet—the notion recognizes that all participants are hybrid and, thus, their forms of materialization are contingent on situated performances. Although the typical conception of articulation is somewhat passive in its locating of agency outside the positioning of nodal points, the notion of summoning offers an active stance, one in which the analyst considers how the networked relations themselves call forth particular (and potentially conflicting) performances.

To investigate *agencement* in startups' pursuit of value, we first describe the setting for this case: An entrepreneurial accelerator in Boulder, Colorado. It is in this context that organizing to cultivate a valuable product unfolds. We start, then, with a description of the accelerator and its mode of influence over claims to value.

AmpVille

The setting for this case study is *AmpVille* (all designations are pseudonyms), a startup accelerator geared toward digital technology startups in Boulder, Colorado. The Denver-Boulder region (Boulder is only about a 30-minute drive from Denver) has received a good deal of attention for its technology- and Internet-based entrepreneurial activity, and Boulder specifically has received accolades for its ability to attract entrepreneurs (e.g., Helm, 2013; Miller, 2010). Brad Feld, a co-founder of both one the most prominent VC firms and startup accelerators in the region, is an outspoken advocate for the Boulder startup "ecosystem"; his book on *Startup Communities* (2012) paints Boulder as unique with respect to its capacity to nurture high-growth entrepreneurship.

Funded by venture capital firms, a bank, and a handful of wealthy individuals, AmpVille gives each startup accepted into its program $20,000 of seed capital in exchange for a 7% equity stake in the business. The cohorts it has hosted have ranged from 8 to 11 startups, and two or three members typically represent each startup (usually the founders, who are also ordinarily the only employees). The program is akin to a semester at a university: Over a period of 12 weeks, startups are presented with a series of educational opportunities, classroom-like instruction, and resources to hone their business cases; most of these are aligned with the "lean startup" model, which dominates entrepreneurship practice (Ries, 2011).

AmpVille's four co-directors (Tony, Steve, Juan, and Emma) understand this as a mentor-based accelerator: Startups are paired with several mentors—"experienced entrepreneurs or investors who actively contribute time, energy, and wisdom to startups" (Feld, 2012, p. 42)—drawn from the local community who influence startups' development. The program also exposes the firms to experts in branding, law, finance, and presentational speaking (i.e., "pitching"). Some of these experts donate their time, but the co-directors decided to pay a firm (AmpVille and each startup split the cost) that specializes in the economic valuation of firms. According to co-director Steve, this is because the AmpVille co-directors discovered that when startups produced their own calculations, even if following a standard protocol, "VCs would take these and say, 'What the

Figure 5.1 AmpVille's central workspace (the left half of the main room)

hell is this?'" In other words, they wouldn't trust an estimate made by a likely biased financial novice.

At the beginning of each class, AmpVille's co-directors assigned teams to two rectangular tables, along with writable wall space, in a room that measured approximately 20 meters long by 10 meters wide (see Figure 5.1). At one end of this room was a large TV used for projecting presentation slides; it functioned much like the front of a university classroom. In the upper right of the photo is a "countdown clock": In bright red LED numbers, this clock displayed the days, hours, and minutes remaining until the aforementioned Demo Day, where each startup pitched its product to potential investors, as well as the assembled community as a whole. Behind the vantage point from which the photo in Figure 5.1 was taken was another large, open workspace, along with smaller private meeting rooms.

Though receiving funds that become equity stakes in the startups it nurtures, an accelerator is a business that requires revenue. That equity stake is the primary mode by which AmpVille can secure its future viability and, as such, the co-directors have a strong interest in developing startups that can "pay off" through acquisitions or IPOs. Juan described AmpVille's stance on building value this way:

> We [co-directors] are here to maximize whatever value they have. And sometimes that isn't clear, sometimes it's very clear, sometimes it's clear the value of a company when, where we know we increased

it when we build some sort of strategic connection, where they now have a contract with this company, or when they bring on a really strong co-founder, or the attraction of users, or start getting revenue, or they run experiments and completely pivot, we are like ok, we have saved you and your investors a lot of time and money, because you were doing something that was not going to be beneficial, or a good business, or whatever. And so we can determine that—we can kind of see where the people, where the companies are at, throughout the program, and we kind of keep track where we see them compared to each other, and often a big part of our discussions, like how hard are they hitting the ground, like, if they haven't had a single bit of traction or progress, are they trying to, are they working really hard, or are they kind of just getting by, hoping things are handed to them, asking for a lot of things but not really making the effort?

Juan indicates here several indicators of value that AmpVille seeks to influence: The startup's connections to other (preferably high-profile) clients, the degree to which it has generated revenue ("traction"), the founders' degree of (observable) effort and initiative, and a startup's promise relative to others in the cohort. Each of these is an element of claims to value that startups can marshal in efforts to attract resources.

Agencies Comprising *Agencement*

As suggested earlier, the first step in the sort of analysis pursued here is to outline the array of agencies configured together in the constitution of the *agencement*. Developing a *product* that promises value, in anticipation of attracting the funding that will support the startups' trajectory, is just the sort of practice that can lay bare the participants implicated in it. Another way of stating our interest here—keeping with our stance of materializing as making elements matter in practice—is this: *What has to materialize in the "product" to support startups' claims to value?* In the interest of simplicity, we abbreviate our description to three agencies (i.e., nodal points), but our presentation of each will show how none are singular: Each is articulated by, and with, an array of additional elements; each is made meaningful in—*made to matter* through—other agencies operating in the *agencement*.

Teams' Skills

A first resource through which startups' claims to value emerged was the qualifications of the *team*, understood as the set of people working to materialize the ideas and bring the business to life. The team, as *product*, became relevant in claims to value in two ways.

A first is in the startups' entry into the accelerator. Startups enter AmpVille only after a stringent application process, and AmpVille runs only three cohorts per calendar year. It typically receives over 200 applications from startups all over the world and, according to one of the co--directors, accepts only around 2% of its applicants—a rate, that was, he claimed (during a welcome speech to a new cohort), more rigorous than admission into Ivy League Universities. Applicants are typically teams of startup founders, usually 2–3 persons, who are in the early stages of business development. Their applications are reviewed by the AmpVille staff and are followed by interviews for those making a "short list." At the application stage, startups tend to be driven by not fully formed ideas for a novel enterprise more than concrete business plans or evidence of viability. This makes sense, since most accelerators' primary (stated) goal is to foster the growth and development of the startups in each cohort.

For the co-directors, the challenge in the application process is discerning the potential value of each startup. Calculating potential value is a particular challenge because a good deal of speculation, on the part of both the founders and the AmpVille evaluators, is built into the ideas at these early stages, and some of the applicants offer little more than ideas. The co-directors ask experts in their personal networks to weigh in on the promise of these ideas, but they also report extracting information from the minds and bodies of the entrepreneurs who are applying. For instance, after noting that each team must complete a 30-question survey, followed by interviews with a co-director and then the larger committee, Juan mentioned that the co-directors operate on

> just your gut feeling . . . sometimes you just feel like, "ok these guys are—something is off about them, it's not quite right." Similarly, we've seen enough entrepreneurs that we know when these guys are moving shit forward, or they're just kind of waiting around to get stuff handed to them, or a lot of their wording, like "we are going to build" versus "we've built something," or "once we've raised money" versus, like, "this is what we're doing"—two different things. You see body language, it's just inevitable, you can't hide little cues of, like, someone turning away or making like a kind of crazy face when somebody's talking. We've had entire conversations around one person's body cue, after a certain statement, whether it was a video interview or a paper interview or in the actual interview, because it shows a lot about the relationship [between the founders], like they are not willing to respect each other.

Juan addresses here how the valuation of startups involves significant intuition, particularly in an attentiveness to symbols (including bodily cues) and assessment of founders' relationships. It is not that the technological elements or the business plan are unimportant, but that these more apparently human and discursive elements are key for AmpVille's principals as they consider which entrepreneurs to invite into the program.

A second way in which "team" became part of the startups' product was in statements about skill attributed to the individual (human) members. Based on the assumption that persons possess expertise, the entrepreneurial challenge is bringing together a set of people with the requisite skills to cover the needs of a developing firm. The AmpVille curriculum encourages thinking of individuals as pieces of a puzzle that, assembled together, become a startup team; this was most explicit in an exercise that extracted personality types from each participant via an "entrepreneurial profile" developed by the Gallup corporation. The profile suggests there are ten talents needed to start and grow a business (e.g., confidence, delegation, determination, willingness to disrupt, independence, ability to manage risk, profit-oriented decision making, salespersonship, ability to build relationships, and desire to locate knowledge); the results of the tool are then given to each team so that they can recognize members' strengths and weaknesses and seek to overcome capability gaps, as well as learn how to best collaborate with one another. In presenting the results to the startups as a spur to conversation, co-director Emma said, "I don't think there's any right pairing, but you need to look at what you and your partners have. Think of it more as a range of interests, and which of you is into those parts of the business. So it's also about knowing whether you have an ability to take something on, but also when you're not the best person to take something on."

The assumption that individuals *have* or *possess* particular and deeply engrained knowledge and habits (i.e., traits) aligns with the lean startup methodology from which AmpVille operates. In lean startup thinking, it is seen as rare that any set of founders will possess the requisite skills to make a startup successful; they may have capacities in technical (e.g., coding) and marketing (e.g., branding), but they often need to attract others to fill out the array of persons beyond the founders of the team. One entrepreneur gave voice to this:

> When you are a brand-new startup, nobody's ever heard of you, you've never had any previous exits, you are a nobody, having a good team helps. I don't know if *validate* is the right word, but it kind of gives you some credibility when you can say that you have a tech person, you have a finance and accounting person, you have a lawyer, you have another person, a marketing person, and each of these people, but as a whole they can lend bits and pieces to the puzzle. . . . So having the balance, having people that can weigh in to a different angle.

Evidence of the skills balance mentioned by this entrepreneur came most clearly in the pitches on Demo Day, where startups' pitches (coached intensively over the program by co-directors, mentors, and a presentational speaking expert) invariably list advisors and mentors whose experiences flesh out the accumulated expertise. The team—typically referred to as "a killer team"—is usually presented on a slide populated with

photos of the team members in casual attire (often in t-shirts emblazoned with the startup's logo), accompanied by verbal descriptions of
the capacities that make each person an outstanding contributor to the
startup. In these pitches, the notion that the team, and the individuals
comprising it, is an important component of the product is unmistakable.

This emphasis on the quality of the team in establishing value suggests
that the product offered by a startup—at least to those who might supply
funding—is not at all limited to digital technology. Yet the quality of the
team is relevant not merely if it covers skill domains, but if evaluators
can assess the likelihood that the entrepreneurs will have the tenacity to
pursue the startup to be viable over a term longer than the 12-week accelerator program, they are more likely to invest in its future. This system
of belief is aided, the logic goes, if entrepreneurs have *failed* in previous
startups, as co-director Steve explained:

> Something that's commonly understood is that it comes down to team,
> more than the idea. And with the team, oftentimes, you're looking at
> what is their experience as an entrepreneur—have they started another
> business before? And whether or not the business has failed or succeeded
> doesn't really matter, because oftentimes you learn more from failure.
> And if you've failed and you want to go again, good for you, that actu-
> ally is a plus. If you've started a business and succeeded with it, that's an
> even bigger plus. . . . But it's tough to know who has the stamina.

An entrepreneur explained his understanding of the importance of team
in the following way, clearly demonstrating the connection with a drive
for funding as an indicator of value:

> The other scenario would be, you've had an exit before, so are you
> are kind of well known, you have a reputation, somehow what you
> have done previously lends the chances of you being successful in the
> future because you are able to—you possess some capability, whether
> it's from the expertise point of view, or it's just the been there, done
> that kind of thing, that you know the ins and outs of the process. That
> makes you a better person to execute on it. Then people are willing
> to throw more money at you quicker, because you've proven yourself.

Another entrepreneur, considering what makes a great startup, replied,

> Team. It's not great product, because if you have a good team that
> recognizes its strengths and weaknesses, you can pretty much do any-
> thing. I think ideas are thought of every day by billions and billions
> of people, and it's up to the right team to execute on those ideas.
> Especially in software, ideas can be copied left and right, so it really
> depends on the individuals you're surrounding yourself with.

Although "product" here is equated with the technological object, the larger point is that entrepreneurs recognize the importance of projecting an image of *individuals* in which investors can place their trust.

One interesting component of individuals—and thus also of teams—is actors' motivations for engaging in a startup. As mentioned earlier (and as is no doubt obvious to the casual observer), successful entrepreneurs can become fabulously wealthy from harvesting the fruits of their labors. An article of faith in the startup world, however, is that those driven by money would not be successful—and, therefore, that their startups were not valuable. This is something to which several entrepreneurs could speak. One mentioned that he was struggling with a co-founder who hadn't made the move to Boulder to participate in AmpVille:

> I heard certain things in our communication, early on, when we first started working together, like "Oh, in four months, we will have this massively generated crowd of people using the app, and we can sell it for so much money, make so much money, the valuation will be crazy." And that kind of talk, it bothers me. . . . I just know that the most successful people in life have not been focused on money. Warren Buffett—you know, he's the wealthiest man in the world— right from the time he was a junior security analyst, he was always focused on excellence, making sure he had a careful eye, trying to detect the best companies that had the best gray matter, which led to success. Those were the ones he would invest in. And it wasn't because "Oh, I'm going to make so much money." It was like, "No, I want to see if this correlates with something in the economy."

Another suggested that diligence in work sits uncomfortably aside the desire for wealth:

> Obviously, everybody thinks their company is going to be the next Tesla or whatever that just blows up out of the water and you are a billionaire overnight. That's definitely something that motivates us— like, hey, there is a financial reward somewhere in here, but you have to work for it, and you can't just sit back. So that may be what drives the day-to-day thing, in that if you aren't doing something right now, you know that one of your competitors is probably passing you up.

A story that made the rounds at AmpVille was about one of its startups, which was invited to pitch to the giant (and, by reputation, avaricious) investment bank Goldman Sachs. The story goes that the founder included, as the last slide in the presentation, his personal "exit strategy" that would ensure him a rather generous payout. The Goldman banker rejected the pitch on that count—that when the entrepreneur mentioned the desire for personal enrichment, that it ruined the presentation. Pitching is a central component of the practice of entrepreneurship at AmpVille, and almost every day during the 12-week session sees a session devoted to it.

At one rehearsal session where mentors provided feedback to the entrepreneurs, an event resonating with the Goldman Sachs story unfolded. After an entrepreneur included a joke about getting rich in her presentation, the mentor inveighed that "investors want to get rich, but they don't care if you do. And they don't want to invest in people who want to get rich." In response to another pitch, a second mentor argued that, while it's important to display experience, entrepreneurs should "avoid saying that one of your founders was successful because he had a big exit [from a previous startup]; it will 'flip the bid' and turn investors off." Early in the session, co-director Tony tells the assembled entrepreneurs that their pitches need to be narratives that include answers to the following prompts, projected on the TV at the front of the room:

I am . . .
I do this . . .
For . . .
So that . . .
Because . . .

Such prompts insert a logic of the *individual* presenter as the driving force of the startup. (Incidentally, he mentions that his own response to the final prompt is "Because entrepreneurship is how positive change happens in the world.") The completion of these phrases provides an opportunity for others to assess the rightness of the claims. In the cases described here, the pursuit of wealth is understood as inappropriate and unspeakable; VCs thus impose a moral tension on entrepreneurs—one that, when coupled with the money the VCs control, shapes the trajectory of the startup.

What, then, is summoned by the particular relations characterizing the nodal point of team? The activity called for—as a component of the practice of materializing value—is the ongoing projection of a startup's ability to complete the challenging journey of developing a valuable product. In articulating the relationships around "team," the *agencement* configures money (in terms of investments), skills (rendered as traits and materialized through online and paper-based tools such as the Gallup entrepreneurial profile), gut feelings (of the co-directors when selecting members of the cohort) experiences, reputations, and personal motivations and passions. It relies on bodily presence (or absence). It depends, too, on its manifestation on t-shirts and photographic representation on Demo Day slides. These are the participants through which *team* can be materialized as an element of a startup's claim to value.

Consequently, *team*, in AmpVille, does not conjure up the messy communicative processes of negotiating the relationships between these participants, nor does it refer to deciding and acting together. Team instead signifies a set of *individuals*. This individualization leads to assessments of whether a desirable range of traits and experiences is covered (the afore-mentioned "skills balance") and whether the members evince the "proper" motivations, both of which are indicators of quality—and, in turn, of the potential for attributions of value. What is summoned from a startup by the articulation of meaning around the node of team, then, are claims regarding a canonical set of personal characteristics arrayed across persons; "team" becomes reduced to its human and psychological manifestations.

(Ferreting Out a) Business Model

Once the AmpVille program begins, a first task for each startup is to make the case for the significance of a particular problem as the ground-ing for a business model. The aforementioned lean startup curriculum starts with the assumption that a business must satisfy a need, it must solve a problem, for its idea to be valuable. Thus, one of the early activi-ties in which each startup participates is the creation, and defense, of a "Value Proposition Canvas" (VPC). The VPC, freely available on the Internet (https://strategyzer.com/canvas/value-proposition-canvas), is a paper artifact upon which entrepreneurs write, in a single sentence, what their business will provide to customers. It requires that the startup identify a typical customer for whom the product will be generated, the needs—the "pain points"—a customer experiences, and an explicit state-ment of how the product alleviates the customer's pain.

This is accompanied by a claim of the partnerships (e.g., with produc-tion, coding, or marketing) necessary to deliver the product, along with a statement of how the startup's offering will be superior to competi-tors' solutions. Subsequent steps are "getting out of the building" to test whether customers would respond to the proposed product, followed by "journey mapping": The completion of an artifact in which startups project each step in the process of satisfying the customer's need. At that first session, though, each startup was given a large copy of the VPC and, over a two-hour period, filled it out while being interrogated by the co--directors. During this session, co-director Emma argued, "Sometimes the terminology we use can guide the way we think about stuff," which led the group to a consideration of the assumptions each startup was mak-ing about (and the language it was using to talk about) its target market. Tony informed the startups that they must be "willing to thrash," to experience confusion, frustration, and disappointment about the promise of their original plans.

Upon completion of this exercise, the VPCs were hung on the wall of each startup's workspace (akin to the brainstorming practice described in Chapter 4), becoming a frequent conversation piece, a boundary object, to explain the intended value of each startup's product to mentors, inves-tors, and other visitors to the space (Figure 5.2).

Figure 5.2 Continually amended artifacts on the wall of the AmpVille workspace

The VPC, then, became the first explicit statement of the intended value provided by each startup. Yet these initial enunciations were not set in stone. Tony introduced the VPC exercise by arguing, "A seed-stage startup means your job is to *find* your business model, not to defend it." Discovery and emergence are encouraged, and this process of finding unfolds over several weeks, as the startups test the extent to which the customers feel the pain the team identified, whether there's a sufficiently sizable market, and whether their product will be understood as a pain reliever. The lean startup artifacts, including the VPCs, often receive modifications in response to those tests, with additional writing and sticky notes displaying changes in value propositions.

One entrepreneur mentioned that their efforts to test whether the customer identified on their VPC would be viable led his team to give hundreds of flyers, with cash vouchers to use on their website, to students at the local university; these flyers encouraged students to log on to the website and become the startup's first paying customers. The following morning, he proudly showed a visitor a counter, created by computer code, which revealed the number of visitors on the site. During the course of a ten-minute conversation, the entrepreneur and the visitor watched as the counter gradually registered zero.

Here is an instance of recalcitrant materiality: Despite the team's efforts to elicit interest and despite its insistence that university students would be enthusiastic about this product, including a provision of money to a target market, the relationship between the anonymous customers, the money provided to them, and the computer code tracking website users generated an outcome unexpected by the entrepreneur: A large green "0" projected on the open program window on the laptop. Glancing at the screen dejectedly, the entrepreneur immediately framed this result as information that they needed to refine their user group, mentioning that the startup might next target stay-at-home housewives, 20 somethings just out of university, or perhaps teenagers.

In this case, the digital technology was intimately connected with the VPC and the entrepreneurs' effort to construct a promising customer persona; these participants are not easily separable in the practice of ferreting out a business model. The activity of "iterating" (making minor changes in the business model, including the user group) illustrated here shows that the performative task is to be able to articulate a customer with motivations, goals, and problems that align with the solution the startup can provide; the interesting element is that this is inextricably bound up with both money and computer technology, as displayed in this instance. Although the lean startup artifacts propose a linear process where the customer's "pain points" exist apart from the product—with the product developed in direct response to that problem—the more common practice is to assert particular customer needs, design a solution for (and technological assessment of) them, and only afterward assess the fit between the two.

Other entrepreneurs described the utility of the VPC and related artifacts as shaping humans' decisions about the startup's trajectory because they bridged past and future:

> These tools are great for discovery. And I think that's what they're meant to do, they're meant to remind you—even the canvas, the value prop—they're meant to remind you of what your core assumptions are, if you're following them, and what strategies you're taking. When it comes to a lot of the post-its on the wall, you see, they're reminders—a lot of people are just visual people, they can't remember everything. . . . And I think if you have them up there to remind you of what your business is centered on, it helps you think about it more.
>
> [Lean startup artifacts including the VPC] are a shrine, kind of an *homage* to what you want to be, may have been, could have been. It's just a way to visualize where you came from—and a lot of people use that as a kind of ethics, or gauge, or morals, just to always view where you've come from, where you're going, or just to look into the past. . . . . . I think the wall can be considered a mentor, too, you know—you can get whiplash from looking at what you used to be.

In the practice of finding and refining the business model, the artifacts were thus more than statements of intent. They were vehicles for making claims about the centrality of a particular problem and the likelihood that customers would surrender money to address that problem. And, in the register of economic performativity's conception of calculation, they also *commensurated*: Funneling all claims through common artifacts enabled easy comparisons for anyone (e.g., VCs and mentors) seeking to compare the potential value of the assembled startups. The artifacts on the wall, in other words, were neither inert objects nor were they possessors of agency on their own; in terms of a relational ontology, they participated in the accomplishment of action that shaped the trajectory of the startups they mentored.

What, then, does the nodal point of *business model* summon from startups? First, it is important to note that a startup's business model does not pre-exist its entry into AmpVille, nor does it emerge fully formed from early attempts to articulate it. Instead, the business model is the ongoing result of what Barinaga (in press) refers to as *tinkering*. A key element of claiming to provide a valuable product in the lean startup methodology is the articulation of a convincing business model, and in AmpVille the business model summons particular activities and relations. The business model requires that startups complete the VPC, make it a dominant presence on the walls of their workspace, and revise it in ongoing fashion via iterating ("thrashing" and revising).

The production of the VPC additionally requires a narration of the prototypical customer, followed by testing (with computerized documentation) to determine whether such customers would form an ample market. The development of a *business model* additionally summons the startup to identify the partners required to bring its solutions to customer problems into the world. And across all these, materializing the business model entails employing, and reflecting upon, the assumptions built into the language used in bringing forth the business model. In the vocabulary of the communicative extension to performativity theorizing introduced in Chapter 3, we see how a business model materializes, how it becomes a site for value emergence only when it has summoned the range of relations suggested here.

Technological Innovations

A third participant in the *agencement* was what might be seen as a traditional conception of *product*: Technological innovations. At AmpVille, most teams were working with some novel appropriation of Internet-based technology; these included developing an online marketplace for small investors to meet small consumer goods providers, sophisticated approaches to inserting advertisements in online content, wearable technology for pets, video enhancements to online dating, an app enabling businesses to easily create and modify spreadsheets, software to deliver targeted video content to consumers, and an app allowing managers to analyze how retail outlets can maximize financial performance. Each startup, then, was working with creative uses of (usually Internet-based, and always computerized) technology, so explaining how their particular approach was valuable, and could be monetized in the context of rapid technological advancements and intense competition, was the task of each startup.

One entrepreneur whose startup was developing an email app for business users noted the challenge here:

> One of the things we found here (at AmpVille) was that people were saying, "It's just an email app; what makes you different?" . . . We could answer it, but then they'd be like, yeah well, so does my thing, mine does that too. So whatever answer we gave, it wasn't enough. So, clearly we were not doing something innovative enough. . . . So we are trying to figure out that blend for the business side to see how the product fits. Here, what we determined was that we had to have something cool and stellar, so that's where the big turn came, it was spurred on by the conversations that we're having here, but it's something that we chose to do. It wasn't like you have to do this or we are not giving you money, it was like "we are not going to get money unless we do something different."

Attracting investment requires, then, an approach to the product in which the novelty and non-substitutability of the technology is evident. For many startups, discovering that uniqueness is a challenging process of discovery.

A common conversation in AmpVille starts with questioning why a particular Internet-based technology firm dominates its market. Whether the focal organization is Facebook, Apple, Twitter, Salesforce, or some other enterprise, the question is how it was able to crowd out the competition and reign supreme in its category. The example par excellence is Google. The reason that the Google search engine became seen as more valuable than others is because of its interface's design simplicity, its avoidance of irrelevant results, and because its (proprietary) page rank algorithm was based on the backward links made to a given web page. That algorithm gave priority to pages with more connections and thereby ordered results in a way desired by users—as opposed to jumbled sets of page results. Unseen is the array of coders, engineers, and project managers who brought Google search to life, materializing the search on the computer screens of users. However, what made Google search both profitable and a staple of everyday life was that users recognized value in appearing high in page rankings, thus producing a cottage industry in what became Search Engine Optimization. It also led Google salespersons to sell the ability to appear in prominent positions in the search, which generated the income that led the company's foray into a host of other technology initiatives and to create an encompassing technology platform.

In other words, technological features do not exhaust the notion of product. What is taken to be a technological *innovation* must, in the practice of startup entrepreneurship, solve problems or create opportunities, and a host of additional (human and nonhuman) agencies are implicated in advancing such claims to value. Consider the following exchange, recorded during a startup's meeting with a mentor. The startup's plan was to use "cookies" to enable micro-segmentation of Internet users (i.e., targeting very small market segments) so the startup could deliver video advertising in a way more accurate than other providers— which would also bring the cost for running video advertisements down to where small businesses could afford it. In this meeting, the founder reported on the development of an algorithm that would enable them to accomplish micro-targeting, but also to generate a large storehouse of data—data that could be sold to other users. The following exchange (E is the entrepreneur; M is the mentor) occurred:

1 E: So, I wanted to introduce you to <name of algorithm>, dude,
2   this was a big part of what we did last week. . . . I took my dog
3   out for a walk, and it all kind of came together for me. So, what
4   I realized was that I had really been obsessing over building the
5   predictive analytic model, but what we really had the opportu-
6   nity to do was build a fairly simple descriptive model that no
7   one's done before, that adds direct value to the platform. So, one
8   of the questions that we've been getting is, "Well, what if the
9   small business owner doesn't know who to target or who his cli-
10   ents are, or something like that?" So, <algorithm> does that. . . .
11   What it is, is, we tie into the client's social feeds—Facebook,
12   Twitter, LinkedIn, what have you, bring that information up, ex-
13   pand at, or augment it against the MPs, the Management Plat-
14   forms, these are data warehouses that do nothing but augment
15   data, then will crunch it through our descriptive algorithm and
16   come out with descriptive assets, so it also will come in and tie
17   their Facebook and Twitter into it, bring that data up, married
18   again some third-party data, crunch it out, and then be able to
19   come back to [a local coffee shop] and say, "Hey, 40% of your
20   engaged audience online are women in this zip code between
21   these ages. We think we should target that automatically, and
22   that will inform the campaign, straight out."
23 M: That's neat.
24 E: It's fucking awesome is what that is.
25 M: Sorry, that's what I meant to say. Neato. Peachy keen.
26 E: Thanks, man, I'm blushing.
27 M: It *is* neat. So that's what you would, um, patent.
28 E: Yes.
29 M: It's a good thing to patent, anyway.

30 E: Yep. But it adds some very specific value into exactly what we are
31   doing.
32   (. . .)
33 M: If I were [a small business owner], I'd be curious, like "Why are
34   you guys interested in my data?"
35 E: But, as we started thinking about this, and a lot of thinking will
36   have to go into this, is do we *tell* them?
37 M: *That* you do it?
38 E: No, no, no. We tell them *that* we do it, but do we tell them what
39   we get out? Because that feels like, hugely valuable in and of
40   itself. Or do we just black box it and say, you click here and we
41   will optimize it. It almost feels like another business, where you
42   can sell that knowledge back to [local coffee shop] and say these
43   are your sweet spots, these are your Goldilocks zones. So, I don't
44   know how that's going to work yet.
45 M: Yeah, I can't answer that either.
46 E: But this is the way we are moving, in that direction.
47 M: Yeah. Once you, once you run it, once you make it, and you are
48   seeing what comes out of it, you'll have a better sense of the value.
49 E: Right.
50 M: A lot of big advertisers would like that too, especially the compa-
51   rable stuff.
52 E: It's pretty cool, it's really cool.
53 M: Is anyone doing it? That's what I wonder, when you go to patent
54   it, does it already exist?
55 E: Ahh, well, so, there's different ways you can patent it. I am sure
56   there is some IP (intellectual property) around this by itself. But
57   how it ties within the system and a campaign workflow, that
58   would be new. You see that?

This exchange is interesting in that it appears to be about what this algorithm can produce—what its role is as a *product*. No algorithm can function without a large amount of data, so drawing upon (constructing a relationship with) clients' social media feeds, along with third-party sources of data, enables the algorithm to do the micro-targeting the startup seeks. In one sense, then, the test of the algorithm was a breakthrough: It convinced the members of the startup that their idea was technologically possible. (There was a coding specialist in the room, an early employee of the startup, who later in the conversation vouched for the feasibility of bringing these elements together in the manner described earlier.)

If we were to consider the algorithm as a stand-alone element, however, it would clearly not qualify as a *product*. It—acknowledging that labeling the algorithm an "it" already effects the sort of ontological distinctions we wish to avoid—can only be considered an innovation, it can only be rendered valuable, when it is articulated with other agencies. Here, those additional agencies are the enthusiasm of the entrepreneur, the possibility of receiving a patent (which, presumably, carries the potential for both fending off competition and for generating additional profits), the potential to use the algorithm for an additional (moneymaking) purpose beyond the startup's original business model, and the mentor's interest. And to return to the invocation of "cool" technology in the quote preceding this, the startup in this episode worked to portray its algorithm as something that would beckon from the mentor the enthusiasm embodied by the entrepreneur. And this articulation is only possible in the situation established by the accelerator's practice of scheduling meetings between startups and mentors in which the startup is able to present its innovative idea to a mentor whose resources are sought.

What does the nodal point of *technological innovations* summon from startups? Technological innovations, as seen here, are materializations of a startup's product that are always partial (as also discussed in Chapter 4's case on creativity), but which call forth claims to value of their coding efforts. Key here is the combination of technology and creativity, an ability to convey to an audience the novelty of technological use along with claims regarding both enthusiasm and the financial benefit of the combination. In other words, that which is taken to be "the" product is not reducible to technological innovations; rather, products become materialized in degrees, as other participants are articulated into a set of relations that portray the startup as possessing a technological innovation that can provide value. That calculation of value depends upon the character of the situation, the divergence from competitor technologies, the portrayed and perceived "coolness" of the innovation, lessons from prominent organizations like Google, and the enthusiasm that animates the actors involved. Communication stitches these elements together, however contingently and temporarily, to produce meanings that guide and direct the trajectory of practice.

Summary

In Chapter 3, we presented a communicative extension to performativity theorizing, and suggested that this extension sees the overdetermination of agencies articulating each nodal point in an *agencement* as containing contradictions that emerge in the practice through which each element is articulated. When examining "the product" as multiple and protean, as constituted by the intersections between and among teams' skills, the (emerging) business model, and technological innovation, startups' trajectories are exposed as bound up in tensions. Those tensions—to which we gestured, but did not make explicit, in the preceding sub-sections— are multiple. For instance, to gain entry into the program, a startup must base its existence on a novel idea for fulfilling a market need but, at the same time, must be able to show the quality of the team pursuing it.

Startups must aim to secure funding (through VC investment, IPO, or acquisition) but, at the same time, must avoid seeking personal wealth for their founders. Startups inhabit a world in which marketplace success is venerated and imitated but, at the same time, failure is an acceptable—even, from the perspective of a longer march, desirable—element of individual entrepreneurs' experience. A startup must possess a convincing account of its intended customers and its ability to solve those customers' problems but, at the same time, must be prepared to "iterate" and "pivot," switching trajectories either modestly or dramatically. The locus of these conflicts and contradictions is the *agencement*, and the tensions only arise in the communicative practice of articulating the meanings of those elements in the pursuit of *value*. In this sense, conflicts and contradictions participate in the constitution of the practice, just as each of the assembled elements do. In other words, because practices are comprised by multiple relations, and because the participants comprising these practices are sociomaterially heterogeneous, tensions and contradictions are endemic to their ongoing materialization.

Articulating the Logic of Practice: The Individualization of Possession

Given our interest in illustrating the utility of a communicative extension to economic performativity theorizing, the *agencement* sketched out earlier is minimal, consisting of a matrix of elements we have called *team skills* (as a collection of individual human characteristics, including the denial of avarice), the *business models* (especially artifacts associated with the lean startup methodology as participants shaping trajectories), and *technological innovation* (as marrying technology with a creative surfacing of possibilities for use). This is clearly a truncated depiction of *agencement*, but focusing on these three nodal points allowed us to show how the relations with an array of other agencies—human (e.g., mentors, co-directors, VCs, "the" customer, reputations, motivations, entrepreneurs' personality traits) and nonhuman (e.g., computer code, locale, patents, big data, an attribution of "coolness")—participated in materializing these central elements of the practice.

Organizing in this context, therefore, is a matter of articulating these agencies, both configuring them and operating from within the configured matrix of agencies, in ways that enable claims to value. In the AmpVille case, the practice of *agencement* fashioned the individual entrepreneurs (more specifically, startups' founders) as the primary calculative agency, the center point of control.

In the practice of establishing value in high-tech startup entrepreneurship, founders are typically portrayed as the composers, engineers, and deciders: The active agents who recognize opportunities "out there" in the market, who design a technological solution, and who assemble the components necessary to create a product superior to those of potential competitors. Although the mentors and co-directors encountered through AmpVille are important sources of information, and though those possessing funding (e.g., VCs) harbor expectations that summon startups to develop in particular directions, it is the entrepreneur who ultimately decides, as the following excerpt from the blog of the aforementioned Brad Feld, the most prominent spokesperson for the Boulder startup community, suggests, in a post directed to entrepreneurs:

> If you ask five mentors the same question you'll get seven different answers. This is especially true early in any relationship, when the mentors are just getting to know you and your company. . . . As the business grows, there are more points of stimuli, more agendas, more exogenous factors, and more potential whiplash. If you don't build your own muscle around collecting, synthesizing, dealing with, and deciding what to do with all the data that is coming at you, then you are going to have massive problems as your company scales up.
>
> (2013)

Feld is asserting that founders—entrepreneurs, both individually and as members of a team—must make decisions in the face of conflicting opinions and sources of influence. In the conventional telling of the story of entrepreneurship, then, human agency is central. And recall the discussion in this chapter's introduction as confirmation that this individualization is not limited to Boulder: The construction of the entrepreneur as cultural hero and overwhelmingly positive socioeconomic force fosters a conception that the individual is, and should be, in charge.

More specifically, ownership is portrayed as the driving force, because the company is understood to be the founders' possession—and thus also their responsibility. The practice considered in this chapter, the pursuit of a valuable product, occurs in the intersections of agencies running through nodal points, from which the individual entrepreneur emerges as the central figure. The centrality of the individual entrepreneur cropped up in assessments of founders' (body) language; evaluations of individuals' experiences, skills, and motivations in the investor pitches; posting ongoing amendments to (and perceiving the influence of) lean startup artifacts; presenting ideas with an enthusiasm and ability to convey "coolness"; and conceiving of creative appropriations of digital technologies. All emphasize the individual entrepreneur as the source of decidability and action. The logic of the practice is the individualization of agency.

Given that the results of wealth generation from entrepreneurship are understood as accruing to individuals rather than groups or communities, such an individualization of agency and authority is perhaps unsurprising. Yet from the perspective of economic performativity, this logic of practice is problematic. It is problematic because it fosters a conception of ownership as uninterrogated assumptive base, but when (or if) the startup attracts investors (including AmpVille's 7% stake in each startup), ownership becomes diluted and thus can emerge as a site of struggle. One founder voiced this struggle as he reported on his response to a VC offer received after his startup completed the AmpVille curriculum:

> They wanted too much of my company—they wanted 30% for half a million [dollars]. And it's like we don't need that much money right now—where we are, we can do a lot of growth, we can get really far on much less money than that. . . . Tony, from AmpVille, has been pressuring me like hell to take the money. They're our shareholders, so we told them, and they're also our advisors still, so we keep them close and informed. . . . But if we had accepted that deal, [the VC firm] would have owned more of the company than [my co-founder].

Because individual founders are understood to be the site of decision (and the beneficiaries of wealth creation), this founder—occupying the sole seat of decidability, as configured by the *agencement*—located reasons to reject the offer, but the quote illustrates how struggles over trajectory implicate (individualized) ownership.

Beyond this, however, an individualized conception of agency neglects the *distribution* of decisional power across the matrix of agencies. This chapter showed how advancing claims to value is a sociomaterial process, rather than merely a discursive one. In one sense, this is obvious since these startups are all developing digital technology businesses. However, the issue is that all claiming of value is always simultaneously social and material—for instance, the assertion that the firms must find a human problem (and a customer persona) makes it seem like value propositions are merely discursive. But if we see material not as "stuff" but as *mattering*—as about the agencies that are made to matter in organizing—we can see that the artifacts are made to matter, the customers are made to matter, the algorithms are made to matter, the legal conception of ownership is made to matter. And thus we can see that communicative relationality does not eradicate notions of human agency but, taking a page from Barad's (2003) concept of agential cuts, asks how it is—by what performances does it become the case—that persons are framed as the principal locus of responsibility and decision in *agencement*.

The topic of interest, then, is figuring out the network of agencies operating here and how they get activated, *materialized*, to produce a particular vision of value. What this implies is that "the product" is not a thing—but neither are the three elements considered here (teams' skills, the business model, and technological innovation). The sources of data upon which the algorithm depended, the VPC as a mentor hanging on the wall that honed the business model, the purportedly measurable skills of team members, the assessments of presence and "proper" motivations, the marshaling of the "cool," the evidence that the startup had "thrashed," and the computer-generated evidence of customer interest are all, as Barad would say, *constitutively entangled*; they are hybrids of what are conventionally taken to be human and nonhuman elements.

Claims to value could not materialize without the involvement of these participants—and these participants could not exist, they could not participate in startup practice, without one another. And when some elements became recalcitrant—when code failed to work, when the customer base failed to respond (as registered through the software interface), when a pitch exposed an entrepreneur's greed, when an app was not meaningfully different from competitors—performances failed. In AmpVille, it is neither ideas nor people nor technological things that inherently have, or *possess*, value; instead, for a seed-stage startup in an accelerator, value is a matter of configured agencies' capacity to make claims to value; these claims provide evidence that the startup can manifest a valuable product and, accordingly, that it is a worthy site for the attraction of resources.

Assessing the "Value" of the Communicative Extension for Economic Performativity Theorizing

This chapter demonstrated how "the product" in startup entrepreneurship is not at all a simple technological object. Product was, instead, shown to be ontologically multiple, materialized by the relational intersections of team, business model, and technological innovation. Startups speculate about what will be technologically possible, marketable, and valuable to funders, just as those funders are engaged in financial speculation in their attraction to startups. Identifying the varied participants configured together shows that the action of the *agencement*—its "agencing"—is both hybrid and precarious. The communicative extension to economic performativity draws attention to the ways in which startups' capacity to advance claims to value hinges upon organizing practices that stitch together myriad agencies; the analysis earlier makes it clear that these claims are not merely accomplished discursively, but are relational accomplishments only possible when the participants are hybrid, open to multiple forms of materialization.

In addition to this conceptual reframing, a benefit of identifying the logic of the practice is that doing so can highlight unanticipated consequences. A key challenge facing entrepreneurs generally is whether they are able to make their claims to value appeal to multiple audiences at the same time: As Stark (2009) suggests, "*Entrepreneurship is the ability to keep multiple evaluative principles in play and to exploit the resulting friction of their interplay*" (p. 15, emphasis in original). In AmpVille, startups enter into a matrix of agencies that present the entrepreneur/owner, as possessor of primary decisional power, as natural and normal. Stark's claim is that developing a valuable product depends upon *ambiguity*, which allows multiple audiences to perceive worth in different terms. Establishing a common curriculum around the lean startup model, encouraging stylistic similarity in pitching, and inculcating a belief in the primacy of the individual entrepreneur (even as a member of a team) may well mitigate against the ability to play multiple "games" in a startup's trajectory. These activities develop a startup as an agent that (or who) can appeal to VCs for funding but may have a limited capacity to interest audiences prizing technical prowess, personal passion, or community contribution in its product (Patriotta, Gond, & Schultz, 2011).

Further, we hold that the notion of summoning, introduced in this chapter and associated with the second communicative extension to relationality introduced in Chapter 3, offers value to organization studies. In the domain of research on technologically dense work practices, entire academic careers have been built on a drive to avoid the paired dangers of technological determinism and human voluntarism, which is only the latest rendition of a long-standing division in social theory (Bourdieu, 1990; Giddens, 1979). The argument here sought to disturb the assumptions undergirding typical varieties of the determinism-voluntarism debate, especially concerning agency as residing in *either* humans *or* technologies. Starting with a vision of nodal points created by *agencement*, the perspective here has shown how the meanings constituting a practice are contingent combinations of (non)human—hybrid agencies reducible to neither human or nonhuman—participants.

The nodal point of *team*, for instance, demanded individual (and individualized) human figures. It also required embodied and embrained knowledge, including psychological "traits" demonstrable through tools like Gallup's entrepreneurial profile—which was, in turn, materialized both through an online interface and the hardware and software making that possible, as well as through the paper report provided to each person in the cohort. *Team* also encouraged scrutiny of members' motivations, urging a rejection of overt greediness, as well as an assessment of the presence or lack of bodies in the site (as depicted by the case of the startup co-founder who had refused to move to Boulder to participate in AmpVille). The meaning of *team* was further articulated in the use of members' previous experiences, whether a successful exit or a startup failure. Efforts to materialize the team also took the form of logo-emblazoned apparel and images of members (and advisors) on Demo Day pitch slides. And, as demonstrated earlier, team is intrinsically connected to technological innovation and the emergence of a business model.

The point in highlighting the articulations creating the meaning(s) of this nodal point is to demonstrate—keeping with our third premise of relationality in Chapter 2—that the contributors to the notion of *product*, including elements typically taken to be human and discursive, might be more profitably understood as sitting at the nexus of a host of simultaneously and irreducibly sociomaterial relations. Participants sometimes have reasons for framing the team, business model, or technological innovations as *either* human or technological (i.e., they enact ontological cuts), but a performative study must also be able to include those interests as participants shaping the *agencement's* logic of practice. And, as noted earlier in the chapter, the notion that communication associated with the nodal point *summons* particular relations and activities suggests that the *agencement's* meaning(s) for a notion like team calls forth the set of materializations observed here, simultaneously commanding each startup to manufacture evidence of value.

Finally, this case illustrates the utility of our communicative augmentation of performativity theorizing for the complex themes of contemporary capitalism. This perspective rejects the position that neoliberalism or financialization (for instance) imposes itself on AmpVille and its startups from a position of exteriority. Keeping with the tenet (from Chapter 2) that reality is multiple, enacted, and flat, the analysis makes clear how practices that might conventionally be coded as "financialized" emerge from the particular configuration of agencies marking the scene such that when observers—including those putatively "in" the startup world—categorize these practices, tokens such as "neoliberalism" or "the new economy" become participants in the *agencement*.

Analysts might pick up on a given logic of practice that aligns with themes of financialization, and might locate its incursion into a practice through elements such as artifacts, actors' motivations, and presence of algorithms. Yet, according to this communicative extension, analysis cannot assume that these materials *carry* financialization, as if an ideology speaks through them (Hall, 1996; Harding, Lee, & Ford, 2014); instead, it must examine how such elements are bound up with other agencies, mutually constituted in the accomplishing of a practice. As a startup's product is materialized, what an observer might term "financialization" can be made to matter as well. In other words, financialization is not to be understood as an overarching structure that creates the conditions of possibility for entrepreneurial communities to exist; it is a categorization produced by meaning-making activity, engineered by specific agents, that participates in both the configuration of a field of horizontal relations and the ongoing (re)accomplishment of (value-producing) practice.

6 Branding Work

Occupational Identity as Affective Economy (aka The Glass Slipper, Take Two)

Branding has come a long way (baby), and it has changed hands. Mention branding these days, and first impressions no longer flash to plantations, prison yards, or even ranches, toward the brutal labor of men searing marks of possession and stigma onto the bodies of other beings. Branding remains the work of establishing identity and identification. It is still consumed with the production of ownership and value, though it now aims to promote rather than prevent circulation, and to enhance rather than merely maintain value. But it has cleaned up and slipped into the suit (or today, business casual) of the marketing and advertising industries. Like many of the objects to which it is applied, the activity of branding was transformed for public consumption, profiting from that twentieth century upgrade known as professionalization. And those *Mad Men* still seduce, it seems.

No longer made of iron or coercively imposed, their product is comparatively immaterial, which is not to deny its materialization. Specifically, *brands* are symbolic condensations and carriers of identity that operate instantaneously and energetically, through elusive jolts of felt activation, for instance, rather than conscious processing. As symbols, brands also take material form, such as a logo or a uniform, and they are imbued not only with meaning but also with material intentions—to generate physiological response, impel behavior, and enhance value, to name a few. In a word, brands are about affect or, more precisely, its "farming." We might say that *branding* is the activity of cultivating and harnessing affective relations of identity in order to yield desired harvests (allusions to ranching resurface).

In advanced capitalism, however, branding is no longer the sole province of handsome suits and furtive boardroom machinations. Experts today tout branding as a decentralized playground, because the brand has become an increasingly fluid and mobile object of knowledge that invites interaction with and contributions to it (Lury, 2004). These days, for example, consumers participate mightily in the production of brands too, serving the so-called social factory with voluntary labor, often in the act of leisure. In this sense, "Brands are a name for cutting into and making manageable an increasingly dynamic production process" (p. 47).

DOI: 10.4324/9781315680705-6

Here the term *branding work* refers to that activity of symbolic manipulation that generates and modifies value through the ongoing creation and rehabilitation of brands. Branding work is widely regarded as a prototypical form of affective labor, a category that has come to denote jobs focused on the regulation of emotional fields. Although the label of branding work is typically applied to paid and tactical labor, it need not be reserved for those who specialize in branding for a living. As suggested earlier, branding work in the twenty-first century is best understood as a distributed activity that enlists myriad participants. Indeed, because it is often performed on the edge or outside of customary employment boundaries, and because it entails the production of commodified cultural content, branding is also commonly cited as an instance of immaterial labor.

This chapter is concerned with a specific kind of branding work, one implicitly addressed from the opening paragraph—namely, that activity by which a set of tasks comes to assume the status of an immediately recognizable "occupation" (see Ashcraft, Muhr, Rennstam, & Sullivan, 2012). Simply put, we take interest in work itself as an object of branding, although it is rarely considered as such. We consider why not, and preview our argument, next.

Why Occupational Identity and Branding?
An (Ir)Rationale and Preview

Why do we commonly treat organizations, but *not* occupations, as foci for identity work and branding? A bountiful literature considers organizations as units that develop identity, image and, more recently, brand, or strategic alignments and condensations of internal and external essence. No parallel literature addresses occupations in this way. Instead, questions of identity and occupation are mostly limited to individual practitioners' dis/identification, while research on the meaning of work examines workers' variable perceptions and experiences, presuming constancy in the nature of a job itself. An impression arises that organizations are identity- vulnerable in some way that occupations are not. We seem to assume that organizations are susceptible to a number of symbolic partners, hence collective identity constructions are necessary to rein them in, whereas occupations are not similarly promiscuous and, so, do not require comparable effort—except for their practitioners, who must navigate the relation between work and other sources of identity.

It is as if the nature and worth of work itself simply *is*, a straightforward matter determined by evident features such as the physical or cognitive demands of tasks and the market for them, level of complexity or knowledge abstraction, requisite education, degree of autonomy, salary and benefits, and so forth. These, after all, are among the burdens of proof for occupations aspiring to elevate their professional standing— burdens of proof *and* rewards for successful persuasion, we should add.

For how do any of these features actually come about, and do imagery and meanings stamped upon the work have anything to do with it?

The short answer, which we develop at length in this chapter, is a resounding yes: To be known and evaluated as an occupation is to endure symbolic associations, which may or may not be articulated and formalized, but in any case are profoundly *felt*, and it is these sensed associations that *move* work's enacted character and value. Discerning the nature and worth of work entails identity maneuvers, in other words. Or to put the matter bluntly, *any* review of work's factual features involves social negotiation. We contend that these maneuvers, even when explicit, operate primarily through affect instead of direct meaning contestation, even when the latter occurs. That is, the meanings that make work *work* must materialize as both sense-able and move-able in order to take hold. Occupational identity is an affective relation, we will argue, all the more so in the days of advanced capitalism. Hence, branding is particularly relevant to contemporary experiences of work.

To clarify, we are not simply saying that *one's* occupational identity exerts affective tugs. This much we already know from abundant research on emotionality in work and organizational life, much of which frames emotion either as the feelings of self-contained individuals at and about work (e.g., stress, burn-out, bullying) or as a distinguishing feature of certain, usually feminized occupations (e.g., emotion, aesthetic, service labor). The claim advanced here recalls the distinction drawn in Chapter 2, between emotion as sifted personal feelings and affect as a transpersonal flow of feeling that evades such capture. Pushing beyond the feelings of practitioners, we are saying that the identity of an occupation *as an entity*—a coherent line of work distinguished by certain qualities—is created and regulated through affect.

It is our specific contention that the character and value of work itself is affectively rather than rationally generated. In other words, occupational identity is born of concrete inhabitations wherein certain bodies, objects, spaces, practices, and meanings come to adhere to one another, and it circulates through nomadic encounters that radiate these sticky yet unfinished associations with felt proof of their inherency. It is this affective production that we call *occupational branding*: practices whereby a line of work becomes branded, or re-branded, as such—readily identifiable occupations possessed of essential character and value, best known through an immediate reflex of feeling, sensed as real rather than otherwise verified. Ashcraft's (2013) conception of the *glass slipper* provides our starting point, and we rework it through a relational ontology in order to explicate occupational identity as an affective economy with tangible returns. Consistent with a decentralized view of branding work, occupational branding may be proprietary, strategic, and compensated, as in the labor of some professional associations, but it is not necessarily so.

In depicting affect as an a-rational force that (dis)organizes occupations, we do *not* mean to awaken tired dualisms between rationality and its supposedly irrational opposites. In fact, we treat rational accounts and coherent narratives of work's identity as integral to its affective composition. These symbolic devices are among the vital materials that bring credible form to vague senses of labor. However, they do so in a particular way: by assuring us that Logos, not Pathos, is the narrator; by moving a malleable identity toward immovable reality *through* narration; and by negating the very sensate roots that lend such narratives life and animation. Put differently, meaning contestation plays a key part in the affective germination of occupational identity, but it does not operate alone, first, or at the disembodied remove it often claims. Struggles over meaning are also mired in the flow of affect.

We thus come to reference arguments about occupational identity as *irrationales*: resources of reasoned meaning that are part of affect's movement—indeed, distinctive tools for its transmission—for they contribute to *felt* proof and *passionate* attachments precisely by denying the power of sensory influence (and this contradiction earns the prefix "ir"). By way of illustration, we are building such an irrationale here, inhabiting the form of disembodied scholarly argument to make a case for, and from, affective flow—more on this point later.

But first, this is how the argument previewed here contributes to current understandings: Whereas Ashcraft's (2013) recent conception claimed the centrality of communication by positioning discursive struggle as *the* constitutive mechanism of occupational identity, we open a different space for communication in this chapter, guided by the affective model developed in Chapter 3. In this model, occupational identities are not so much social constructions of working subjectivities as they are *worldings* of labor, inhabited associations rife with intensities that turn ordinary tasks into scenes of living. Communication, then, is not so much a battle for meaning as a mode of energetic encounter and transfer. It is how the various intensities that make jobs into habitable occupations come into contact and travel, bouncing from scene to scene and morphing along the way. Ultimately, we develop with greater specificity the first trajectory that Chapter 3 identified as following from this revision: meaning as material that gathers, condensates, and circulates.

Occupational identity is a pressing issue at this historical moment, if for no other reason than the staggering growth of income inequality amid late capitalism, as outlined in Chapter 1. Appraisals of the relative character and worth of jobs weigh heavily in the explosion of income inequality, and people of color and white women are overwhelmingly concentrated in lines of work that draw lower valuation—a phenomenon known as *occupational segregation* (e.g., Charles & Grusky, 2004; Cohen & Huffman, 2003; Tomaskovic-Devey, 1993). Regarded in this light, income inequality is not half of the alarming story. Enmeshed with wage gaps linked to occupational segregation are the differential distribution of voice, risk, opportunity, sleep, mental and physical health and health care, exposure to violence, access to quality food and housing, to resources of all kinds, experiences of dignity and shame, of authority and deference, intergenerational and community thriving, security and precarity, even life expectancy, and more.

Occupational identity is a leading vector of inequality, a powerful vein through which asymmetries accumulate, stick together, and saturate the ordinary. As we will show, occupations *occupy*—lives, spaces, and temporalities well beyond workplace demands, compelling and conditioning relational performances of power, day in and day out. These relentless, contagious, embodied experiences swell, and sometimes fester, into simmering currents of feeling that can far outrun any rational declarations of self- or group- interest. The recent U.S. elections, and associated divides between professional and working classes, raced and gendered bodies, attest to this phenomenon in vivid color, as do similar surges of nationalist populism around the globe. We ignore the affective politics of occupational identity at our peril.

Accompanying these escalating inequalities is the rise of "truthiness" (thanks to Stephen Colbert for the pithy expression). We lack space to trace here the complex relations between advanced capitalism and the so-called post-truth era, though others are trying (e.g., Harsin, 2015; McCright & Dunlap, 2010; Roper, Ganesh, & Zorn, 2016). Suffice it to say, affect plays an increasingly vital role in the production of facts, or should we say certainty, unseating trust in conventional institutions and information sources, and favoring impressions of style over substantive debate. Consider the prevalent preoccupation with the "optics" of things, or their implications for brand. With regard to occupational identity, proof of merit and accountable record fall by the wayside as the pivotal question becomes: Does s/he *seem* presidential (or managerial, professional, like "executive material," an engineer, and so on)? Arguably, whether something looks or feels true *matters* more than ever in a growing number of arenas. And it is affect that delivers this felt proof, which is incontrovertible for its visceral resonance.

It is no longer safe to assume, (as) if it ever was, that the nature and value of occupations is rooted in rational soil. Occupational branding occurs, and is gaining steam, we suggest, precisely because it is not. We do not mean this as some nostalgic projection of a normative future, but, rather, as an invitation to come to terms with what appears to be evolving.

The Glass Slipper: A Case for the Materiality of Communication at Work

As hinted by our justification for attending to occupational identity and branding, we are especially interested in the claim that occupations assume distilled identities, or brands, in accord with the company they keep. Ashcraft (2013) argues that decades of research on occupational segregation deliver convincing evidence: The fate of an occupation depends in significant part on the embodied social identities with whom it becomes associated. Historically, for example, the most reliable way to professionalize is to align a set of tasks with elite (usually, white and well-educated) men and masculinities. Conversely, the surest way to downgrade the worth of work is emasculation through links to women, feminization, or racialized others. The history of branding thus comes full circle, as bodies branded in the old sense (i.e., stigmatized) leave a definitive stamp on the character of the tasks they perform. Likewise, the privilege of *un*branded bodies—those that manage to escape specific marks and, thus, appear universally human—imprints their labor too.

Not only do people derive identity from their work, then; work derives identity from affiliated people. But *how*, more precisely, does this happen? Engaging extant theories of occupational segregation, Ashcraft (2013) makes a case for communication as an alternate explanation, contending that symbolic practices across many cultural locales constitute occupational identity. Her view of communication is akin to that outlined at the outset of Chapter 3: the distributed social activity of (re)constructing durable, yet also pliant, meanings that bring about palpable consequences. Specifically, the identity of an occupation arises through ongoing discursive struggle over two entangled questions: What is this line of work, and who does it?

Several key features of this discursive struggle merit mention. First, it *transpires in multiple sites*, often detached or only loosely connected, such as family socialization, education and training, employing organizations, professional associations, popular cultural representations, and so on. Second, it *may be more or less concentrated and strategic*. Imagine a formal professionalization campaign versus organic identity formation, as when jokes about the stereotypical practitioners of a job (e.g., lawyers, car salesmen) are widely circulated. These first two features suggest a third, reminiscent of our opening depiction of branding work: It *is decentralized and open to a wide range of participants*, including constituents with direct or indirect investment and passersby with little to none, although differential influence is likely. Fourth, it *may be more or less acute in certain periods*—a frenzy of contested meaning when a job is new or metamorphosing, for example, yet only moderate maintenance or fairly stabilized meaning at other times. However, Ashcraft contends that, in some degree, the social construction of occupations in relation to practitioners is occurring all the time in mundane communication. Fifth, though seemingly immaterial, the discursive struggle *carries high material stakes*. This is not to say that every representation matters—plenty will be localized and fleeting, evaporating with an exchange or two—but those which find their way into circulation are likely to ripple with material effects.

Finally, Ashcraft (2013) introduces the metaphor of a *glass slipper* to capture the tangible meanings that emerge from this discursive struggle over occupational identity. In effect, a glass slipper is *both* a constructed, crystallized, and conditioned message that "this occupation is the natural province of these sorts of people" *and* the host of physical and institutional arrangements and material dis/advantages which proceed from that symbolic attachment. Ashcraft is clear that "these sorts of people" is a highly situated, intersectional construction that is not about gender and race in some separate or generic way (e.g., women's work), but that enlists specific embodied social identities—a strain of white middle-class "polite" femininity with a regional twist, for instance, or "nerd" masculinity linked to white and Asian men with certain body types, technical talents, and social ineptitudes.

We can confidently say, for example, (a) that the glass slipper of commercial aviation in the U.S. has long favored men who appear white, heterosexual and fatherly, educated, professionally authoritative (e.g., clean-cut, well-spoken, calm and confident), and technically or scientifically skilled; (b) that this symbolic attachment was strategically invented in the late 1920s to mid-1930s, when the promiscuous popular image of pilots—ranging wildly from rough, rowdy men to dainty, high-society women—received a thorough makeover to persuade the public that airline flying was a safe and legitimate profession; (c) that this glass slipper materialized in a range of supporting configurations and practices that became deeply institutionalized; and (d) that not only airline pilots but also the character of airline flying as a job gained extraordinary benefit from this symbolic attachment between work and particular bodies (for a detailed account, see Ashcraft & Mumby, 2004). Airline pilots provide but one of innumerable illustrations, though not all would be so grandiose or definitive.

In sum, while we think of privilege and discrimination as something granted to, or hurled against, *people*, it is also directed toward *occupations*, and affects their very constitution, largely *on the basis* of their alignment with particular social identities.

Weighing the Glass Slipper Through Relationality: The Persistent Primacy of Discourse

Although the glass slipper account may appear to embrace the sociomateriality of occupational identity, a closer look is illuminating. To be sure, social and material are interwoven in this conception. For example, social identities are thoroughly embodied and interactive, not only cognitive, and definitely not discrete, targets of identification. Certainly, the very notion of a glass slipper evokes something artificial *and* actual, fabricated through the "magic" of symbolic labor yet making real waves in the world.

But it is in that last point—and, especially, the way it claims the material impact of meaning—that the glass slipper departs from the relational ontologies explored in this book. Recall in Chapter 3, for example, where affect theory approaches meaning's materiality quite differently. There, discourse *is* material, another kind of stuff that occupies bodies and animates scenes with the voltage of encounter. Language, interpretation, and meaning matter, but they do not enjoy ontological priority.

In contrast, the glass slipper puts meaning first by announcing that social construction is what *makes* the difference, which then comes to matter. The relationship between work and embodied social identities is up for *symbolic* grabs, and material configurations crop up around whatever meaning wins. Admittedly, occupational identity is more contestable in some moments than others, and it is not open to all conceivable constructions. Materiality is posited as the reason why—an exigency or limit for discursive activity that foments and forecloses opportunity. Materiality is thus acknowledged as influential, but the juiciest action unfolds through discursive activity, the vigor of which is further proven through subsequent material formations. Occupational identity is *first* about human signification constituting embodied subjectivities, and *then* about materialization.

Discursivity thus emerges as the realm of invention, with materiality as its henchman, a brute enforcer of sorts. We are reminded of the classical division of labor—"managers plan, workers implement the plan"—and the dualisms it activates, such as brain-brawn, civilized-primitive, and human-beast. No wonder, then, that "materiality itself is always already figured within a linguistic domain as its condition of possibility" (Barad, 2003, p. 801), ensuring an "implicit reinscription of matter's passivity" (p. 809).

While we are dwelling on occupations, it is worth noting that what we might call the *discursive classes*[1]—knowledge workers (e.g., scholars, especially communication researchers), media personnel (e.g., journalists and pundits), branding specialists, and others whose job it is to influence realities through argument, narrative, symbol, the written or spoken word or image—harbor a particularly keen investment in this version of the discourse-materiality relation. In other words, this relation is not merely an intellectual question; it is an occupational validation, as we will soon see, and one that has enjoyed great success in recent times. No wonder that many who identify against the discursive classes, and with traditional material labor, feel neglected.

In sum, the glass slipper model not only retains some separation of social and material, even as it proclaims their enmeshment; it also renders social construction primary in every sense of the term: principal, initial, and fundamental. The making of meaning through discursivity is the main show, and it is figured as cause, while materiality is left to play the supporting roles of input, constraint, and effect. A linear, sequential causality persists, and humans—especially the discursive classes—stay firmly in the driver's seat, even as human capacities for subjectivity, interpretation, and action are caught up in their own discursive matrix. Strangely, that matrix remains disembodied, despite explicit concern for embodied social identities as the stuff of discursive struggle. It is as if discursive calculations respond to and provoke material exigencies, yet somehow are not of the sensate world.

Affect and the Jurisdiction Contest: Putting the "Occupy" Back in "Occupation"

But, candidly, why bother with such a critique? Does it really matter if we err on the side of paying lavish due to discourse, as the heart and soul of communication, if that move creates new leverage for addressing real problems of work? What tangible benefit can a more fully relational conception of communication offer, anyway? A closer examination of the discursive struggle that manufactures glass slippers—and, specifically, how we are assured of its *discursive* character—can help to answer these questions. Following relationality, what better way to consider them than through the enactment of this very struggle.

To begin addressing occupational identity as a collective rather than individual formation, Ashcraft (2013) leans on Abbott's (1988) formulation of the system of professions. In particular, she picks up on the point that the nature of work "does not speak for itself" but, rather, is "an open, priceless question" answered through *jurisdiction contests*, wherein various constituents of an interoccupational field "vie for control over the meaning of work by advocating and disputing the nature of tasks and the expertise they require" (p. 14). In other words, people speak for work, and they do so through fairly predictable forms of argument. Granted, some material features of tasks can make certain arguments a stretch, but many features are surprisingly symbolically elastic. Jurisdiction claims sound solidly discursive, then—a linguistic version of branding in the old sense: "This turf belongs to us." In fact, the glass slipper is just such an argument, so it may prove instructive to read it on its own terms, as welcomed in the final paragraph (Ashcraft, 2013, p. 27).

The glass slipper operates as a jurisdiction claim for the discipline of communication, declaring that communication theorizing is a better way of understanding the evolution of work as well as explaining and intervening in the problem of occupational segregation. It stakes this claim on behalf of what we might call a "transitional" model of communication, one increasingly aware of the relation between human interaction and materiality yet still invested in demonstrating the relative muscle of discourse and, so, not fully given over to the sociomateriality of relational ontologies. There are many possible reasons for this attachment to the primacy of discourse, perhaps the intellectual moment of the glass slipper's articulation, caught between linguistic and ontological turns, or the sheer momentum of disciplined habit.

The point is not to settle on a stimulus, but to illuminate what all of the possible candidates reveal: that the glass slipper, like all scholarly arguments, is a product of knowledge work that enacts the interoccupational relations from which it arises. Indeed, interdisciplinary relations exemplify Abbott's (1988) notion of an interoccupational field, wherein practitioners argue that "X is *this*, not *that*, sort of phenomenon and, thus, properly our turf." Any intellectual position that aspires to make an interdisciplinary splash, gaining voice and influence for one (sub)field over another, involves painstaking consideration of audience, stage, and speech, so to speak—a patently rhetorical endeavor.

As theories go, the glass slipper is unusual only for its meta-operation. That is, it seeks for the discipline of communication just what it asserts all occupations aspiring to claim new territory pursue: control over relevant meanings. Moreover, it does so precisely *by making that assertion*. Put another way, it positions discourse as integral to our knowledge of work and related problems by engaging in the very discursive struggle it designates as pivotal. The performativity of theory indeed: staking a claim *for* discourse by staking a claim *through* discourse. Clever, perhaps (or not)—and certainly typical of the discursive classes—but so what?

We raise this and ensuing observations not to gaze at the navel of one minor provocation to an academic turf war, but because it allows us to pick more carefully through the claim that jurisdiction contests are *primarily* discursive. In one sense, the example is stacked: In the work of scholarship, especially in the social sciences and humanities, articulating persuasive arguments is not simply something done *on behalf of* a task, to boost the status of the work; it *is* the actual task, the ticket required to enter this work at all. And yet, even in a line of work where argument is the core game, the claim to its chiefly discursive character begins to crumble.

An argument needs, at minimum, a conscious brain, words, a tongue or paper, situated and embodied activities such as reading, thinking, typing, conversing, and revising, preferably with an audience of some kind, at least projected. Or "it" cannot exist, as currency or anything else. Actually, to materialize in the late-capitalist academy, a good argument requires much more: forms and norms of legitimate (read: publishable and well-placed) scholarship; keyboards, screens, hardware, and software; email and other digital information systems and devices; journals and their editorial personnel, policies, and practices, their global distribution, consumption, ranking and impact factors; managerial accounting systems that continually intensify expectations for faculty publication records—and we are just warming up to the neoliberal worlding of scholarly knowledge production (see Ashcraft, 2017).

Yet already, we can see that scholarly argument, among the most obviously discursive of struggles, is thoroughly material, and cannot take shape but through material forms. Its surface or presentational form appears linguistic, but it is nested in an intricate, multi-material infrastructure that is absolutely critical to its life and force. From the embodied, interactive incubation of ideas, to typesetting on the page, to the buzzing networks of institutions and invisible colleges, argument is a sociomaterial activity and apparatus. If thrown from that dynamic infrastructure—cut and pasted from a journal to an opinion column, for example—it must find new material form and footing to survive. A brief detour through the concrete life of an argument, and it becomes the product of multiple and hybrid agencies entangling, rather than the exclusive property or invention of a human mind. Thus far, this material reading of argument resembles the discussion of *agencement* in Chapter 3, but additional texture will arrive if we extend the detour a bit further.

Argument is enabled by the sociomaterial elements and practices named earlier, but it is *animated* by the forces of their encounter, their capacity *to affect* and *be affected*. Only this evolving contact and its indeterminate fallout can explain the shape and direction in which argument—or any*thing*—takes off. Argument gestates, or comes gushing out, through impressions that gather and stew in bodies and artifacts steeped in the varied intimate scenes of their discipline, faltering on the foreign ground of others, spilling into the jumbled geopolitical networks of interdisciplinary relations (if fortunes allow), bumping into the differential distribution of wages, teaching loads, support, exposure, time and space to read and write, language privilege—a remarkable density of relational intensities replayed again and again, even in the minute regulatory exchanges of the review process. Argument is a thing of encounter.

A reflexive illustration might help. When what is now the glass slipper sought a place on the coveted page, multiple "blind" commentators from two top-ranked American journals sniffed a disciplinary outsider through her use of theories and styles linked to another continent, a presumed foreignness invoked to recommend English language coaching to this native speaker. Feeling the familiar spank of otherness—the one that spawned this blasted idea in the first place—yet still resolved to plant one small flag for a lesser discipline, she eagerly purged her prose of its dripping excess and watched the whittled argument take on a life of its own. Once her private conviction—a thrilling and verbose retort to the nagging question of why one settles to make half as much to do twice as much in a feminized field (let's say communication), when they might have jumped to greener pastures where big boys roam (say, management)—now this wayward argument performed gymnastics on screen (or were those backflips typed by her own hand?) in a shameless effort to please others—namely, reviewers from the bright green field of management who (quite usefully) requested a catchy concept to tame the drifting idea. "How about the glass slipper!" she chortled aloud, two glasses of wine into a sleepless overseas flight to deliver a talk justifying the project at a fancy dinner with the business patrons supporting her visiting appointment in a faraway school of economics, a lucky arrangement not lost on her skeptical communication colleagues back home, and one on which she had better make good.

Lest it feel needlessly jarring, the dizzy, ambivalent, *stream*-of--consciousness writing style is meant to perform the affective maze it narrates. As indicated in Chapter 3, affective reflexivity is not *self*-reflexivity but, rather, a post-human practice intended to interrupt stable subjectobject relationships in order to trace-by-doing "the ontological politics evolving as a body of research mingles with other (not necessarily human) bodies in practice" (p. 88). The relevant question now is what, if anything, we can learn from such an *exercise*.

Here, the review process is not as we often think of it, not a disembodied textual exchange over a single manuscript. It is, all at once, an outgrowth, refraction, and re-enactment of occupational relations of intensity, which brings renewed vibration, and perhaps some new pulse, to those energetic relations. In this sense, the review process escapes the confines of Manuscript Central, or whatever virtual body claims to safely shield it, and deposits residue in journals and upon scholarly biographies ("Her work has been published in . . . "), lurks around at conferences (in "meet the editor" panels and countless informal war stories), whispers doubt and motivation in the ears of aspiring authors, and even hitches a plane ride to haunt loosely related activity on the other side of the world. Especially in interdisciplinary venues, the review process is a nexus of personal and occupational branding such that one builds their own reputation by performing as a disciplinary spokesperson. The journal review "complex," we might say—that complex tangle of moving intensities that animate the production of published knowledge—is an occupational habitat: Scholars dwell in the review process, and it takes up residence in us.

Nor does the argument stick to its assigned role as mere ideas under review. It is likewise born of intensities exuding from particular histories of sociomaterial interaction. However, it is a device for re-packaging those energies in cerebral wrapping such that relational intensities are worked upon *as* the ideas are tussled over, as in the vignette earlier. The notion of irrationales is useful precisely for this reason: It opens up the feeling textures of arguments (like this one), how they become material for the conduction of affect—a kind of briefcase in which to smuggle illicit feeling.

Notice that we have landed on a clear example of how relationality regards the materiality of communication quite differently than the original glass slipper account. Argument is a classic communicational mode. Accepting its purely discursive character, the glass slipper claims that jurisdiction claims are a constitutive practice proven in material effects. In contrast, relationality surfaces the material infrastructure of argument and shows how, through sociomaterial practice, argument becomes some*thing* with evolving form and trajectory, changing as it collides with others, running away from and acting back on its alleged author. **As communication, argument is constitutive not because it *makes* the world, but because it is *of* the world,** a vibrant participant in affective contact and transfer. No wonder we form passionate attachments and aversions to argument; no wonder (jurisdiction) claims *feel* right and wrong. We suggest that this sensate worldliness, and not discursivity alone, is the "heart and soul" of communication.

In sum, jurisdiction contests arise *from*, but never rise *above*, bodies in perpetually indeterminate contact. These bodies may be fleshly, textual, organic, ideational, technological, institutional, linguistic; they may be hybrids intersecting all of the aforementioned and more. Jurisdiction claims propagate not only as talking points on tongue or page, but as desire, an unrequited sense of entitlement, repetitive slumps of indignity, a knot in the chest or stomach, meager bank accounts or crushing college debt, fantasized identities, beckoning tools of the trade, resentment and envy, dedication that ought to pay off, booze-fueled epiphanies and depressions, rules and regulations, opportunities sensed or missed, hot pressures breathing down sweating necks. Jurisdiction contests are not only embodied; they are affective, enlivened by the variable energies that come along with dwelling in them. Jurisdiction contests are, in a word, *inhabitations* of power and longing.

This is the *thing* about occupations: Inhabitation goes both ways. Work comes to inhabit the bodies that inhabit work (no matter how disidentified some may feel). Thus, our opening claim that occupations *occupy*, not merely in the sense of passing time (e.g., he, or that office, is occupied right now), but in the sense of *moving*, and *moving in* (e.g., she is consumed, *preoccupied*, with writing this chapter). Occupations literally inhabit—and, at times, possess—bodies, objects, and spaces, the way you know with high confidence that "this is an engineering office," or "this is a salon, not a barber shop," or "she must be the secretary," upon simply walking in. The way we fling about the phrase "occupational hazard" to evoke not only physical dangers of labor but also the decided risk of succumbing to personal habits formed through our line of work. The way that rhythmic motions of labor become engrained in our bodies, as when a massage therapist knows through touch that a client works on a computer all day, while their own bodies bear the pains born of soothing others. An occupation (as line of work) is an occupation (as being occupied), though its intensity modulates and affects bodies differently.

With particular regard to human bodies, we can say that occupations dwell in us. They leave marks upon us, just as we come to live in, and make a life by, their provisions. So it is not just that the embodied social identities associated with a line of work imprint meaning onto the tasks they perform, as the glass slipper maintains. The relation between work and bodies is reciprocal, more like *mutual inhabitation*. This means that bodies also come to bear the marks of branded work, that the branding of work *affects* the bodies in its path.

Before developing this point, we close this section by returning to the question that launched it: What difference might it make for occupational identity if we pursue a relational conception of communication over familiar models that maintain the primacy of discourse? It is not that discourse no longer matters, nor that humans lose their will. Rather, we *sense* how human language, interpretation, and meaning are caught up in the sensate world, which exceeds their capacity and control, and which activates and rides along their movement. Discursive cause and material effect do not quite hold up in this world, but their simultaneous enactment does. In *fleshing out* the "occupy" in occupation, we might come to know—by heart—how occupations, in the dual sense, affect us all.

Occupations of Identity as Affective Economy: Communicating the Work-Body Relation

The idea that "occupation" goes both ways—what we called *mutual inhabitation* earlier (i.e., bodies dwell in occupations *and* vice versa)— suggests the utility of examining the work-body relation more closely. We begin with bodies designated human, as they are the focus of the original glass slipper model. Thus far, we have followed its claim that lines of work become recognized as distinctive occupations through association with certain practitioners, but we have not yet specified how that alignment comes to pass or develops over time.

Ashcraft (2013) condenses three reigning theories in occupational segregation research. The first holds that *the bodies of actual practitioners determine the nature of work*. In this view, tasks are open to multiple meanings, and how they are ultimately regarded depends on who does them. In simple terms, nursing is seen as the emotional, and therefore less technical, labor of caring largely because it is dominated by women. A second position reverses this claim, asserting that *the nature of work regulates who will come to do it*. Here, tasks have intrinsic properties that are readily amenable to cultural coding, which then summons particular people to the job: Nursing entails caring and soothing, hence it is women's work. The third theory incorporates elements of both, placing them in recursive relation. *The nature of work forms around its usual practitioner* (drawing on the first), *and more and less valuable occupations are reserved for certain social identities* (drawing on the second). Working from both ends—that is, discriminating against (or privileging) both bodies *and* jobs, and doing so to one *by* doing so to the other—these twin processes keep feeding one another until the material organization of work becomes solidified. Through this lens, nursing continually struggles for professional status because overwhelmingly women do it, and nursing is mostly reserved for women men because it is a lower quality job relative to other medical specialties. Apparent here is the sensibility, and irony, of attempts to interrupt such vicious cycles by interjecting valued bodies, as in campaigns for men in nursing.[2]

Specifying key difficulties with each position, Ashcraft introduces a fourth theory based on the glass slipper: *The work-body relation is determined through discursive struggle*. This explanation is said to resolve the snags of the other three yet retain their respective foci as open empirical questions. Namely, how are (socially differentiated) physical bodies, task features, and the material organization of work made to matter in a given occupational context? And how they are made to *matter* is settled by social construction, as explicated earlier. Notice that the first three theories treat materiality, in varied forms, as the decisive force, downplaying or denying the role of discourse, whereas the fourth position reduces materiality to discursive fodder, albeit the raw material that the social has to work with.

Without retracing our extended critique of this "discourse first" stance, we home in on two problems faced by theory four once we acknowledge occupation as a mutual inhabitation. On the one side (i.e., bodies occupy occupations), discursive struggles over the work-body relation are themselves embodied, already submerged in affective streams of sociomaterial practice. As we have shown, for example, jurisdiction contests stem from, and stay nested within, worldings of work in progress. On the flip side (i.e., occupations occupy bodies), human forms are *affected* by occupational inhabitations. They are not merely symbolic fodder for constructing occupational identity. They are moved and shaped—emotionally, cognitively, habitually, ideologically, economically, physiologically—by the affective flows of occupation in which they (quite literally) find themselves. Occupational hazards are real, because "occupation" leaves tangible marks on human bodies. The brand is returned, so to speak.

The failing of the fourth theory is therefore this: By elevating discourse above the sensate world, it cannot address occupations as inhabited by *and* inhabiting bodies. We need a better explanation of how the work-body relation *moves*, reciprocally, in the multiple senses drawn out in Chapter 2: how it *affects*, *travels*, and *modulates*. An adequate explanation would need to account for its constitution through affective contact and transmission, as Chapter 3 proposed. We need, in short, a theory of the work-body relation as *communicable*. Fortunately, help is on hand.

Ahmed's (2004, 2014) conception of affective economies provides a useful launch pad, starting with the deceptively simple query, "what sticks?" Her central concern is one of *association*, and she is particularly interested in the formation and circulation of powerful, durable associations, such as those animating *movements* of racial identity and hatred. For Ahmed, then, the question of stickiness is about both sticking *together* and sticking *around*. Put otherwise, how do compelling connections between things— especially signs and bodies—get going? How do associations germinate and propagate, and with what consequences for implicated bodies?

Ahmed observes that the most potent associations rarely arise from reasoned discourse or coherent narrative. Sure, overt logics may crop up on their behalf, especially under pressure. These defensive logics usually pronounce themselves the viable origin or cause of an association, rather than the afterthought and smokescreen they are (another "reason" to approach such logics as irrationales). Nonetheless, truly vigorous associations gain force and momentum precisely from their vague *and* sharply felt character. They are unarticulated yet unmistakable. So how exactly do they work?

In such formations, *adherence* becomes a kind of *coherence*. Various signs begin to cling together, and to certain bodies, thereby forming the appearance or effect of a collective. Ahmed describes such hybrids as a *metonymic slide*, wherein signs that stand in for each other congregate as huddled figures, and the constant gliding between them "constructs a relation of resemblance between the figures" (2014, p. 44). Present one or two of the figures, and their associates are cued on scene as well, as if stuck to their heels. Collective identities become activated and activate the bodies in their path. For example, signs such as terrorist, fundamentalism, Islam, Arab, repressive, primitive, and so forth not only cluster together; it is the constant slipping from one to the next that builds intensities—in this case, of fear and hate—which galvanize a white nationalistic "we" under siege from the perpetual threat of "their" invasion. Ahmed (2004, pp. 131–132, original emphasis) elaborates,

> Indeed, the slide of metonymy can function as an implicit argument about the causal relations between terms (such as *Islam* and *terrorism*) within the making of truths and worlds, but in such a way that it does not require an explicit statement. The work done by metonymy means that it can remake links—it can stick words like *terrorist* and *Islam* together—even when arguments are made that seem to unmake those links.

This capacity to "argue" through *felt*, rather than *said*, associations is what makes sticky signs more forceful than any irrationale that may come to their defense, no matter how cogent. Articulated claims and overt stories can be contested, but how to argue with what *feels* true?

Exactly as this suggests, Ahmed argues that affect does the work of binding figures together. It is the glue that sticks signs to one another and attaches them to bodies. Against the prevailing view of emotion as the property of subjects (e.g., fearful, hateful white nationalists) or objects (i.e., dark bodies deemed ominous), Ahmed (2014) insists that it is the *non*residence of affect—its constant *circulation* "between signifiers in relationships of difference and displacement"—that lends it potency (p. 44). Specifically, Ahmed treats affect as a sociomaterial adhesive that generates, through movement, a sense-able tackiness of meaning that is not merely metaphorical. Metonymic slides, in other words, form and gain intensity through encounter.

Contact with clustering signs creates *impressions*, by which she means more than an ambiguous sense of things. She means, rather, that metonymic slides exert actual impact and leave tangible traces. What kind of impression particular associations will make on a human body—whether and how they will stick, for how long, where they will go, what other figures they might attract—depends on that body's accrued history of encounter and imprint. Our lived orientations become trajectories, rendering some associations more vivid, intimate, and gripping, whereas others easily evaporate or roll off the skin (Ahmed, 2006). Abridged, histories of contact are telling such that repetitive encounters become a kind of trigger.

Ahmed (2004) cautions that these accumulated impressions left by affective circulation do not belong to individual psyches, as commonly conceived. They are social, and exceed particular bodies: "The movement between signs does not have its origin in the psyche, but is a trace of how histories remain alive in the present" (p. 126). Indeed, metonymic slides get rolling by summoning historical associations, even as they may conceal or deny links to earlier moments and scenes. Historical links among signs and bodies can be conjured precisely because they are shared, not so much in the sense of shared meaning, but that material traces of their circulation linger on.

Moreover, signs and bodies cannot hang together unless their connection is reiterated; they must continue to tour as a group for the associational slide to endure. Another way to say this is that affect produces stickiness through persistent contact, which enables the "transference of affect" from one figure in a metonymic slide to the next—a transmission that is agentic yet not bound in customary relations of subject-object and cause-effect: "A relation of 'doing' in which there is not a distinction between passive or active" (Ahmed, 2014, p. 91). The tackiness of signs bound through affect inclines them to pick up other figures as they travel, and to retire those that lose adhesive in the course of encounter. As Ahmed (2004, p. 123) explains in the context of racial formations, "The impossibility of reducing hate to a particular body allows hate to circulate in an economic sense, working to differentiate some others from other others, a differentiation that is never 'over,' as it awaits for others who have not yet arrived."

Affective adherence, then, is all about movement. Metonymic slides move sideways (i.e., transferring from one figure to another) as well as backward and forward (i.e., summoning histories projected toward futures). They travel from one scene to the next, linking signs and bodies here as well as there. They activate and regulate feeling that animates bodies in action and leave impressions upon them. And they do all this through communication as re-defined in Chapter 3: the continual process of sociomaterial encounter and transmission.

That this communicational movement is *economic*, or functions *like* an economy, is critical for Ahmed. For one thing, metonymic slides generate and accumulate value through circulation itself, not through any positive value inherent to those figures in circulation. In this way, Ahmed (2014) reframes the notion of *materialization* affectively, as *intensification*: The more certain relations are enacted, *moving* within and across the varied scenes they bring to life, the more intensity they gather. In this becoming, more than "the real" is achieved; the *value* of that version of the real is also gathering, and palpable *investments* in it are getting made such that its demise "is felt as a kind of living death" (p. 12). Ahmed also prefers an economic frame because she asserts that affect circulates by charging objects (e.g., signs, bodies, texts, artifacts, hybrid figures thereof) that touch and trigger as they change hands and places. It is repetitive and distributed contact with these saturated commodities that transfers and modulates feeling, *not* some sort of raw emotional contagion whereby we come to feel the same fear, hate, or longing.

For Ahmed, then, *affective economy* is more of an analogy that illuminates how affect produces associations that "stick" in a manner akin to the capitalist generation of value. Extending her conception into the realm of work, we suggest that **affective economies of occupational identity generate** *actual* **economic value.** Specifically, the branding work that brands work—as "this, not that" kind of labor—operates through metonymic slides, those implicit yet powerfully felt associations between signs and bodies that *move* through mutual inhabitation. The metonymic slides of occupation connect (and detach) figures in relations of resemblance (and differentiation), yielding collectives of recognizable character that gain steam through travel, and generating dispersed intensities of feeling that translate into tangible value (or devaluation) for the occupation itself. Simply put, occupations *capitalize* on (or depreciate by) affective economies, these sticky "occupations" of identity. We contend that **the glass slipper can be productively reframed in these terms—as a metonymic slide that generates economic value by affective association or adherence, as the branding work by which work becomes coherently branded.**

To illustrate briefly, we return to the example of commercial aviation featured in the original formulation of the glass slipper (see Ashcraft, 2013). There, a strategic symbolic attachment between airline flying and a particular kind of male body (e.g., white, educated, clean-cut, heterosexual and paternal) was *first* discursively produced (through the social constructions of a jurisdiction contest) and *then* materialized (in embodied performances, followed by deeper institutionalizations). Interestingly, Ashcraft indicates that the introduction of a crew *uniform* proved integral to the symbolic makeover of both airline pilots and their labor. Ahmed might have a "field day" with this minor observation, and it could be instructive to join her.

By now a well-worn commodity, the airline pilot uniform came about in a sweeping industry effort to assure a nervous public that flying was a safe and reliable mode of transportation (the stake of airlines), and that pilots were knowledgeable, dependable, even elite professionals (the stake of the nascent pilot union) (for more detail, see Ashcraft & Mumby, 2004). It is worth stressing that the uniform responded to pervasive anxiety; it was *designed* as an affective device, an object imbued with the comforts of manly competence and authority. Several airlines fashioned the uniform around the model of a sea captain—a dark, trim officer's suit complete with epaulets of rank and an ornamented commander's cap to match. This is the uniform that found its way into circulation and persists with little variation to this day.

Already, we can sense an affective economy of occupational identity evolving: With this single object—a uniform—associations from past and parallel scenes (e.g., fascination with aerospace meets military masculinity meets transportation) are evoked to enact certainty in the new and faltering scene of commercial aviation. Saturated with the affective residue of prior circulations, the object is ready to adhere (to) new figures with only minor adjustments. But it must, and will, be inhabited and circulated over and over again for this new version to "stick," *together* and *around*—for airline pilots to swell with confident pride inside its cloth, for passengers to "relax and enjoy the flight" upon its sight, for all other airline employees to honor it with deferential display, for Hollywood to glorify it, for Congress to be seduced by union lobbyists adorned in it, for young boys to harbor longings to wear it, and for young girls to learn to swoon at its imagining. Each of these inhabitations, and countless more, gather intensity through circulation. The signs are magnetized, glide back and forth, move around, and attract new associates: *airline pilot, officer, professional, discipline, authority, dignity, respect, knowledge, technical and sexual prowess, tall and handsome, strong and silent, manliness.* The metonymic slide attaches to, and remakes, certain bodies, forming the effect of a collective by association, a recognizable "occupation," inhabit*ed* and inhabit*ing.*

By accumulating affect, the uniform accumulates (or, depending on the quality of intensities, loses) value, not only energy, momentum, and force, as Ahmed would have it but also identity-based economic value, or brand. The object condenses or encapsulates—and carries into circulation—not only an occupational identity but also a mode of feeling about that identity. Repetitive contact with the uniform leaves impressions, sensory responses that become a tacit warrant for commercial aviation safety and the standing of the flying trade. Albeit not in these terms, airlines and the pilot union knew this, and *banked* on it (figuratively and literally—see how *investment* began at once), when they collaborated to put pilots in uniform. The ensuing transformation "set you up separate and distinct with high qualifications and high in the economic set up of this country. That is worth plenty," said the founder of the pilot union in an early address to his constituents (as cited in Hopkins, 1998, pp. 17–18). And at least some pilots today sense it, when they describe seeing women in the crew uniform: "It does hurt just a tad. It pricks something," said one, struggling to share the feelings of embarrassment and deflation that flood him when the uniform gets detached from a narrow slice of men.[3] If the metonymic slide is interrupted, occupational brand value is eroded.

Upon further scrutiny, however, the uniform is not a *single* object at all. It is only part of an occupational object world. To do its affective work, it needed the concurrently developed intercom between cockpit and cabin that intensified its authority with mystery and invisibility, the closely guarded cockpit with its dizzying bells and whistles and other masculinist artifacts (e.g., ritual pornography for the next crew to find), the black "nav(igation) kit" to showcase its requisite technical materials, and the many "runways" for uniformed swagger afforded by airport spaces and attendant rules of passage, not to mention the support of innumerable institutions. It also needed surrounding figures from which to differentiate, for instance, "stewardesses" clad in their feminized, sexualized uniform, performing wife-mother and object of desire, accessible in the cabin to attend to the bodily needs of pilots and passengers while their husband-father counterparts are left alone to carry out the complicated business of the cockpit. In a word, occupational object worlds are thoroughly relational. The circulation of any object takes the participation of a sociomaterial village. The branding work that brands work, then, is not limited to human participants, and need not entail their strategic effort or will, though it often does.

Crucial to our purposes, it is the mutual inhabitation of occupational object worlds and the *movement* that entails—the distributed repetitions of contact and impression that we have called *communication*—that makes for an occupational world*ing*. These worldings well escape the borders claimed by any work*place*. Consider just this example: A pilot's daughter, whose research interests in gender and work are indelibly carved by the cumulative intensity of his countless departures and returns, and who endeavors now to rewrite the glass slipper, recalls with intoxicating clarity the pungent smell of a uniform never intended for her, moments ago as she wrote of its history. She remains occupied by his occupation, just as it occupied him and enveloped a family. Her labor, such as the irrationale built by this chapter, keeps the circulation alive in the act of examining it. "Occupation" can be an affective inheritance, it seems.

Returning at long last to theories of the work-body relation, we are equipped to propose a fifth position: *The work-body relation is constituted through metonymic slides that accumulate intensity and (de)generate brand value through communication, defined as the circulation of mutual inhabitations.*

Conclusion

We have come a long way (baby?), and the journey could use some review. The primary aim of this chapter has been to re-conceptualize the branding work it takes to brand work. Because occupations are so rarely addressed from a branding angle, we lingered over why it could be fruitful to do so, and why occupational branding is a consequential contemporary practice (see also Ashcraft et al., 2012). We then turned to Ashcraft's (2013) initial formulation of how occupational identities arise through social construction, yielding durable (but also presumably breakable) glass slippers that align lines of work with particular social identities. A closer look at this framework revealed the hierarchical relations it fosters between discourse and materiality such that human symbolic activity calls the shots, and material formations mostly do its bidding, occasionally throwing up roadblocks and inducements. The cost of this discursive supremacy is that the communication which constitutes occupational identity becomes oddly disembodied, a practice performed apart from the sensate world, even as it entails the social construction of bodies. Lost is a robust sense of how occupations, including arguments and narratives about them, are both inhabited and inhabiting. Yet occupations become living worlds and perceptible brands only through such mutual inhabitation.

In an effort to revive the "occupy" in occupation, and thereby address communication as embroiled in the sensate world, we turned to Ahmed's (2004, 2014) conception of affective economies. Through this relational account, the glass slipper transforms into a metonymic slide that accumulates intensity and generates brand value through circulation. Here, communication is not the making of meaning, but the movement of felt associations through repetitive contact and transfer, encounter and impression. In this sociomaterial rendition of the glass slipper, discourse is no longer in the lead, with materiality in second place. Instead, they are staged simultaneously, and together, as the work-body relation is affectively constituted through communicative transmission.

Indeed, this was another goal of the chapter: to explore how theorizing communication through relational ontology, especially affect theory, might make a difference to practices of work. For the central work practice of many of our readers—that is, the conduct of scholarly inquiry—the turn toward relationality taken here signals several implications. Briefly, communication defined as affective transfer requires expansion of the customary *observational* apparatus of qualitative research, which emphasizes sight and sound (e.g., visible behavior, speech) at the expense of other powerful sensations and modes of transfer (e.g., smell, touch). Moreover, analyses of affective economies draw qualitative research beyond interpretation and critique as we know them, with their quests for *co*herent meaning, and toward an associational logic of *ad*herence.

The guiding question shifts from what makes sense (i.e., how do human participants negotiate meaning?) to what sticks (i.e., what signs and figures become bundled and intensified through circulation, and how are human and nonhuman participants affected?). Such inquiry thus addresses the question of *what makes sense* with a "fuller-bodied" read of the phrase. Accordingly, analyzing affective economies requires delving into the sociomaterial histories of signs—specifically, of their clustering and sliding around occupational object worlds, and of the differential impressions they leave on inhabiting and inhabited bodies (e.g., those variously hailed as protagonist, foil, and object), as well as on the valuation of work.

Thinking beyond these methodological implications, what if—as we have tried to demonstrate here—the character and value of work itself is affectively rather than rationally made, and communication is the means of its sociomaterial production? So what if human bodies are imprinted by occupation in the process? We have already opened a case for how such claims *affect* our knowledge of social and material inequalities, such as those wrought by occupational segregation. Understanding how occupational identities arise and gain intensity and value through circulation, and their profound impact with and upon human bodies, is critical to understanding relations of power not only in contexts of work, but in other societal arenas as well. At the outset, for example, we hinted at the ways in which repetitive injuries of occupational identity may contribute to swells of feeling that ignite currents of political unrest. The subsequent analysis fleshed out how occupational worldings radiate well beyond the workplace, through inhabitation and inheritance, catching fire in resentments and longings directed elsewhere, which can animate a wide range of present scenes and desired futures. To the extent that communication is the vehicle for this movement, we *feel* that critical affect studies of the communicative transmission of occupational identity are a vital endeavor.

Even as we continue to reference occupational "identity," readers may notice that identity has changed along the way—from some central and enduring character or essence of an entity, from coherent narratives that establish stable meanings of self, to unarticulated and ambiguous yet acutely felt associations such that *ad*herence performs the work once credited to *co*herence. The emphasis on brand is critical to this shift, because it highlights how occupational identities that stick operate like a reflex, an uncontrollable jerk of a knee upon activation. They are immediately felt, rather than reflex*ive*ly derived, connections between work and bodies.

The creation and dissemination of such automatic responses have long been a welcomed outcome, if not an overt aim, of conventional professionalization campaigns. However, condensations of occupational essence that elicit predictable reflexes of feeling have become all the more important in the "truthy" age of late capitalism. Others have tracked key shifts in the notion, administration, and practice of professions during this period, which have contributed to the erosion of traditional modes and tactics of professionalization, even as the quest to professionalize has mushroomed, courting arenas of labor once well beyond its reach (e.g., Fournier, 1999; Malin, 2000; Suddaby, Cooper, & Greenwood, 2007). The upshot, some say, is the decline of the professions, or at least intensified challenges to their stability as institutions, amid an explosion of claims to professional status. Coupled with the rise of branding as a neoliberal imperative and its proliferation as a generic filter (e.g., "but what are the implications for his brand?"), we should expect occupational branding to be all the more typical of our times.

Thus far, we have developed only the first trajectory of an affective redefinition of communication, as proposed in Chapter 3—namely, examining the material circulation of meaning. The second trajectory awaits attention: that is, exploring material sign systems beyond human symbolism that may also participate in occupational identity. In Chapter 3, we briefly considered Brennan's (2004) case for the transmission of affect through various material "languages," such as chemical and electrical communication.

Interestingly, Ahmed (2014, see pp. 218–219) explicitly distinguishes her approach from Brennan's (2004) by emphasizing the economic circulation of affective objects *as opposed to* the transmission of affect via physiological contagion. What this overlooks is that the alleged opposition may simply be a difference in the operation of different kinds of signs. Whereas Ahmed takes interest in the circulation of human symbolism, Brennan is concerned with the circulation of physical signs that are not typically read *as* signs. She takes them as such in an effort to open up commonalties across material modes of communication. Perhaps, then, hormones are a different communicative vehicle for affective transfer—another kind of object that is not exactly commodified, but is nonetheless conductive. Brennan contends that hormones are *communicative* precisely for the complexity of the process whereby affective transfer is mediated (i.e., like symbolic language, it requires a great deal of bodily interpretation, or "reading" signs).

In one passage, for instance, Brennan (2004, pp. 85–86) muses about a comparative study of ministers and performers:

> The latter were found to have higher levels of testosterone, which led to the primitive conclusion that choice of occupation was determined by hormone levels, a sociobiological conclusion flying in the face of social variables affecting this and other steroids. What would make more sense of the findings of this study is the notion that the occupational choice of the minister led to more transformation or repression of testosterone-associated effects (aggression, overconfidence, sexual arousal) as a matter of occupational course, whereas the same effects in the entertainer are indistinguishable from those evoked in the course of performance. Being—or identifying—with those in receipt of adulation raises levels of testosterone . . . [whereas an occupation that requires] monitoring the affects associated with testosterone means those affects have less hold.

However we evaluate this provocative claim, it raises a prospect worth fuller consideration: that chemical communication and other material sign systems may participate in the production of occupational identity. Despite her disagreements with Brennan, Ahmed concurs that affective economies shape bodies, not only at the level of emotions or surface markings such as appearance and comportment, but in musculature and health. In a later work, for instance, she invokes repetitive strain injury and cites a lump on her right ring finger from writing to exemplify the impressions labor makes upon a body, or how we take the shape of our occupations: "we get stuck in certain alignments as an effect of this work" (Ahmed, 2010, p. 247).

A question that begs study, then, is the extent to which occupations brand (in the sense of imprint) human bodies, and through what modes of communication. Such inquiry would materialize the second trajectory proposed by Chapter 3, but more profoundly, could materialize the very notion of a "line" of work—no longer the figurative pathways of vocation, trade, or calling, but trajectories of the real that leave substantial traces in their wake and take flight in unforeseen directions.

Unlike the original, the revised glass slipper formulated in this chapter is *not* meant as a jurisdiction claim. It is simply an argument—admittedly an *ir*rationale—for what relational ontology can *do* in the world. Really, it is a yearning for other worlds we might do with it.

Notes

1. We are indebted to Pete Simonson, our colleague and Ashcraft's partner, for this insight. Much gratitude to Pete for his multiple readings of, and helpful commentary on, this chapter and, specifically, for the lively conversations about who is most/best served by claims to the social construction of reality. The argument presented here is relational indeed.
2. E.g., www.discovernursing.com/men-in-nursing#.WFraNy0rKUk.
3. Versions of this feeling, expressed here by only one of Ashcraft's airline pilot interviewees, were also echoed by many others. This first articulation caught her off guard, however, perhaps because it was her father speaking.

7 Conclusion

The Value(s) of Communicative Relationality

Almost a quarter century ago, Law (1994) proclaimed a "bonfire of the certainties": social changes that disrupt beliefs in organizational stability and unity, a shakeup of the field's fundaments, a commitment to perspectival pluralism, and a continual interrogation of ontological and epistemological commitments—all of which could lead the field in one of two directions. In the first, the field would divide into federations that offer safe harbor from the threat brought about by the elimination of certainty, allowing the pursuit of putatively better explanations of the "problem of organization." There would be a paradigmatic balkanization of the field, and different units would pursue different aims and would operate based on different criteria. In Law's (favored) second direction, the field, as a whole, would eschew confident answers altogether in favor of surfacing questions and uncertainties, with an eye toward a continual destabilization of existing theories while shedding light on that which they conceal, in the service of generating new narratives of organizing. As is often the case with such predictions, the options were never mutually exclusive; both futures have appeared to some extent. Reed (2006), for instance, saw evidence for *both* a return to orthodoxy and vibrant critical debates about conceptual foundations; work published since this 2006 recognition seems to confirm his conclusion.

In this context, we offer this book not so much to challenge traditional foundations, nor simply as a mechanism to surface additional questions and uncertainties (though there are hints at, and disavowals of, both in the preceding pages), but primarily to outline an alternative. Scholars of organization have long struggled with questions about how to engage with constant transformations in working and organizing, along with questions about how to navigate the long-standing divisions between symbolic and material domains. Our marshaling of relational approaches, honed as they were by communication theory, can provide an itinerary for the scholar seeking resources for engagement with such questions. The benefit of this marshaling has been the depiction of an array of conceptual possibilities, grounded by a set of five commitments yoking them together, and a set of demonstrations of the empirical purchase these perspectives provide.

DOI: 10.4324/9781315680705-7

Throughout the preceding chapters, we sought to advance a claim. In response to our guiding question from Chapter 1 (*What have work and organization become under contemporary capitalism—and how should organization studies approach them?*), we acknowledged that a multitude of paths for analysis exist, especially given the array of problems around (and factors participating in) working and organizing mentioned in Chapter 1. Our claim was that finding a single scheme that would capture the complexity of factors producing the "new economy" was ill advised (not to mention likely impossible), and that engaging with perspectives that could generate novel insights, heuristic value, and new lines of inquiry was a more fruitful path. We thus chose to pursue questions associated with the *communicative* organization of production, consumption, and accumulation in contemporary capitalism.

In Chapter 2, we advanced several versions of relational ontologies (as well as five premises these bodies of thought share); the third chapter described our efforts to augment those perspectives with an eye toward the book's guiding question. In that chapter, we proposed a set of three approaches that built upon, and extended, Chapter 2's relational ontologies. We captured these efforts under the banner of *communicative relationality*, a term that indicated the capacity of communication to serve an explanatory role in endeavors to transcend discursive-material dualisms in organization studies. The three conceptions of communicative relationality, based on divergent conceptions of communication, differ markedly. But, across the three, the fusion of contemporary communication theory and relational ontologies tendered conceptual tools with the capacity to guide analyses into modes of mattering in working and organizing.

In this sense, we see our development of communicative relationality as an alternative story—not one superior to existing stories, but one whose unconventional plotlines and protagonists tell a useful tale with respect to working and organizing in late capitalism. Our three case study chapters—on creativity and the becoming of an idea in Chapter 4, the emergence of "the product" in digital startup entrepreneurship in Chapter 5, and the examination of occupational branding work in both academic writing and airline pilots in Chapter 6—illustrated the appeal of the approaches developed in the earlier chapters. In this final chapter, we draw out implications for those who might be tempted to travel the route sketched in the preceding pages.

The "Work" of Communication

The premise of this book is that, if the organization studies field is to develop responses to the question about working and organizing in late capitalism guiding our investigation, that communication must become a central figure. In a dual sense, this is true. First, the content and tenor of work associated with the "new economy" has increasingly become *communicative labor*, a mode of activity that depends on working with what has been typically understood as the realm of *immaterial* goods: knowledge work, service-oriented work, branding, and even academic labor (Discenna, 2011; Mosco & McKercher, 2009; Rennstam & Ashcraft, 2014). Throughout, we troubled the implied division of the material and immaterial, and argued that relational ontologies, refined and extended through encounters with sophisticated conceptions of communication, carry the potential to develop novel insights on the accomplishment of working and organizing in this rapidly shifting scene.

An interest in developing novel insights on working and organizing leads to the second sense of "the work of communication," one in which *work* involves shifting organization studies' sense of communication as both a phenomenon and a mode of explanation. Rethinking communication, we have argued throughout, engenders the possibility of engaging with the messy complexity associated with contemporary capitalism developed in Chapter 1—and, especially, creates possibilities for studying the problems associated with it. Chapter 2 presented several versions of relational ontologies—versions of performativity, sociomateriality, ANT, and affect theory—apposite for investigating what we termed a dizzying array of factors and forces associated with contemporary work and organization. Communication was rendered not merely a mode of expression of pre-existing cognitions, nor an activity occurring within already-existing systems; instead, it became the site and surface of working and organizing, the intricate sociomaterial process by which working and organizing relations are *real*-ized. "Materializing" communication in this sense was the project of Chapter 3, in which we offered communicative extensions to lines of relational thinking, portraying communication as relating/linking/connecting, as writing the trajectory of practice, and as constitutive transmission.

The next three chapters provided evidence of the "work" communicative relationality can perform; they proffer a sense of the payoffs possible when pursuing the thinking portrayed in Chapter 3 (as well as the challenges provoked by such studies). As we mentioned at the end of that third chapter, the case studies exhibit an array of approaches available to those who wish to pursue communicative relationality. Chapter 4's detailed empirical analysis demonstrates that, even when human discursive activity is not decentered, communicative relationality occasions a substantial and innovative reframing of working and organizing. Interrogating literature on creativity—a concept that is a cornerstone of, but also serving as a cipher for, the knowledge work key to contemporary capitalism—Chapter 4 delivered an analysis of the becoming of an idea, from its inception to its prototypification. Positioning "idea" in active, agential terms, we showed how creativity manifests itself through its embodiment in an idea, which is itself far from a passive recipient of human intention and cognition. Our analysis of the case of Museomix demonstrated how the idea always materialized itself in a multiplicity of ways: In its emergence on artifacts employed in a brainstorming session, in its capacity to attract audiences' interest, in its production of alignments between other agencies in the scene, and its facility in altering situations. The version of communicative relationality deployed in this chapter produced a unique understanding on the existence of (an) idea: seeing creativity not as the outcome of individual or shared cognition, but as a complex and precarious relational process revolving around the (equally complex and precarious) emergence and existence of an idea that must be empirically followed through an array of communicative manifestations to be understood.

Chapters 5 and 6 emanate somewhat more directly from problems (very different problems, to be sure) associated with late capitalism. While they do not provide a single clear path through the thicket of factors identified in Chapter 1, they each place somewhat less emphasis on talk. Each represents an effort to conceive of agency as the conjoint accomplishment of a heterogeneous mix of participants, though they move in very different directions. Chapter 5's investigation of digital technology entrepreneurship at the startup accelerator AmpVille employed the second extension to relational theorizing introduced in Chapter 3. Augmenting economic performativity with articulation theorizing in a way that responds to criticisms lodged by Butler (2010), that second perspective offered a route by which analysts can attend to the logic of a practice and its trajectory, as well as to the alignments and contradictions marking the *agencement* (conceived as both a network of participants and locus of agency). The work of communication displayed in the AmpVille case was about the ways in which a model of startup entrepreneurship imposed by the accelerator's curriculum summoned from startups claims about product that *could be*—were *promised* to be—received as valuable by potential funders. The version of product that emerged was one marked not merely by a digital tool, but was a conglomeration of team, business model, and technological innovation—all of which were made to matter (i.e., materialized) in the practice of developing a valuable product.

For anyone with even a passing interest in entrepreneurship, this set of participants (i.e., nodal points) would be hardly surprising; what is perhaps more interesting is that the version of communicative relationality deployed in this chapter showed how each participant was better understood as a sociomaterial hybrid constituted by the myriad of relations articulating its meaning(s) in the practice. The analysis then showed, with respect to the contours of contemporary capitalism, how the communicative practices catalyzed by this particular network of agencies emphasized the sort of individualism endemic to entrepreneurship and its privatized accumulation of wealth—a practice contributing to the yawning economic inequality characteristic of late capitalism. The novelty emanating from this analysis is not, however, merely in calling attention to individualism running through startup practice (a point also made in Chapter 4's discussion of creativity); it is also in showing "the product" to be a tenuous accomplishment not reducible to human activity—one requiring the communicative stitching together of multiple agencies in advancing claims to value.

Chapter 6, employing a vision of communicative transmission built on affect theorizing, considered occupational branding as manifest in academic publishing and commercial aviation. Branding, we argued, refers to the symbolic work that cultivates and capitalizes on the affective relations associated with identity; it produces what Arvidsson and Peitersen (2013) call an "affective proximity" between the embodied person and the (dis) embodied brand. The work of communication here is in the creation of symbolic associations around an occupation, the affective labor through which the occupation is realized, and in the defining of the occupation as an object eligible to shape experience. Communication is not only what occurs in the negotiation of occupational status, nor is it merely what is observable "on the job"; communication, here, is a mode by which actors engage with, and transfer, affect. Bodies, signs, scenes, and energies bunch together, they inhabit one another. And although academic writers and airline pilots encounter somewhat different affective economies, branding work carries the potential to generate economic value when associations between signs and bodies accumulate affect in the service of a brand. The novelty offered by an analysis like this reframes branding, moving it from the domain of product marketing and injecting it fully into the process by which value is materialized in effect economies, occupational or otherwise.

Across these cases and the versions of communicative relationality on which they draw, we note that *meaning* appears—or is materialized—rather differently. Chapter 4, building on the first vision of communicative relationality offered in Chapter 3, presented communication as occurring when acts of relating/linking/connecting occur; the presence of symbolism and human minds is not required. Meaning, as a central component of social action, is demoted from its traditional perch in this posthumanist-influenced perspective. As Martine and Cooren (2016) present it, "Speaking in terms of communication rather than in terms of discourse and meaning thus allows us to highlight the *relational* nature of our world without resorting to concepts that have been traditionally associated with a human-centered perspective" (p. 151; emphasis in original).

An alternative engagement with meaning is offered in Chapter 5, which aligned with communication's interest in writing the trajectory of practice, the second vision of communicative relationality. In that chapter, we depicted meaning as the ongoing product of the relations that enmesh a myriad of (non)human participants. Bringing together economic performativity and articulation theorizing, meaning becomes the result of the multiple relational forces that position a nodal point in an *agencement*—with the concomitant understanding that it is the *agencement*, rather than the putatively autonomous individual human—that is the seat of agency.

And Chapter 6 recouped a conception of communication as constitutive transmission, informed by the affect theorizing presented in the third model in Chapter 3. As a third alternative regarding communicative relationality, this approach renders communication not as a struggle over meanings conducted discursively, but as about the conveyance of energies and the constitution of metonymic slides: confederations of sociomaterial figures through which affect is transferred. Meaning, then, does not evaporate; it inhabits the practices of encounter and transmission in practices such as branding, but its conventional (i.e., discursive and human-centered) manifestation cannot be the analytical focal point in an investigation led by communicative relationality.

We have presented, then, three conceptions of communicative relationality that offer sharply contrasting approaches to (and radical departures from conventional accounts of) meaning. What unites these perspectives is that they beckon analysts to attend to *how* adherence, alignment, stickiness, articulation, stitching, and coming-together-ness are *accomplished*. Although organization theory has long venerated versions of connection and integration (e.g., Cyert & March, 1963; Simon, 1997; Thompson, 1967), the field has shown comparatively less interest in understanding the intricacies of the accomplishment of connection (Kuhn, 2012). In the next section, we outline several methodological claims regarding *how* analysts might pursue the *how*.

Methodological Implications for Organization Studies

One of the central planks in our development of the three perspectives on communicative relationality is that studying practice, as a "unit" of analysis—as opposed to cognitions, discourses, organizations, is essential. This is not a completely novel stance: theorists of (social) practice such as Gherardi (2012), Leonardi (2015), Nicolini (2012), Schatzki, Knorr-Cetina, and von Savigny (2001), and (in the realm of a process ontology) Hernes (2014) have been arguing the same for a long time. Simply asserting that practice should form the basis of the epistemological and empirical, therefore, is not enough. What is needed, instead, is a honing of the notion of practice to align with the principles, the non-foundational premises, outlined in Chapter 2.

Doing so would begin with a recognition that practice never presents itself to researchers as an objective and unambiguous "thing":

> Practice always needs to be brought to the fore, it needs to be made visible, articulated, and turned into an epistemic object in order to enter discourse. Practice can never be apprehended in an unmediated way and the notion that practice is "just what people do" is a return to a naive form of empiricism (Schatzki et al., 2001). Articulating practice therefore requires discursive work and material activity: another practice.
>
> (Nicolini, 2009, p. 196)

Nicolini is arguing that analysts must develop sophisticated method-ological techniques for making sense of practice. If, as we suggested throughout the preceding chapters, practice always involves a fluid mix of ontologically heterogeneous agencies, analyses (and analysts) require additional sensibilities to grasp both the many participants in practice and the complexities of the phenomena accomplished in practice.

A route into engagement with practice in the sense of the relational ontologies presented here is a consideration of what Fox and Alldred (2015, 2017) call the "research assemblage," the conglomeration of researcher, data, methods, and contexts. Relationality demands that analysts think (and feel, and relate) not simply in terms of relations rather than substances, but that they develop empirical techniques that provide insight into the prac-tices about which those sensitivities speak. A demand for contemplation of research techniques summons from analysts a desire to reject the sort of separation of discursive and material domains, along with the prioritiza-tion of one over the other, described in this book. The events, phenomena, objects, states, or practices we examine should be understood as enmeshed in their own multiplicitous network, their own affect economy, which is intimately bound up with the phenomenon the analyst seeks to understand.

Fox and Alldred (2015, 2017) encourage scholars to recognize that, in seeking to understand a given event, phenomenon, object, state, or practice, that our research activities are likely to comprise their own set of relations (researcher stance, tenor of interactions with the site, research instruments, theories, etc.), which interact with the *explanandum* in the production of an *explanans*. In other words, relational inquiry summons scholars to identify hybrid networks and the practices in which they participate, to examine the flow of affect and the capacities the flows enable (or how meanings exceed a given practice to saturate others), and to pay heed to the materializations—the modes of mattering—of particular events and affect economies. Analysts must, then, acknowledge that the voices of (non)human participants, each a composite "being," are not always present in words and thus cannot sim-ply be captured by traditional applications of observational or interview techniques; sensitivity to multiple modes of mattering are thus required (Mazzei, 2010), and forms of shadowing oriented to objects, as demon-strated in Chapter 4 (see also Czarniawska, 2007; Vásquez, Brummans, & Groleau, 2012) can be useful techniques in this regard.

The claims here are not so much a call for new methodological tech-niques, nor an assertion that existing methods are inadequate; instead, they insist on the doing of research differently. Accordingly, interviews can be a valuable approach, but what "interviewing" becomes is a matter of methodological and epistemological performativity. For instance, Nicolini's (2009) description of an "interview to the double"—where an interviewer asks an interviewee to imagine that he or she has a "double," a clone, who will replace him or her tomorrow; the respondent then must tell the dou-ble all the detailed information so that no one will be able to discern the difference—can be useful in its elicitation of narratives providing insight on the practical concerns, including others' expectations, that guide practice, along with the local lexicon of accountability guiding a particular practice.

And although we have taken up only qualitative techniques in this book (it is a predilection we share), we can envision quantitative approaches to relationality as well, particularly those operationalizing complex sociomaterial networks (Contractor, Monge, & Leonardi, 2011); we also would do well to remember the inventive engagement with quantitative measures in Bourdieu's (1984) work. In any case, to be in step with communicative relationality, an analyst using any methodological approach must be attuned to relationality's assertions regarding multiplicity and hybridicity of agencies, contingencies of entities, indivisibility of sociomateriality, performativity of theory, complexity of causality, and arbitrariness of practice trajectories.

These attunements are necessary but not sufficient for the approach to inquiry we advocate. What is additionally demanded of those pursuing relational ontologies is, first, to be attentive to the micropolitics of the research process in the emergence of explanations. Connolly (2010) offers useful guidance in this regard with his elaboration of the micropolitics of perception. Cautioning against an intellectual tendency to treat linguistic, symbolic and, specifically, conceptual activity as autonomous from embodiment, mood, memory, anticipation, and other layers of experience, he treats these instead as imbricated "circuits of inter-involvement" (p. 183), whose rich history is imbued with various social disciplines that "find expression in the color of perception itself. Power is coded into perception" (p. 190). He suggests ways of intervening in these communicative dynamics by slowing down and opening up the affective textures of perception, thereby creating opportunities for its disruption.

Beyond the researcher's practices of discernment, attending to the micropolitics of the research process entails turning outward as well, to consider how various actors (which are, again, always composites of human and nonhuman elements, not all of them present in the sites we study) affect and are affected by the depictions we produce (Fox & Alldred, 2015). Important here is the quality of relations among practices often deemed separate—namely, how practices of scholarly perception move, and are moved by, those practices and agencies under investigation. In addition, sensitivity to the micropolitics of research requires tempering intellectual quests for rationality and coherence with simultaneous appreciation for the disorderly. For example, alongside our desires to locate a logic of practice (see the second version of communicative relationality in Chapter 3, and the associated analysis in Chapter 5), we also sought to acknowledge the irreducible queerness, the seemingly illogical and a-rational character of the practices we study (see the third version of communicative relationality in Chapter 3 and the associated analysis in Chapter 6).

Barad (2012) makes it clear that we must be prepared to grasp the queerness, the strangeness, of the domain of the "natural"—and is concerned that we too often bend conceptions of the natural to social desires. She argues that much of the so-called natural world is stranger than we acknowledge:

> The discourse on 'crimes against nature' always already takes liberty in the confidence that Nature is herself a good Christian, or at least traffics in a kind of purity that the human has been excluded from ever since the Edenic fall of man. But what if Nature herself is a commie, a pervert, or a queer?
>
> (p. 29)

Barad's posthumanist ethico-onto-epistemology makes questions of knowing coextensive with questions of being, a move that challenges analysts to decenter the human in conceptions of agency and intention and to prioritize difference over identity (such that identity is on par with other materials of existence rather than *the* constitutive force) in examinations of how and why practices engender the distinctions upon which their perpetuation relies (Hein, 2016). In the end, what relational ontologies offer is not a set of new techniques, but a reconfiguring of their use: "a re-imagining of what method might *do*, rather than what it *is* or *how to do* it" (St. Pierre, Jackson, & Mazzei, 2016, p. 105; emphasis in original).

The technologies we employ in observing phenomena therefore *matter*; they too can be part of the assemblage of agencies enacting agential cuts. For Barad, "knowing is a matter of part of the world making itself intelligible to another part" (2003, p. 829), and making intelligible is not a capacity limited to humans. Intelligibility, and therefore meaning, thus have, according to Barad (2007, 2014) to be understood relationally, posthumanistically, because they concern not only human beings but also parts of the world humans might *re-present*—i.e., make present and materialize in their discussions. Making themselves intelligible to each other means that they would manage to (com)prehend each other—that is, *seize* each other's interest or becoming—that is, somehow *articulate* with each other. Any relation is a form of *prehension*, a form of grasping, grabbing, or seizing, which also means that symbolic language is not necessarily at stake in this kind of phenomenon.

What are these technologies? They are not, unsurprisingly, limited to electronic devices. They include the researcher's mode of engagement with participation in a scene, the mode of capturing data (along with what is considered to be data in the first place), the drawing of boundaries around a phenomenon, the mode of depicting it, the theories that guide sensemaking, and the attention to the emergence of distinctions (Clarke, 2005; Hodder, 2012). Technologies, therefore, both evince and involve *political* choices: active interventions that impact not only the research product but also the phenomenon in question. Likewise, the expectation that order, or organization, will characterize a given phenomenon is a *choice*, and therefore the capacity to see disorder and the production of proposals for how to address it are also political choices (Cooper, 1986).

As hinted in our discussion of research micropolitics, then, traditional conceptions of reflexivity are insufficient. A key question arising from a relational vision of method(ology) is how researchers are to apprehend these entanglements, especially given efforts to critique and transcend representationalism: the dominant practice in our research and writing in which material "realities" are accessible only through the discursive enactments (representations) actors, including researchers, make of them (MacLure, 2013). Our revision of communication through affect theory, for example, offered one foray into enacting post-human reflexivity in the research process. The mode of reflexivity attempted in Chapter 6 was less concerned with confessional tales of the self, or even with accounting for the researchers' identity positionality, as if this could be counted on to persist in the same way across encounters. Rather, we aspired to object-ify the researcher as one feeling, sensing body-vessel caught up with other (kinds of) bodies, both moving and moved by the occupational worldings in which she *finds herself* (notice again, how identities become contingent effects rather than precursors of relations, and reflexive focus remains on the quality of relations unfurling).

Such an approach, which follows Stewart's (2007) orientation to ordinary affects reviewed in Chapters 2 and 3, is but one among many emerging (Harris, 2013, 2017). Barad, for instance, also seeks to purge social science's representationalism by urging a thoroughgoing considering of the politics implied in how analysts approach, and make sense of, research sites. She insists that the researcher does not merely reflect the world, and the researcher should not understand herself as making an incursion into a site (as if it's a domain distinct from the ongoing flow of reality); instead, the researcher should be seen as a participant in material-discursive phenomena and, therefore, as an agency making a difference (i.e., mattering) in the conduct of a phenomenon. Researchers, just like others inhabiting a practice, make attributions of agency—to persons aligned with particular forms of knowledge, machines, genes, cultures, laws, beliefs, and the like—when they endeavor to develop causal explanations about working and organizing.

Finally, the claims of relationality advocate a conception of causality that diverges markedly from that to which organization studies scholars have become accustomed. There are no social facts here, no generative mechanisms, no predetermined boundaries, no dominating ideologies—none of these can be said to exist outside of their being made to matter in discursive-material mattering. There is no search for Aristotelian formal, final, efficient, or material causes (Fairclough, 2005)—actions at t_0 do not necessarily have a linear or even easily discernable connection to those occurring at t_1 and t_2; as Callon and Law (1997) argue, "action cannot [be] explained, in a reductionist manner, as a firm consequence of any particular previous action" (p. 179). There are no ontologically distinct levels of analysis, one impinging on (or causing changes in below, or building upwards to) another. Instead, cause is inseparable from action: The aim is to supplant a view that sees pre-existing things that possess agency, that act and bump into one another, with a conception of relations forming the very "things" to which we attend (as in the fifth premise of Chapter 2). It is to trace, and not assume, the flattened relations across surfaces, phenomena, events, connected by the multiplicity of agencies implicated in complex sociomaterial practice.

The Trajectory of Communicative Relationality

The extensions to relational ontologies offered here hold the potential to alter some foundational assumptions implicated in organization studies' conceptions of working and organizing. First, returning to our discussion of the definitions of work in Chapter 1, relationality can be a resource to make visible the many agencies involved in working and organizing that are erased or ignored in conventional accounts. What labor had to be done (and erased) to enable the labor witnessed (Smith, 1990)? Some of the activity here might be the sorts of invisible work—domestic labor, child care, homemaking—required to (re)produce both public work roles and the economy (-ies). Other erasures tend to be an obliviousness to the types of activity, as well as the sorts of agents, involved in carrying out practices of organizing (e.g., Star & Strauss, 1999).

The versions of communicative relationality presented in this book allow analysts to tell different stories about working and organizing, stories that highlight the activity and agencies obscured when analysts foreground humans and their cognitive and discursive action. In like manner, Leonardi and Rodriguez-Lluesma (2012) suggest that understanding organizational practices in sociomaterial terms reminds researchers that technology is not only important during times of implementation, but that a wide array of tools is central to all organizational processes. It is not merely the case, then, that the material domain is lively and agential, but that employing perspectives that foreground sociomaterial connection and refuse a priori ontological distinctions in the study of working and organizing can highlight the previously unnoticed but, nevertheless, vital contributors to practice.

Second, many organization studies sub-fields envision working and organizing as the province of the *individual person*. Autonomous and atomistic individuals populate many accounts of work, where human actors make choices about—reasoned evaluations regarding—whether they will work and the contracts they are willing to enter, what sense their labor makes, and how the work can be rendered meaningful with respect to pre-existing identities. Work is, thus, treated as an individual possession and an individual activity. Sensemaking, in these literatures, is an act of social cognition shaped by interpersonal, organizational, occupational, and societal influences, but the focus (the unit of analysis) generally remains individuals' identifications, predispositions, beliefs, and the like.

The problem of organizing, too, is often framed as a matter of marshaling the consent of individual members/employees to participate in a system that benefits some individuals more than others (e.g., Alvesson & Willmott, 2002; Fleming & Spicer, 2007; Kuhn, 2008). By way of contrast, investigations of work guided by communicative relationality would insist that the sovereign individual be unseated as the wellspring of decisional power, that understanding working requires an understanding of an assortment of (non)human agencies. Literature on meaningful work, for instance (e.g., Bunderson &Thompson, 2009; Chalofsky, 2003), might move away from studying individualized choice-making, instead examining the agencies articulated together to position a particular form of activity as worthwhile with respect to reticulated (social) practices; it might examine the flow of (and attribution of value to) affect in the conglomeration of bodies, signs, and scenes; it might frame "work" itself as a figure, an agency, that summons particular relations in its own becoming.

A third trajectory is to employ communicative relationality as a mode of interrogating value. Each of our case study chapters, in one way or another, examined the notion of value. Value has long been a token deployed in understandings of organizations and the economy, but it is one rarely probed in detail. Thinking from French conventionalists (e.g., Boltanski & Thévenot, 1991; Bourdieu, 1986) and anthropologists (e.g., Graeber, 2005) have revealed value to be a multifaceted concept— one bound up with, and thus not external from, practice. Relational ontologies offer a vision of value not only as coupled with the interpersonal connections involved in communicative labor (FitzPatrick, Varey, Grönroos, & Davey, 2015), but as generated, sustained, and transformed in the sociomaterial (i.e., communicative) practices of working and organizing. Value is a site of both production and struggle, a not simply discursive resource that participates in the manifestation of other agencies in a practice (Kuhn & Rennstam, 2016; Nelson, 2001; Skeggs & Loveday, 2012).

In the end, then, this book represents a form of storytelling about working and organizing in contemporary capitalism. Rather than try to clean up the complexity of late capitalism via simplicity, the charge is to be able to say something about a particular phenomenon and the participants emerging in the practice and which, together, accomplish it. We have portrayed the "new economy" not as a system as conventionally understood (as in, for instance, management and organization studies textbooks); instead, the system, the market, or society is reframed as a multifarious and flattened assortment of interconnected practices. The overarching lesson is that, as Whitehead (1920) argued over a century ago, connection is everywhere. But those ubiquitous connections materialize only through, and in, practice (Harman, 2013), meaning that unique scholarly engagements with, as well as forms of intervention into, working and organizing require approaching assembly and constitution otherwise. The plotlines we have articulated in this book, the forms of storytelling we advocated, proffer just this sort of novelty to organization studies.

References

Aakhus, M., Ballard, D., Flanagin, A. J., Kuhn, T., Leonardi, P., Mease, J., & Miller, K. (2011). Communication and materiality: A conversation from the CM Café. *Communication Monographs, 78*, 557–568. doi:10.1080/036377 51.2011.618358

Abbott, A. (1988). *The system of professions: An essay on the division of expert labor*. Chicago: University of Chicago Press.

Adler, P. S. (2001). Market, hierarchy, and trust: The knowledge economy and the future of capitalism. *Organization Science, 12*, 215–223.

Ahmed, S. (2004, Summer). Affective economies. *Social Text-79, 22*(2), 117–139.

Ahmed, S. (2006). *Queer phenomenology: Orientations, objects, others*. Durham, NC: Duke University Press.

Ahmed, S. (2010). Orientations matter. In D. Coole & S. Frost (Eds.), *New materialisms: Ontology, agency, and politics* (pp. 234–257). Durham, NC: Duke University Press.

Ahmed, S. (2014). *The cultural politics of emotion* (2nd ed.). Edinburgh: Edinburgh University Press.

Ailawadi, K. L., & Keller, K. L. (2004). Understanding retail branding: Conceptual insights and research priorities. *Journal of Retailing, 80*(4), 331–342. doi:10.1016/j.jretai.2004.10.008

Allon, F. (2010). Speculating on everyday life: The cultural economy of the quotidian. *Journal of Communication Inquiry, 34*, 366–381.

Alvesson, M. (2000). Social identity and the problem of loyalty in knowledge-intensive companies. *Journal of Management Studies, 37*, 1101–1123.

Alvesson, M. (2001). Knowledge work: Ambiguity, image, and identity. *Human Relations, 54*, 863–886.

Alvesson, M., & Willmott, H. (2002). Identity regulation as organizational control: Producing the appropriate individual. *Journal of Management Studies, 39*, 619–644.

Amabile, T. M. (1996). *Creativity in context*. Boulder, CO: Westview.

Anderson, A. R., & Warren, L. (2011). The entrepreneur as hero and jester: Enacting the entrepreneurial discourse. *International Small Business Journal, 29*, 589–609. doi:10.1177/0266242611416417

Andrejevic, M. (2013). Estranged free labor. In T. Scholz (Ed.), *Digital labor: The internet as playground and factory* (pp. 149–164). New York: Routledge.

Araujo, L., & Kjellberg, H. (2015). Enacting novel agencements: The case of Frequent Flyer schemes in the US airline industry (1981–1991). *Consumption Markets & Culture, 19*, 92–110. doi:10.1080/10253866.2015.1096095

Arvidsson, A. (2005). Brands: A critical perspective. *Journal of Consumer Culture, 5*, 235–258.

Arvidsson, A., & Peitersen, N. (2013). *The ethical economy: Rebuilding value after the crisis*. New York: Columbia University Press.

Ashcraft, K. L. (2005). Resistance through consent?: Occupational identity, organizational form, and the maintenance of masculinity among commercial airline pilots. *Management Communication Quarterly, 19*, 67–90.

Ashcraft, K. L. (2013). The glass slipper: 'Incorporating' occupational identity in management studies. *Academy of Management Review, 38*(1), 6–31. doi:10.5465/amr.10.0219

Ashcraft, K. L. (2017). 'Submission' to the rule of excellence: Ordinary affect and precarious resistance in the labour of organization and management studies. *Organization, 24*(1), 36–58.

Ashcraft, K. L., & Kuhn, T. K. (in press). Agential encounters: Performativity and affect meet communication in the bathroom. In B. Brummans (Ed.), *The agency of organizing: Perspectives and case studies*. New York: Routledge.

Ashcraft, K. L., Kuhn, T., & Cooren, F. (2009). Constitutional amendments: 'Materializing' organizational communication. In A. Brief & J. Walsh (Eds.), *The Academy of Management Annals* (Vol. 3, pp. 1–64). New York: Routledge.

Ashcraft, K. L., Muhr, S. L., Rennstam, J., & Sullivan, K. R. (2012). Professionalization as a branding activity: Occupational identity and the dialectic of inclusivity-exclusivity. *Gender, Work and Organization, 19*(5), 467–488.

Ashcraft, K. L., & Mumby, D. K. (2004). *Reworking gender: A feminist communicology of organization*. Thousand Oaks, CA: Sage.

Audretsch, D. B. (2002). The dynamic role of small firms: Evidence from the US. *Small Business Economics, 18*, 13–40.

Austin, J. L. (1962). *How to do things with words*. Oxford: Blackwell.

Axelrod, R., & Cohen, M. D. (1999). *Harnessing complexity: Organizational implications of a scientific frontier*. New York: The Free Press.

Axley, S. R. (1984). Managerial communication in terms of the conduit metaphor. *Academy of Management Review, 9*, 428–437.

Axley, S. R. (1996). *Communication at work: Management and the communication-intensive organization*. Westport, CT: Quorum Books.

Banet-Weiser, S. (2012). *Authentic: The politics of ambivalence in a brand culture*. New York: NYU Press.

Barad, K. (2003). Posthuman performativity: Toward an understanding of how matter comes to matter. *Signs, 28*, 801–831.

Barad, K. (2007). *Meeting the universe halfway: Quantum physics and the entanglement of matter and meaning*. Durham, NC: Duke University Press.

Barad, K. (2012). Nature's queer performativity. *Women, Gender and Research, 1–2*, 25–53.

Barad, K. (2014). Diffracting diffraction: Cutting together-apart. *Parralax, 20*(3), 168–187. doi:10.1080/13534645.2014.927623

Barinaga, E. (in press). Tinkering with space: The organizational practices of a nascent social venture. *Organization Studies*. doi:10.1177/0170840616670434

Barker, J. R. (1993). Tightening the iron cage: Concertive control in self-managing teams. *Administrative Science Quarterly, 38*, 408–437.

Barker, J. R. (1999). *The discipline of teamwork: Participation and concertive control*. Thousand Oaks, CA: Sage.

Barley, S. R., & Kunda, G. (1992). Design and devotion: Surges of rational and normative ideologies of control in managerial discourse. *Administrative Science Quarterly, 37*, 363–399.

Barnes, B. (1983). Social life as bootstrapped induction. *Sociology, 17*, 525–545.

Barthes, R. (1981). *Camera lucida*. New York: Hill and Wang.

Baudrillard, J. (1998 [1970]). *The consumer society* (C. Turner, Trans.). London: Sage.

Bencherki, N. (2012). Mediators and the material stabilization of society. *Communication and Critical/Cultural Studies, 9*(1), 101–106.

Bencherki, N. (2016). How things make things do things with words, or how to pay attention to what things have to say. *Communication Research and Practice, 2*, 272–289. doi:10.1080/22041451.2016.1214888

Bencherki, N., & Cooren, F. (2011). Having to be: The possessive constitution of organization. *Human Relations, 64*, 1579–1607.

Bennett, J. (2010). *Vibrant matter: A political ecology of things*. Durham, NC: Duke University Press.

Bennis, W. G., & Slater, P. (1964). *The temporary society*. New York: Harper and Row.

Benoit-Barné, C., & Cooren, F. (2009). The accomplishment of authority through presentification: How authority is distributed among and negotiated by organizational members. *Management Communication Quarterly, 23*, 5–31.

Bernthal, B. (in press). Investment accelerators. *Stanford Journal of Law, Business, & Finance*.

Bertilsson, J., & Cassinger, C. (2011). Governing consumers through freedom. In A. Bradshaw, C. Hackley, & P. Maclaran (Eds.), *European advances in consumer research* (Vol. 9, pp. 412–416). Duluth, MN: Association for Consumer Research.

Beunza, D., & Stark, D. (2004). Tools of the trade: The socio-technology of arbitrage in a Wall Street trading room. *Industrial and Corporate Change, 13*(2), 369–400. doi:10.1093/icc/dth015

Beverungen, A., Otto, B., Spoelstra, S., & Kenny, K. (2013). Free work. *Ephemera, 13*, 1–9.

Beyes, T., & Steyaert, C. (2011). Spacing organization: Non-representational theory and performing organizational space. *Organization, 19*, 45–61. doi: 10.1177/1350508411401946

Bidhé, A. (2010). *A call for judgment: Sensible finance for a dynamic economy*. Oxford: Oxford University Press.

Blackler, F. (1995). Knowledge, knowledge work and organizations: An overview and interpretation. *Organization Studies, 16*, 1021–1046.

Boltanski, L., & Chiapello, E. (2005). *The new spirit of capitalism* (G. Elliott, Trans.). London: Verso.

Boltanski, L., & Esquerre, A. (2015). Grappling with the economy of enrichment. *Valuation Studies, 3*(1), 75–83. doi:10.3384/VS.2001-5592.153175

Boltanski, L., & Thévenot, L. (1991/2006). *On justification: Economies of worth* (C. Porter, Trans.). Princeton, NJ: Princeton University Press.

Bourdieu, P. (1984). *Distinction: A social critique of the judgment of taste* (R. Nice, Trans.). Cambridge, MA: Harvard University Press.

Bourdieu, P. (1986). The forms of capital. In J. Richardson (Ed.), *Handbook of theory and research for the sociology of education* (pp. 241–258). New York: Greenwood.

Bourdieu, P. (1990). *The logic of practice*. Stanford, CA: Stanford University Press.

Brabham, D. C. (2012). The myth of amateur crowds: A critical discourse analysis of crowdsourcing coverage. *Information, Communication & Society, 15*(3), 394–410. doi:10.1080/1369118x.2011.641991

Brabham, D. C. (2013). *Crowdsourcing*. Cambridge, MA: MIT Press.

Brabham, D. C., Ribisl, K. M., Kirchner, T. R., & Bernhardt, J. M. (2014). Crowdsourcing applications for public health. *American Journal of Preventive Medicine, 46*, 179–187. doi:10.1016/j.amepre.2013.10.016

Brennan, T. (2004). *The transmission of affect*. Ithaca, NY: Cornell University Press.

Bröckling, U. (2015). *The entrepreneurial self: Fabricating a new type of subject*. Los Angeles, CA: Sage.

Brophy, E., Cohen, N. S., & de Peuter, G. (2016). Labor messaging: Practices of autonomous communication. In R. Maxwell (Ed.), *The Routledge companion to labor and media* (pp. 315–326). New York: Routledge.

Brown, W. (2015). *Undoing the demos: Neoliberalism's stealth revolution*. New York: Zone Books.

Brummans, B. H. J. M. (2007). Death by document: Tracing the agency of a text. *Qualitative Inquiry, 13*, 711–727.

Bruni, A. (2005). Shadowing software and clinical records: On the ethnography of non-humans and heterogeneous contexts. *Organization, 12*, 357–378. doi:10.1177/1350508405051272

Bryman, A. (2004). *The Disneyization of society*. Thousand Oaks, CA: Sage.

Bunderson, J. S., & Thompson, J. A. (2009). The call of the wild: Zookeepers, callings, and the double-edged sword of deeply meaningful work. *Administrative Science Quarterly, 54*, 32–57. doi:10.2189/asqu.2009.54.1.32

Burke, R. (1981). Work and play. *Ethics, 82*(October), 33–47.

Butler, J. (1993). *Bodies that matter: On the discursive limits of sex*. London: Routledge.

Butler, J. (1997). *Excitable speech: A politics of the performative*. New York: Routledge.

Butler, J. (2000). *Gender trouble* (10th Anniversary ed.). London: Routledge.

Butler, J. (2004). *Precarious life: The power of mourning and nonviolence*. London: Verso.

Butler, J. (2010). Performative agency. *Journal of Cultural Economy, 3*, 147–161. doi:10.1080/17530350.2010.494117

Butler, J. (2015). *Notes toward a performative theory of assembly*. Cambridge, MA: Harvard University Press.

Cabantous, L., & Gond, J.-P. (2011). Rational decision making as performative praxis: Explaining rationality's Éternel Retour. *Organization Science, 22*(3), 573–586. doi:10.1287/orsc.1100.0534

Çalişkan, K., & Callon, M. (2010). Economization, part 2: A research programme for the study of markets. *Economy and Society, 39*, 1–32.

Callon, M. (1986). The sociology of an actor-network: The case of the electric vehicle. In M. Callon, J. Law, & A. Rip (Eds.), *Mapping the dynamics of science and technology* (pp. 19–34). London: Palgrave Macmillan.

Callon, M. (1998). Introduction: The embeddedness of economic markets in economics. In M. Callon (Ed.), *The laws of the market* (pp. 1–57). Oxford: Blackwell.

Callon, M. (2008). Economic markets and the rise of interactive agencements: From prosthetic agencies to habilitated agencies. In T. Pinch & R. Swedberg (Eds.), *Living in a material world: Economic sociology meets science and technology studies* (pp. 29–56). Cambridge, MA: MIT Press.

Callon, M. (2010). Performativity, misfires, and politics. *Journal of Cultural Economy, 3*(2), 163–169. doi:10.1080/17530350.2010.494119

Callon, M., & Latour, B. (1981). Unscrewing the big Leviathan: How actors macro-structure reality and how sociologists help them to do so. In K. Knorr-Cetina & A. V. Cicourel (Eds.), *Advances in social theory and methodology: Toward an integration of micro- and macro-sociologies* (pp. 277–303). Boston, MA: Routledge & Kegan Paul.

Callon, M., & Law, J. (1997). After the individual in society: Lessons on collectivity from science, technology, and society. *Canadian Journal of Sociology, 22*(2), 165–182.

Callon, M., & Law, J. (2005). On qualculation, agency, and otherness. *Environment and Planning D: Society and Space, 23*(5), 717–733. doi:10.1068/d343t

Callon, M., & Muniesa, F. (2005). Economic markets as calculative devices. *Organization Studies, 26*, 1229–1250.

Carayannis, E. G., Dubina, I. N., & Campbell, D. F. J. (2011). Creative economy and a crisis of the economy? Coevolution of knowledge, innovation, and creativity, and of the knowledge economy and knowledge society. *Journal of the Knowledge Economy, 3*(1), 1–24.

Cardwell, E. (2015). Power and performativity in the creation of the UK fishing-rights market. *Journal of Cultural Economy, 8,* 705–720. doi:10.1080/1753 0350.2015.1050441

Carlone, D. (2008). The contradictions of communicative labor in service work. *Communication and Critical/Cultural Studies, 5,* 158–179.

Carter, C., Clegg, S., & Kornberger, M. (2010). Re-framing strategy: Power, politics and accounting. *Accounting, Auditing & Accountability Journal, 23,* 573–594. doi:10.1108/09513571011054891

Castells, M. (1996). *The rise of the network society* (Vol. 1). Oxford: Blackwell.

Cauthen, N. K. (2011, March 11). *Scheduling hourly workers: How last minute, "just in time" scheduling practices are bad for workers, families, and businesses.* New York: Demos.

Cederström, C., & Spicer, A. (2014). Discourse of the real kind: A postfoundational approach to organizational discourse analysis. *Organization, 21,* 178–205.

Chalofsky, N. (2003). An emerging construct of meaningful work. *Human Resource Development International, 6,* 69–83.

Charles, M., & Grusky, D. B. (2004). *Occupational ghettos: The worldwide segregation of women and men.* Stanford, CA: Stanford University Press.

Clarke, A. E. (2005). *Situational analysis: Grounded theory after the postmodern turn.* Thousand Oaks, CA: Sage.

Clough, P. T., & Halley, J. (Eds.). (2007). *The affective turn: Theorizing the social.* Durham, NC: Duke University Press.

Coates, J. C. (2015). Corporate speech and the First Amendment: History, data, and implications. *Constitutional Commentary, 30,* 223–275.

Cochoy, F. (2014). A theory of 'agencing': On Michel Callon's contribution to organizational knowledge and practice. In P. Adler, P. du Gay, G. Morgan, & M. Reed (Eds.), *The Oxford handbook of sociology, social theory, and organization studies: Contemporary currents* (pp. 106–124). Oxford: Oxford University Press.

Cochoy, F., Trompette, P., & Araujo, L. (2016). From market agencements to market agencing: An introduction. *Consumption Markets & Culture, 19,* 3–16. doi:10.1080/10253866.2015.1096066

Cohen, P. N., & Huffman, M. L. (2003). Occupational segregation and the devaluation of women's work across labor markets. *Social Forces, 81*(3), 881–908.

Cohen, S. (2013). What do accelerators do?: Insights from incubators and angels. *Innovations, 8*(3/4), 19–25.

Collinson, D. L. (2003). Identities and insecurities: Selves at work. *Organization, 10,* 527–547.

Connolly, W. E. (2010). Materialities of experience. In D. Coole & S. Frost (Eds.), *New materialisms: Ontology, agency, and politics* (pp. 178–200). Durham, NC: Duke University Press.

Contractor, N. S., Monge, P., & Leonardi, P. M. (2011). Multidimensional networks and the dynamics of sociomateriality: Bringing technology inside the network. *International Journal of Communication, 5,* 682–720.

Contractor, N. S., Wasserman, S., & Faust, K. (2006). Testing multitheoretical, multilevel hypotheses about organizational networks: An analytic framework and empirical example. *Academy of Management Review, 31,* 681–703.

Coole, D., & Frost, S. (Eds.). (2010). *New materialisms: Ontology, agency, and politics.* Durham, NC: Duke University Press.

Cooper, R. (1986). Organization/disorganization. *Social Science Information*, 25, 299–335.

Cooper, R. (2005). Relationality. *Organization Studies*, 26, 1689–1710. doi:10.1177/0170840605056398

Cooren, F. (2000). *The organizing property of communication*. Philadelphia, PA: John Benjamins.

Cooren, F. (2004). Textual agency: How texts do things in organizational settings. *Organization*, 11, 373–393.

Cooren, F. (2006). The organizational world as a plenum of agencies. In F. Cooren, J. R. Taylor, & E. J. V. Every (Eds.), *Communication as organizing: Empirical and theoretical explorations in the dynamic of text and conversation* (pp. 81–100). Mahwah, NJ: Lawrence Erlbaum.

Cooren, F. (2008). The selection of agency as a rhetorical device: Opening up the scene of dialogue through ventriloquism. In E. Weigand (Ed.), *Dialogue and rhetoric* (pp. 23–38). Amsterdam: John Benjamins.

Cooren, F. (2009). The haunting question of textual agency: Derrida and Garfinkel on iterability and eventfulness. *Research on Language and Social Interaction*, 42, 42–67. doi:10.1080/08351810802671735

Cooren, F. (2010). *Action and agency in dialogue: Passion, incarnation and ventriloquism*. Philadelphia, PA: John Benjamins.

Cooren, F. (2015). In medias res: Communication, existence, and materiality. *Communication Research and Practice*, 1, 307–321. doi:10.1080/22041451.2015.1110075

Cooren, F. (2016). Ethics for dummies: Ventriloquism and responsibility. *Atlantic Journal of Communication*, 24, 17–30. doi:10.1080/15456870.2016.1113963

Cooren, F., Bencherki, N., Chaput, M., & Vasquez, C. (2015). The communicative constitution of strategy-making: Exploring fleeting moments of strategy. In D. Golsorkhi, L. Rouleau, D. Seidl, & E. Vaara (Eds.), *The Cambridge handbook of strategy as practice* (2nd ed., pp. 365–388). Cambridge: Cambridge University Press.

Cooren, F., Brummans, B. H. J. M., & Charrieras, D. (2008). The coproduction of organizational presence: A study of Médecins Sans Frontières in action. *Human Relations*, 61(10), 1339–1370.

Cooren, F., & Fairhurst, G. T. (2009). Dislocation and stabilization: How to scale up from interactions to organization. In L. L. Putnam & A. M. Nicotera (Eds.), *Building theories of organization: The constitutive role of communication* (pp. 117–152). New York: Routledge.

Cooren, F., Kuhn, T., Cornelissen, J. P., & Clark, T. (2011). Communication, organization, and organizing: An overview and introduction to the special issue. *Organization Studies*, 32, 1149–1170.

Corman, S. R. (1996). Cellular automata as model of unintended consequences of organizational communication. In J. Watt & A. VanLear (Eds.), *Dynamic patterns in communication processes* (pp. 191–212). Thousand Oaks, CA: Sage.

Corman, S. R., Kuhn, T., McPhee, R. D., & Dooley, K. J. (2002). Studying complex discursive systems: Centering resonance analysis of communication. *Human Communication Research*, 28, 157–206.

Cova, B., & Dalli, D. (2009). Working consumers: The next step in marketing theory? *Marketing Theory*, 9, 315–339.

Cova, B., Dalli, D., & Zwick, D. (2011). Critical perspectives on consumers' role as 'producers': Broadening the debate on value co-creation in marketing processes. *Marketing Theory*, 11, 231–241.

Crouch, C. (2011). *The strange non-death of neo-liberalism*. Cambridge: Polity.

Cushen, J., & Thompson, P. (2016). Financialization and value: Why labour and the labour process still matter. *Work, Employment & Society, 30*, 352–365.

Cyert, R. M., & March, J. G. (1963). *A behavioral theory of the firm*. Englewood Cliffs, NJ: Prentice-Hall.

Czarniawska, B. (2007). *Shadowing and other techniques for doing fieldwork in modern societies*. Malmo, Sweden: Liber.

Dale, K., & Latham, Y. (2015). Ethics and entangled embodiment: Bodies—materialities—organization. *Organization,22*,166–182. doi:10.1177/1350508 414558721

Dalkian, G. (2013). *90% of tech startups fail*. Retrieved from www.wamda. com/2013/02/90-percent-of-tech-startups-fail-infographic

Daniels, A. K. (1987). Invisible work. *Social Problems, 34*(5), 403–415.

Davis, G. F. (2009). *Managed by the markets: How finance re-shaped America*. New York: Oxford University Press.

Deetz, S. A. (1992). *Democracy in an age of corporate colonization: Developments in communication and the politics of everyday life*. Albany, NY: State University of New York Press.

Deetz, S. A. (2003). Reclaiming the legacy of the linguistic turn. *Organization, 10*, 421–429.

DeLanda, M. (2011). *Philosophy and simulation: The emergence of synthetic reason*. London: Continuum.

DeLanda, M. (2016). *Assemblage theory*. Edinburgh: Edinburgh University Press.

Deleuze, G., & Guattari, F. (1987). *A thousand plateaus: Capitalism and schizophrenia* (B. Massumi, Trans.). Minneapolis, MN: University of Minnesota Press.

Dempsey, S., & Carlone, D. (2014). Autonomist Marxism and the contributions of generative dialogue. In J. S. Hanan & M. Hayward (Eds.), *Communication and the economy: History, value and agency* (pp. 45–66). New York: Peter Lang.

Derrida, J. (1988). *Limited Inc*. Evanston, IL: Northwestern University Press.

Derrida, J. (1993). *Aporias* (T. Dutoit, Trans.). Stanford, CA: Stanford University Press.

Dewey, J. (1939). *Theory of valuation*. Chicago: University of Chicago Press.

Discenna, T. A. (2011). Academic labor and the literature of discontent in communication. *International Journal of Communication, 5*, 1843–1852. doi:1932–8036/2011FEA1843

Doogan, K. (2005). Long-term employment and the restructuring of the labour market in Europe. *Time & Society, 14*, 65–87.

Doogan, K. (2009). *New capitalism?: The transformation of work*. Cambridge: Polity.

Doolin, B., & Lowe, A. (2002). To reveal is to critique: Actor-network theory and critical information systems research. *Journal of Information Technology, 17*, 69–78.

Dore, R. (2008). Financialization of the global economy. *Industrial and Corporate Change, 17*, 1097–1112.

Dourado, E., & Koopman, C. (2015, Dec. 10). *Evaluating the growth of the 1099 workforce*. Arlington, VA: Mercatus Center, George Washington University: Retrieved from www.mercatus.org/publication/evaluating-growth-1099-workforce.

Drucker, P. (1992). *The age of discontinuity: Guidelines to our changing society*. London: Heineman.

du Gay, P. (1996). *Consumption and identity at work*. London: Sage.

du Gay, P., & Morgan, G. (2013). Understanding capitalism: Crises, legitimacy, and change through the prism of the New Spirit of Capitalism. In P. du Gay & G. Morgan (Eds.), *New spirits of capitalism?: Crises, justifications, and dynamics* (pp. 1–42). Oxford: Oxford University Press.

Dyer-Witheford, N. (2001). Empire, immaterial labor, the new combinations, and the global worker. *Rethinking Marxism, 13*(3/4), 70–80.

Emirbayer, M. (1997). Manifesto for a relational sociology. *American Journal of Sociology, 103*, 281–317.

Emirbayer, M., & Mische, A. (1998). What is agency? *American Journal of Sociology, 103*(4), 962–1023. doi:10.1086/231294

Engeström, Y. (1999). Activity theory and individual and social transformation. In Y. Engeström, R. Miettinen, & R. Punamäki (Eds.), *Perspectives on activity theory* (pp. 19–38). New York: Cambridge University Press.

Engeström, Y., Engeström, R., & Kerosuo, H. (2003). The discursive construction of collaborative care. *Applied Linguistics, 24*(4), 286–315.

Erkturk, I., Froud, J., Johal, S., Leaver, A., & Williams, K. (2007). The democratization of finance?: Promises, outcomes, and conditions. *Review of International Political Economy, 14*, 553–575.

Fairclough, N. (2005). Discourse analysis in organization studies: The case for critical realism. *Organization Studies, 26*, 915–939.

Fairhurst, G. T., & Cooren, F. (2009). Leadership as the hybrid production of presence(s). *Leadership, 5*(4), 469–490. doi:10.1177/1742715009343033

Faulkner, P., & Runde, J. (2012). On sociomateriality. In P. M. Leonardi, B. A. Nardi, & J. Kallinikos (Eds.), *Materiality and organizing: Social interaction in a technological world* (pp. 49–66). Oxford: Oxford University Press.

Fauré, B., Brummans, B. H. J. M., Giroux, H., & Taylor, J. R. (2010). The calculation of business, or the business of calculation? Accounting as organizing through everyday communication. *Human Relations, 63*(8), 1249–1273.

Feld, B. (2012). *Startup communities: Building an entrepreneurial ecosystem in your city.* New York: Wiley.

Feld, B. (2013). *The positive benefit of mentor whiplash.* Retrieved from www.feld.com/archives/2013/07/the-positive-benefit-of-mentor-whiplash.html

Fenwick, T. (2010). Re-thinking the 'thing': Sociomaterial approaches to understanding and researching learning in work. *Journal of Workplace Learning, 22*, 104–116.

Fevre, R. (2007). Employment insecurity and social theory: The power of nightmares. *Work, Employment & Society, 21*, 517–535.

Fine, B., & Harris, L. (1979). *Rereading Capital.* London: Macmillan.

Fish, A., & Srinivasan, R. (2011). Digital labor is the new killer app. *New Media and Society, 14*, 137–152. doi:10.1177/1461444811412159

FitzPatrick, M., Varey, R. J., Grönroos, C., & Davey, J. (2015). Relationality in the service logic of value creation. *Journal of Services Marketing, 29*(6/7), 463–471. doi:10.1108/JSM-01-2015-0038

Fleetwood, S. (2005). Ontology in organization and management studies: A critical realist perspective. *Organization, 12*, 197–222.

Fleetwood, S. (2014). Bhaskar and critical realism. In P. Adler, P. du Gay, G. Morgan, & M. Reed (Eds.), *The Oxford handbook of sociology, social theory, and organization studies: Contemporary currents* (pp. 182–219). Oxford: Oxford University Press.

Fleming, P., & Banerjee, S. B. (2015). When performativity fails: Implications for Critical Management Studies. *Human Relations, 69*, 257–276. doi:10.1177/0018726715599241

Fleming, P., & Spicer, A. (2007). *Contesting the corporation: Struggle, power, and resistance in organizations.* Cambridge: Cambridge University Press.

Fleming, P., & Sturdy, A. (2011). 'Being yourself' in the electronic sweatshop: New forms of normative control. *Human Relations, 64*, 177–200.

Fligstein, N., & Calder, R. (2015). Architecture of markets. In R. Scott & S. Kosslyn (Eds.), *Emerging trends in the social and behavioral sciences* (pp. 1–14). New York: Wiley.

Florida, R. (1991). The new industrial revolution. *Futures, 23*, 559–576. doi:10.1016/0016-3287(91)90079-H

Florida, R. (2003). Cities and the creative class. *City & Community, 2*(1), 3–19.

Flyverbom, M., & Rasche, A. (2015, December 2). *Big data as governmentality—Digital traces, algorithms, and the reconfiguration of data in international development.* Humanistic Management Network, (42/15). Copenhagen.

Ford, C. M. (1996). A theory of individual creative action in multiple social domains. *Academy of Management Review, 21*, 1112–1142.

Foroohar, R. (2016). *Makers and takers: The rise of finance and the fall of American business.* New York: Crown Business.

Forum (2006) Perspectives on Teresa Brennan's *The Transmission of Affect. Women: A Cultural Review, 17*(1), 103–117. doi: 10.1080/09574040600628724

Foster, J., & Metcalfe, J. S. (2001). Modern evolutionary economic perspectives: An overview. In J. Foster & J. S. Metcalfe (Eds.), *Frontiers of evolutionary economics: Competition, self-organization and innovation policy* (pp. 1–18). Cheltenham: Edward Elgar.

Fournier, V. (1999). The appeal to 'professionalism' as a disciplinary mechanism. *The Sociological Review, 47*(2), 280–307.

Fox, J. (2009). *The myth of the rational market: A history of risk, reward, and delusion on Wall Street.* New York: Harper Business.

Fox, J. (2015). The rise of the 1099 economy. *Bloomberg View.* Retrieved from www.bloombergview.com/articles/2015-12-11/the-gig-economy-is-showing-up-in-irs-s-1099-forms

Fox, N. J., & Alldred, P. (2015). New materialist social inquiry: Designs, methods and the research-assemblage. *International Journal of Social Research Methodology, 18*, 399–414. doi:10.1080/13645579.2014.921458

Fox, N. J., & Alldred, P. (2017). *Sociology and the new materialism: Theory, research, action.* London: Sage.

Frege, G. (1948). Sense and reference. *The Philosophical Review, 57*(3), 209–230.

French, S., Leyshon, A., & Wainwright, T. (2011). Financializing space, spacing financialization. *Progress in Human Geography, 35*, 798–819. doi:10.1177/0309132510396749

Friedman, A. L. (2000). Microregulation and post-Fordism: Critique and development of regulation theory. *New Political Economy, 5*, 59–76. doi:10.1080/13563460050001989

Friedman, G. (2014). Workers without employers: Shadow corporations and the rise of the gig economy. *Review of Keynesian Economics, 2*(2), 171–188.

Froud, J., Haslam, C., Johal, S., & Williams, K. (2000). Shareholder value and financialization: Consultancy promises, management moves. *Economy and Society, 29*, 80–110. doi:10.1080/030851400360578

Fuchs, C., & Trottier, D. (2013). The Internet as surveilled work play place and factory. In S. Gutwirth, R. Leenes, P. de Hert, & Y. Poullet (Eds.), *European data protection: Coming of age.* (pp. 33–57). Dordrecht: Springer.

Gage, D. (2012). The venture capital secret: 3 out of 4 start-ups fail. *Wall Street Journal.* Retrieved from http://online.wsj.com/news/articles/SB10000872396390443720204578004980476429190

Ganesh, S., & Wang, Y. (2015). An eventful view of organizations. *Communication Research and Practice, 1*, 375–387. doi:10.1080/22041451.2015.1110290

Garfinkel, H. (1967). *Studies in ethnomethodology.* Englewood Cliffs, NJ: Prentice-Hall.

Garfinkel, H. (2002). *Ethnomethodology's program: Working out Durkheim's aphorism*. Lanham, MD: Rowman & Littlefield Publishers.

Gehman, J., Treviño, L. K., & Garud, R. (2013). Values work: A process study of the emergence and performance of organizational values practices. *Academy of Management Journal, 56*(1), 84–112. doi:10.5465/amj.2010.0628

Gherardi, S. (2012). *How to conduct a practice-based study: Problems and methods*. Cheltenham: Edward Elgar.

Gherardi, S. (2016). To start practice theorizing anew: The contribution of the concepts of agencement and formativeness. *Organization, 23,* 680–698. doi:10.1177/1350508415605174

Giddens, A. (1976). *New rules of sociological method*. New York: Basic Books.

Giddens, A. (1979). *Central problems in social theory*. Berkeley, CA: University of California Press.

Gill, R., & Pratt, A. (2008). In the social factory?: Immaterial labour, precariousness and cultural work. *Theory Culture and Society, 25*(7–8), 1–30.

Goede, M. de (2005). *Virtue, fortune and faith: A genealogy of finance*. Minneapolis, MN: University of Minnesota Press.

Gond, J.-P., Cabantous, L., Harding, N., & Learmonth, M. (2015). What do we mean by performativity in organizational and management theory?: The uses and abuses of performativity. *International Journal of Management Reviews, 18,* 440–463. doi:10.1111/ijmr.12074

Gossett, L. M. (2002). Kept at arm's length: Questioning the organizational desirability of member identification. *Communication Monographs, 69,* 385–404.

Graeber, D. (2005). Anthropological theories of value. In J. G. Carrier (Ed.), *A handbook of economic anthropology* (pp. 439–454). Cheltenham: Edward Elgar.

Grant, R. M. (1996). Toward a knowledge-based theory of the firm. *Strategic Management Journal, 17,* 109–122.

Green, F. (2009). Subjective employment insecurity around the world. *Cambridge Journal of Regions, Economy, and Society, 2,* 343–363.

Greene, R. W. (2004). Rhetoric and capitalism: Rhetorical agency as communicative labor. *Philosophy and Rhetoric, 37*(3), 188–206.

Grey, C. (1994). Career as a project of the self and labour process discipline. *Sociology, 28,* 479–497.

Griffin, M. (1996). Literary studies +/- literature: Friedrich A. Kittler's media histories. *New Literary History, 27*(4), 709–716.

Grose, T., & Kallerman, P. (2015). *The 1099 economy: Elusive, but diverse and growing*. In What's the Future of Work [weblog], https://medium.com/the-wtf-economy/the-1099-economy-elusive-but-diverse-and-growing-5233dad6e1bf

Grossberg, L. (1982). Intersubjectivity and the conceptualization of communication. *Human Studies, 5,* 213–235.

Guerard, S., Langley, A., & Seidl, D. (2013). From performance to performativity in strategy research. *M@n@gement, 16,* 264–276.

Hall, S. (1996). Who needs 'identity'? In S. Hall & P. du Gay (Eds.), *Questions of cultural identity* (pp. 1–17). Thousand Oaks, CA: Sage.

Harding, N., Lee, H., & Ford, J. (2014). Who is 'the middle manager'? *Human Relations, 67,* 1213–1237. doi:10.1177/0018726713516654

Hardt, M., & Negri, A. (2000). *Empire*. Cambridge, MA: Harvard University Press.

Hardt, M., & Negri, A. (2004). *Multitude*. New York: Penguin.

Hargadon, A., & Bechky, B. A. (2006). When collections of creatives become creative collectives: A field study of problem solving at work. *Organization Science, 17,* 484–500.

Harman, G. (2013). *Bells and whistles: More speculative realism*. Winchester: Zero Books.

Harman, G. (2016). *Immaterialism: Objects and social theory*. Cambridge: Polity.

Harris, K. L. (2013). *Organizing sexual violence: Communicative, intersectional dilemmas around mandated reporting*. (Doctoral dissertation). Available from ProQuest Dissertations and Theses Database. (UMI No. 3607312).

Harris, K. L. (2017). Re-situating organizational knowledge: Violence, intersectionality, and the privilege of partial perspective. *Human Relations, 70*(3), 263–285.

Harsin, J. (2015). Regimes of posttruth, postpolitics, and attention economies. *Communication, Culture & Critique, 8*, 327–333.

Harvey, D. (2005). *A brief history of neoliberalism*. Oxford: Oxford University Press.

Harvey, D. L., & Reed, M. (1997). Social science as the study of complex systems. In L. D. Kiel & E. Elliott (Eds.), *Chaos theory in the social sciences: Foundations and applications* (pp. 295–324). Ann Arbor, MI: University of Michigan Press.

Healy, K. (2015). The performativity of networks. *European Journal of Sociology, 56*, 175–205.

Hein, S. F. (2016). The new materialism in qualitative inquiry: How compatible are the philosophies of Barad and Deleuze? *Cultural Studies <—> Critical Methodologies, 16*(2), 132–140. doi:10.1177/1532708616634732

Helm, B. (2013). How Boulder became America's startup capital. *Inc. Magazine, 35*, 54–64.

Hemmings, C. (2005). Invoking affect: Cultural theory and the ontological turn. *Cultural Studies, 19*(5), 548–567.

Hennion, A. (2007). Those things that hold us together: Taste and sociology. *Cultural Sociology, 1*, 97–114. doi:10.1177/1749975507073923

Heritage, J. (1984). *Garfinkel and ethnomethodology*. New York: Polity.

Hernes, T. (2014). *A process theory of organization*. New York: Oxford.

Ho, K. (2009). *Liquidated: An ethnography of Wall Street*. Durham, NC: Duke University Press.

Hodder, I. (2012). *Entangled: An archaeology of the relationships between humans and things*. Malden, MA: Wiley-Blackwell.

Hodson, R., & Sullivan, T. A. (1995). *The social organization of work*. Belmont, CA: Wadsworth.

Hoffman, D. L., & Radojevich-Kelley, N. (2012). Analysis of accelerator companies: An exploratory case study of their programs, processes, and early results. *Small Business Institute Journal, 8*(2), 54–70.

Holmer Nadesan, M. (1996). Organizational identity and space of action. *Organization Studies, 17*, 49–81.

Holmes, D. R. (2014). *Economy of words: Communicative imperatives in central banks*. Chicago: University of Chicago Press.

Hopkins, G. E. (1998). *The airline pilots: A study in elite unionization*. Cambridge, MA: Harvard University Press.

Huang, L., & Pearce, J. (2015). Managing the unknowable: The effectiveness of early-stage investor gut feel in entrepreneurial investment decisions. *Administrative Science Quarterly, 60*, 634–670. doi:10.1177/0001839215597270

Hultin, L., & Mähring, M. (2017). How practice makes sense in healthcare operations: Studying sensemaking as performative, material-discursive practice. *Human Relations, 70*, 566–593. doi:10.1177/0018726716661618

Iedema, R. (2007). On the multi-modality, materiality and contingency of organization discourse. *Organization Studies, 28*, 931–946.

Ingold, T. (2008). When ANT meets SPIDER: Social theory for anthropods. In C. Knappet & L. Malafouris (Eds.), *Material agency: Towards a non-anthropencentric approach* (pp. 209–215). New York: Springer.

Introna, L. D. (2009). Ethics and the speaking of things. *Theory, Culture & Society*, 26, 25–46. doi:10.1177/0263276409104967

Irani, L. (2015). Difference and dependence among digital workers: The case of Amazon Mechanical Turk. *South Atlantic Quarterly*, 114(1), 225–234. doi:10.1215/00382876-2831665

James, W. (1912/1976). *Essays in radical empiricism.* Cambridge, MA: Harvard University Press.

Jarzabkowski, B., & Pinch, T. (2013). Sociomateriality is 'The New Black': Accomplishing repurposing, reinscripting and repairing in context. *M@n@gement, 16*, 579–592.

Jensen, M. C., & Meckling, W. (1976). Theory of the firm: Managerial behavior, agency costs, and ownership structure. *The Journal of Financial Economics, 3*, 305–360.

Jessop, B., & Sum, N.-L. (2006). *Beyond the regulation approach: Putting capitalist economies in their place.* Cheltenham: Edward Elgar.

Johnson, P., Wood, G., Brewster, C., & Brookes, M. (2009). The rise of postbureaucracy: Theorists' fancy or organizational praxis? *International Sociology, 24*, 37–61. doi:10.1177/0268580908100246

Jones, C., & Spicer, A. (2009). *Unmasking the entrepreneur.* Cheltenham: Edward Elgar.

Kalleberg, A. L. (2009). Precarious work, insecure workers: Employment relations in transition. *American Sociological Review, 74*, 1–22.

Kantor, J. (2014, August 13). Working anything but 9 to 5: Scheduling technology leaves low-income parents with hours of chaos. *New York Times*, A1–A15. Retrieved from www.nytimes.com/interactive/2014/08/13/us/starbucks-workers-scheduling-hours.html?_r=0

Kaplan, M. (2010). The Rhetoric of hegemony: Laclau, radical democracy, and the rule of tropes. *Philosophy and Rhetoric, 43*(3), 253–283. doi:10.1353/par.0.0061

Kärreman, D., & Rylander, A. (2008). Managing meaning through branding: The case of a consulting firm. *Organization Studies, 29*, 103–125.

Kautz, K., & Jensen, T. B. (2013). Sociomateriality at the royal court of IS: A jester's monologue. *Information and Organization, 23*(1), 15–27. doi:10.1016/j.infoandorg.2013.01.001

Keller, K. L., & Lehmann, D. R. (2006). Brands and branding: Research findings and future priorities. *Marketing Science, 25*, 740–759.

Kempner, R. (2013). Incubators are popping up like wildflowers . . . but do they actually work? *Innovations, 8*(3/4), 3–6.

Kittler, F. A. (1999). *Gramophone, film, typewriter.* Stanford, CA: Stanford California Press.

Kittler, F. A. (2010). *Optical media.* Cambridge: Polity Press.

Knorr-Cetina, K. (1999). *Epistemic cultures: How the sciences make knowledge.* Cambridge, MA: Harvard University Press.

Kochan, T. A., & Barley, S. R. (Eds.). (1999). *The changing nature of work and its implications for occupational analysis.* Washington, DC: National Research Council.

Kohn, E. (2013). *How forests think: Toward an anthropology beyond the human.* Berkeley, CA: University of California Press.

Korczynski, M., Shire, K., Frenkel, S., & Tam, M. (2000). Service work in consumer capitalism: Customers, control, and contradictions. *Work, Employment & Society, 14*, 669–687.

Kornberger, M., Justesen, L., Madsen, A. K., & Mouritsen, J. (2015). Introduction: Making things valuable. In M. Kornberger, L. Justesen, A. K. Madsen, & J. Mouritsen (Eds.), *Making things valuable* (pp. 1–17). Oxford: Oxford University Press.

Kosnik, A. de (2013). Fandom as free labor. In T. Scholz (Ed.), *Digital labor: The internet as playground and factory* (pp. 98–111). New York: Routledge.

Krippner, G. R. (2011). *Capitalizing on crisis: The political origins of the rise of finance*. Cambridge, MA: Harvard University Press.

Kuhn, T. (2008). A communicative theory of the firm: Developing an alternative perspective on intra-organizational power and stakeholder relationships. *Organization Studies, 29*, 1227–1254.

Kuhn, T. (Ed.). (2011). *Matters of communication: Political, cultural, and technological challenges to communication theorizing*. New York: Hampton.

Kuhn, T. (2012). Negotiating the micro-macro divide: Communicative thought leadership for theorizing organization. *Management Communication Quarterly, 26*, 543–584.

Kuhn, T., & Burk, N. (2014). Spatial design as sociomaterial practice: A (dis)organizing perspective on communicative constitution. In F. Cooren, E. Vaara, A. Langley, & H. Tsoukas (Eds.), *Language and communication at work: Discourse, narrativity, and organizing* (pp. 149–174). Oxford: Oxford University Press.

Kuhn, T., & Jackson, M. (2008). Accomplishing knowledge: A framework for investigating knowing in organizations. *Management Communication Quarterly, 21*, 454–485.

Kuhn, T., & Rennstam, J. (2016). Expertise as a practical accomplishment among objects and values. In J. Treem & P. Leonardi (Eds.), *Where is expertise?: Communication and organizing in the information age* (pp. 25–43). Oxford: Oxford University Press.

Kumar, K. (1995). *From post-industrial to post-modern society: New theories of the contemporary world*. Malden, MA: Blackwell.

Kuratko, D. F. (2005). The emergence of entrepreneurship education: Development, trends, and challenges. *Entrepreneurship Theory and Practice, 29*(5), 577–598. doi:10.1111/j.1540-6520.2005.00099.x

La Berge, L. C. (2015). How to make money with words: Finance, performativity, language. *Journal of Cultural Economy, 9*, 43–62. doi:10.1080/1753035 0.2015.1040435

Laclau, E. (2005). *On populist reason*. London: Verso.

Laclau, E., & Mouffe, C. (1985). *Hegemony and socialist strategy: Towards a radical democratic politics*. London: Verso.

Laet, M. de, & Mol, A. (2000). The Zimbabwe bush pump: Mechanics of a fluid technology. *Social Studies of Science, 30*, 225–263.

Lambert, S. J., Haley-Lock, A., & Henly, J. R. (2012). Schedule flexibility in hourly jobs: Unanticipated consequences and promising directions. *Community, Work & Family, 15*, 293–315. doi:10.1080/13668803.2012.662803

Lamont, M. (2012). Toward a comparative sociology of valuation and evaluation. *Annual Review of Sociology, 38*, 1–21.

Langley, A., & Tsoukas, H. (2010). Introducing 'Perspectives on Process Organization Studies.' In T. Hernes & S. Matlis (Eds.), *Process, sensemaking, and organizing* (pp. 1–26). Oxford: Oxford University Press.

Langley, P. (2008). *The everyday life of global finance: Saving and borrowing in America*. Oxford: Oxford University Press.

Latour, B. (1986). Visualization and cognition: Thinking with hands and eyes. *Knowledge and Society: Studies in the Sociology of Culture Past and Present, 6*, 1–40.

Latour, B. (1987). *Science in action: How to follow scientists and engineers through society*. Cambridge, MA: Harvard University Press.

Latour, B. (1996). On interobjectivity. *Mind, Culture, and Activity, 3*(4), 228–245.

Latour, B. (2004). Nonhumans. In S. Harrison, S. Pile, & N. Thrift (Eds.), *Patterned ground: Entanglements of nature and culture* (pp. 224–227). London: Reaktion Books.

Latour, B. (2005). Reassembling the social: An introduction to actor-network theory. Oxford: Oxford University Press.

Latour, B. (2013). *An inquiry into modes of existence: An anthropology of the moderns* (C. Porter, Trans.). Cambridge, MA: Harvard University Press.

Latour, B., & Woolgar, S. (1979). *Laboratory life: The construction of scientific facts.* Princeton, NJ: Princeton University Press.

Law, J. (1986). Laboratories and texts. In M. Callon, J. Law, & A. Rip (Eds.), *Mapping the dynamics of science and technology* (pp. 35–50). London: Palgrave Macmillan.

Law, J. (1994). Organization, narrative, and strategy. In J. Hassard & M. Parker (Eds.), *Toward a new theory of organizations* (pp. 248–268). London: Routledge.

Law, J. (2009). Actor network theory and material semiotics. In B. S. Turner (Ed.), *The new Blackwell companion to social theory* (pp. 141–158). London: Blackwell.

Law, J., & Singleton, V. (2013). ANT and politics: Working in and on the world. *Qualitative Sociology, 36,* 485–502. doi:10.1007/s11133-013-9263-7

Lazear, E. M. (2005). Entrepreneurship. *Journal of Labor Economics, 23,* 649–680.

Lazonick, W., & O'Sullivan, M. (2000). Maximizing shareholder value: A new ideology for corporate governance. *Economy and Society, 29,* 13–35.

Lazzarato, M. (1996). Immaterial labour. In M. Hardt & P. Virno (Eds.), *Radical thought in Italy: A potential politics* (pp. 133–147). Minneapolis, MN: University of Minnesota Press.

Lazzarato, M. (2004). From capital-labour to capital-life. *Ephemera, 4,* 187–208.

Leonardi, P. (2011). When flexible routines meet flexible technologies: Affordance, constraint, and the imbrication of human and material agencies. *MIS Quarterly, 35,* 147–167.

Leonardi, P. M. (2012). Materiality, sociomateriality, and socio-technical systems: What do these terms mean? How are they different? Do we need them? In P. Leonardi, B. A. Nardi, & J. Kallinikos (Eds.), *Materiality and organizing: Social interaction in a technological world* (pp. 25–48). Oxford: Oxford University Press.

Leonardi, P. M. (2013). Theoretical foundations for the study of sociomateriality. *Information and Organization, 23,* 59–76.

Leonardi, P. M. (2015). Studying work practices in organizations: Theoretical considerations and empirical guidelines. *Annals of the International Communication Association, 39,* 235–273. doi:10.1080/23808985.2015.11679177

Leonardi, P. M. (2017). How to build high impact theories of organizational communication: Strategies of discovery and reconceptualization. *Management Communication Quarterly, 31,* 123–129. doi:10.1177/0893318916675426

Leonardi, P. M., & Barley, S. R. (2008). Materiality and change: Challenges to building better theory about technology and organizing. *Information and Organization, 18,* 159–176.

Leonardi, P. M., & Barley, S. R. (2010). What's under construction here?: Social action, materiality, and power in constructivist studies of technology and organizing. In J. Walsh & A. Brief (Eds.), *The Academy of Management Annals* (Vol. 4, pp. 1–51). Philadelphia, PA: Taylor & Francis.

Leonardi, P. M., & Rodriguez-Lluesma, C. (2012). Sociomateriality as a lens for design: Imbrication and the constitution of technology and organization. *Scandanavian Journal of Information Systems, 24,* 79–88.

Leyshon, A., & Thrift, N. (2007). The capitalization of almost everything: The future of finance and capitalism. *Theory Culture and Society, 24,* 97–115.

Licoppe, C. (2010). The 'performative turn' in science and technology studies: Towards a linguistic anthropology of 'technology in action.' *Journal of Cultural Economy, 3,* 181–188. doi:10.1080/17530350.2010.494122

Lilley, S., Lightfoot, G., & Amaral, M. N. P. (2004). *Representing organization: Knowledge, management, and the information age.* Oxford: Oxford University Press.

Linstead, S., & Pullen, A. (2006). Gender as multiplicity: Desire, displacement, difference and dispersion. *Human Relations, 59*(9), 1287–1310. doi:10.1177/0018726706069772

Lloyd, M. (1999). Performativity, parody, politics. *Theory, Culture & Society, 16,* 195–213.

Locke, J. (1690/1959). *An essay concerning human understanding* (Vol. 1 and 2). New York: Dover Publications.

Loxley, J. (2007). *Performativity.* London: Routledge.

Lucas, K. (2011). The working class promise: A communicative account of mobility-based ambivalences. *Communication Monographs, 78,* 347–369. doi:10.1080/03637751.2011.589461

Lury, C. (2004). *Brands: The logos of the global economy.* London: Routledge.

Lynn, G. (1992). Multiplicitous and inorganic bodies. *Assemblage, 19,* 32–49.

McCright, A. M., & Dunlap, R. E. (2010). Anti-reflexivity: The American conservative movement's success in undermining climate science and policy. *Theory Culture and Society, 27,* 100–133.

McDaniel, J. P., Kuhn, T., & Deetz, S. A. (2008). Voice, participation, and the globalization of communication systems. In J. V. Ciprut (Ed.), *Democratizations: Comparisons, confrontations, and contrasts* (pp. 281–300). Cambridge, MA: MIT Press.

McDonough, T., Reich, M., & Kotz, D. M. (Eds.). (2010). *Contemporary capitalism and its crises: Social structure of accumulation theory for the 21st century.* Cambridge: Cambridge University Press.

MacKenzie, D. (2007). Is economics performative?: Option theory and the construction of derivatives markets. In D. MacKenzie, F. Muniesa, & L. Siu (Eds.), *Do economists make markets?: On the performativity of economics* (pp. 54–86). Princeton, NJ: Princeton University Press.

MacKenzie, D. (2011). The credit crisis as a problem in the sociology of knowledge. *American Journal of Sociology, 116*(6), 1778–1841. doi:10.1086/659639

MacKenzie, D., & Millo, Y. (2003). Constructing a market, performing theory: The historical sociology of a financial derivatives exchange. *American Journal of Sociology, 109,* 107–145.

MacKenzie, D., Muniesa, F., & Siu, L. (Eds.). (2007). *Do economists make markets?: On the performativity of economics.* Princeton, NJ: Princeton University Press.

MacLure, M. (2013). Researching without representation? Language and materiality in post-qualitative methodology. *International Journal of Qualitative Studies in Education, 26*(6), 658–667. doi:10.1080/09518398.2013.788755

McRobbie, A. (2010). Reflections on feminism, immaterial labour, and the post-Fordist regime. *New Formations, 70,* 60–76. doi:10.3898/NEWF.70.04.2010

Malin, N. (Ed.). (2000). *Professionalism, boundaries, and the workplace.* London: Routledge.

March, J. G. (2005). Parochialism in the evolution of a research community: The case of organization studies. *Management and Organization Review, 1,* 5–22. doi:10.1111/j.1740–8784.2004.00002.x

Marens, R. (in press). Laying the foundation: Preparing the field of business and society for investigating the relationship between business and Inequality. *Business & Society.* doi:10.1177/0007650316679990

Markose, S. M. (2005). Computability and evolutionary complexity: Markets as Complex Adaptive Systems (CAS). *The Economic Journal, 115*(504), F159–F192. doi:10.1111/j.1468-0297.2005.01000.x

Martine, T., & Cooren, F. (2016). A relational approach to materiality and organizing: The case of a creative idea. In L. Introna, D. Kavanagh, S. Kelly, W. Orlikowski, & S. Scott (Eds.), *Beyond interpretivism?: New encounters with technology and organization* (pp. 143–166). Cham, Switzerland: Springer.

Mason, P. (2015). *Postcapitalism: A guide to our future.* New York: Farrar, Straus and Giroux.

Massumi, B. (1995). The autonomy of affect. *Cultural Critique, 31*(Autumn), 83–109.

Massumi, B. (2015). *Politics of affect.* Cambridge: Polity.

Mayer-Schönberger, V., & Cukier, K. (2013). *Big data: A revolution that will transform how we live, work, and think.* London: John Murray.

Mazzei, L. A. (2010). Thinking data with Deleuze. *International Journal of Qualitative Studies in Education, 23*(5), 511–523. doi:10.1080/09518398.2 010.497176

Meijer, I. C., & Prins, B. (1998). How bodies come to matter: An interview with Judith Butler. *Signs, 23*(2), 275–286.

Mensch, G. O. (1993). A managerial tool for diagnosing structural readiness for breakthrough innovations in large bureaucracies (technocracies). In R. L. Kuhn (Ed.). *Generating creativity and innovation in large bureaucracies.* (pp. 257–282). Westport, CT: Quorum Books.

Miller, C. C. (2010, May 13). Boulder, Colo., a magnet for high-tech start-ups. *New York Times,* p. 1.

Miller, P., & Bound, K. (2011). The startup factories: The rise of accelerator programmes to support new technology ventures (SF/72). Retrieved from www. nesta.org.uk

Misak, C. (2013). *The American pragmatists.* Oxford: Oxford University Press.

Mol, A. (1999). Ontological politics: A word and some questions. *The Sociological Review, 47,* 74–89. doi:10.1111/j.1467–954X.1999.tb03483.x

Mol, A. (2002). *The body multiple: Ontology in medical practice.* Durham, NC: Duke University Press.

Mol, A. (2014). Other words: Stories from the social studies of science, technology, and medicine. *Cultural Anthropology website.* Retrieved from https:// culanth.org/fieldsights/472-other-words-stories-from-the-social-studies-of-science-technology-and-medicine

Mol, A., & Law, J. (2004). Embodied action, enacted bodies: The example of hypoglycaemia. *Body & Society, 10*(2–3), 43–62. doi:10.1177/1357034X04042932

Mosco, V., & McKercher, C. (2009). *The laboring of communication: Will knowledge workers of the world unite?* Lanham, MD: Lexington.

Mumby, D. K. (2005). Theorizing resistance in organization studies: A dialectical approach. *Management Communication Quarterly, 19,* 19–44.

Mumby, D. K. (2016). Organizing beyond organization: Branding, discourse, and communicative capitalism. *Organization, 23,* 884–907. doi:10.1177/ 1350508416631164

Muniesa, F. (2004). Assemblage of a market mechanism. *Journal for the Center of Information Studies, 5*(3), 11–19.

Muniesa, F. (2011). Is a stock exchange a computer solution?: Explicitness, algorithms and the Arizona Stock Exchange. *International Journal of Actor-Network Theory and Technological Innovation, 3*(1), 1–15. doi:10.4018/ jantti.2011010101

Muniesa, F. (2014). *The provoked economy: Economic reality and the performative turn.* London: Routledge.

Mutch, A. (2013). Sociomateriality—Taking the wrong turning? *Information and Organization, 23,* 28–40. doi:10.1016/j.infoandorg.2013.02.001

Neff, G. (2012). *Venture labor: Work and the burden of risk in innovative industries*. Cambridge, MA: MIT Press.

Nelson, J. A. (2001). Value as relationality: Feminist, pragamtist, and process thought meet economics. *Journal of Speculative Philosophy, 15*(2), 137–151. doi:10.1353/jsp.2001.0021

Nicolini, D. (2009). Articulating practice through the interview to the double. *Management Learning, 40*, 195–212. doi:10.1177/1350507608101230

Nicolini, D. (2012). *Practice theory, work, and organization: An introduction*. Oxford: Oxford University Press.

Nicotera, A. M. (2013). Organizations as entitative beings: Some ontological implications of communicative constitution. In D. Robichaud & F. Cooren (Eds.), *Organization and organizing: Materiality, agency, and discourse* (pp. 66–89). New York: Routledge.

Nöth, W. (1995). *Handbook of semiotics*. Bloomington, IN: Indiana University Press.

Nussbaum, M. C. (1997). Flawed foundations: The philosophical critique of (a particular type of) economics. *The University of Chicago Law Review, 64*, 1197–1214. doi:10.2307/1600214

Nyberg, D. (2009). Computers, customer service operatives and cyborgs: Intra-actions in call centres. *Organization Studies, 30*, 1181–1199.

Nyberg, D., & Wright, C. (2016). Performative and political: Corporate constructions of climate change risk. *Organization, 23*, 617–638.

O'Donnell, M. (2010). Editor's introduction: The structure/agency 'problem.' In M. O'Donnell (Ed.), *Structure and agency. Part I: Modernity, sociology and the structure/agency debate* (pp. xxiii–lxvi). Los Angeles, CA: Sage.

OECD (Organisation for Economic Co-operation and Development). (1996). *The knowledge-based economy*. Retrieved 7 Feb. 2011 from www.oecd.org/sti/sci-tech/1913021.pdf.

Olins, W. (2003). *Wally Olins on brand*. London: Thames & Hudson.

Orlikowski, W. J. (2007). Sociomaterial practices: Exploring technology at work. *Organization Studies, 28*, 1435–1448.

Orlikowski, W. J., & Scott, S. V. (2008). Sociomateriality: Challenging the separation of technology, work and organization. In J. P. Walsh & A. P. Brief (Eds.), *The Academy of management annals* (Vol. 2, pp. 433–474). New York: Routledge.

Orlikowski, W. J., & Scott, S. V. (2014). What happens when evaluation goes online? Exploring apparatuses of valuation in the travel sector. *Organization Science, 25*, 868–891. doi:10.1287/orsc.2013.0877

Orlikowski, W. J., & Scott, S. V. (2015). Exploring material-discursive practices. *Journal of Management Studies, 52*(5), 697–705. doi:10.1111/joms.12114

O'Sullivan, S. (2001) The aesthetics of affect: thinking art beyond representation. *Angelaki, 6*(3), 125–135.

Ouchi, W. G. (1980). Markets, bureaucracies, and clans. *Administrative Science Quarterly, 25*, 129–141.

Patriotta, G., Gond, J.-P., & Schultz, F. (2011). Maintaining legitimacy: Controversies, orders of worth, and public justifications. *Journal of Management Studies, 48*, 1804–1836. doi:10.1111/j.1467-6486.2010.00990.x

Peck, J. (2010). *Constructions of neoliberal reason*. Oxford: Oxford University Press.

Peirce, C. S. (1991). *Peirce on signs: Writings on semiotic*. Chapel Hill, NC: University of North Carolina Press.

Perelman, C. (1982). *The realm of rhetoric*. Notre Dame, IN: University of Notre Dame Press.

Perelman, C., & Olbrechts-Tyteca, L. (1969). *The new rhetoric: A treatise on argumentation*. Notre Dame, IN: University of Notre Dame Press.

Perry-Smith, J. E., & Shalley, C. E. (2003). The social side of creativity: a static and dynamic social network perspective. *The Academy of Management Review, 28*, 89–106.

Peters, J. D. (1999). *Speaking into the air: A history of the idea of communication.* Chicago: University of Chicago Press.

Peters, T. (1999). *The Project50: Fifty ways to transform every task into a project that matters.* New York: Random House.

Phelan, P. (1998). *Unmarked: The politics of performance.* New York: Routledge.

Philipsen, G. (1975). Speaking 'like a man' in Teamsterville: Culture patterns of role enactment in an urban neighborhood. *Quarterly Journal of Speech, 61*, 13–22.

Phillips, J. (2006). Agencement/assemblage. *Theory Culture and Society, 23*, 108–109.

Pickering, A. (1995). *The mangle of practice: Time, agency, and science.* Chicago: University of Chicago Press.

Piette, A. (2016). *Separate humans: Anthropology, ontology, existence.* Milan, Italy: Mimesis International.

Pinchot, G. (1985). *Intrapreneuring: Why you don't have to leave the corporation to become an entrepreneur.* New York: Joanna Cotler.

Pleios, G. (2012). Communication and symbolic capitalism: Rethinking Marxist communication theory in the light of the information society. *Triple C: Cognition, Communication, Cooperation, 10*(2), 230–252.

Porter, M. (1980). *Competitive strategy: Techniques for analyzing industries and companies.* New York: Free Press.

Powell, W. W., & Snellman, K. (2004). The knowledge economy. *Annual Review of Sociology, 30*, 199–220. doi:10.1146/annurev.soc.29.010202.100037

Power, M. (1997). *The audit society: Rituals of verification.* Oxford: Oxford University Press.

Puar, J. (2012). Precarity talk: A virtual roundtable with Lauren Berlant, Judith Butler, Bojana Cvejic, Isabell Lorey, and Ana Vujanovic. *The Drama Review, 56*, 163–177.

Putnam, L. L., & Nicotera, A. M. (Eds.). (2009). *Building theories of organization: The constitutive role of communication.* New York: Routledge.

Reddy, M. (1979). The conduit metaphor—A case of frame conflict in our language about language. In A. Ortony (Ed.), *Metaphor and thought* (pp. 284–324). Cambridge: Cambridge University Press.

Reed, M. (2006). Organizational theorizing: A historically contested terrain. In S. Clegg, C. Hardy, T. Lawrence, & W. Nord (Eds.), *The SAGE handbook of organization studies* (2nd ed., pp. 19–54). Thousand Oaks, CA: Sage.

Rendell, M., & Brown, J. (2014). *The future of work: A journey to 2022.* Retrieved from www.pwc.com/gx/en/issues/talent/future-of-work/journey-to-2022.html

Rennstam, J. (2012). Object-control: A study of technologically dense knowledge work. *Organization Studies, 33*, 1071–1090.

Rennstam, J. (2013). Branding in the sacrificial mode: A study of the consumptive side of brand value production. *Scandinavian Journal of Management, 29*, 123–134.

Rennstam, J., & Ashcraft, K. L. (2014). Knowing work: Cultivating a practice-based epistemology of knowledge in organization studies. *Human Relations, 67*, 3–25.

Riach, K., Rumens, N., & Tyler, M. (2016). Towards a Butlerian methodology: Undoing organizational performativity through anti-narrative research. *Human Relations, 69*, 2069–2089. doi:10.1177/0018726716632050

Rice, J. E. (2008). The new 'new': Making a case for critical affect studies. *Quarterly Journal of Speech, 94*(2), 200–212.

Ries, E. (2011). *The lean startup: How today's entrepreneurs use continuous innovation to create radically successful businesses.* New York: Crown Business.

Riley, D. (2005). *Impersonal passion: Language as affect.* Durham, NC: Duke University Press.

Ritzer, G., & Jurgenson, N. (2010). Production, consumption, prosumption: The nature of capitalism in the age of the digital 'prosumer.' *Journal of Consumer Culture, 10*(1), 13–36. doi:10.1177/1469540509354673

Roberts, J. (2005). The power of the 'imaginary' in disciplinary processes. *Organization, 12,* 619–642.

Roberts, J. M. (2012). Poststructuralism against poststructuralism: Actor-network theory, organizations and economic markets. *European Journal of Social Theory, 15,* 35–53.

Roediger, D. R. (1999). *The wages of whiteness: Race and the making of the American working class.* New York: Verso.

Roper, J., Ganesh, S., & Zorn, T. E. (2016). Doubt, delay, and discourse: Skeptics' strategies to position climate change as contentious. *Science Communication, 38,* 776–799. doi:10.1177/1075547016677043

Rorty, R. (1979). *Philosophy and the mirror of nature.* Princeton, NJ: Princeton University Press.

Roscoe, P., & Chillas, S. (2014). The state of affairs: Critical performativity and the online dating industry. *Organization, 21,* 797–820. doi:10.1177/1350508413485497

Russell, B. (1935/2004). *In praise of idleness and other essays.* New York: Routledge.

Schatzki, T. R., Knorr-Cetina, K., & Von Savigny, E. (Eds.). (2001). *The practice turn in contemporary theory.* London: Routledge.

Schau, H. J., Muñiz, A. M., & Arnould, E. J. (2009). How brand community practices create value. *Journal of Marketing, 73*(5), 30–51. doi:http://dx.doi.org/10.1509/jmkg.73.5.30

Schegloff, E. A., & Sacks, H. (1973). Opening up closings. *Semiotica, 7,* 289–327.

Schild, H. (2017). Big data and organizational design: The brave new world of algorithmic management and computer augmented transparency. *Innovation: Organization and Management, 19*(1), 23–30. doi:10.1080/14479338.2016.1252043

Schramm, W. (1954). How communication works. In W. Schramm (Ed.), *The process and effects of mass communication* (pp. 3–26). Urbana, IL: University of Illinois Press.

Schulz, J., & Robinson, L. (2013). Shifting grounds and evolving battlegrounds: Evaluative frameworks and debates about market capitalism from the 1930s through the 1990s. *American Journal of Cultural Sociology, 1,* 373–402.

Seigworth, G. J., & Gregg, M. (2010). An inventory of shimmers. In M. Gregg & G. J. Seigworth (Eds.), *The affect theory reader* (pp. 1–25). Durham, NC: Duke University Press.

Sennett, R. (1998). *The corrosion of character: The personal consequences of work in the new capitalism.* New York: Norton.

Sennett, R. (2005). The culture of work. In C. Calhoun, C. Rojek, & B. Turner (Eds.), *The Sage handbook of sociology* (pp. 129–134). Thousand Oaks, CA: Sage.

Sennett, R. (2006). *The culture of the new capitalism.* New Haven, CT: Yale University Press.

Sennett, R. (2008). *The craftsman.* New Haven, CT: Yale University Press.

Sewell, G., & Wilkinson, B. (1992). 'Someone to Watch Over Me': Surveillance, discipline and the just-in-time labour process. *Sociology, 26,* 271–289. doi:10.1177/0038038592026002009

Shalley, C. E. (1991). Effects of productivity goals, creativity goals, and personal discretion on individual creativity. *Journal of Applied Psychology, 76*, 179–185.

Shane, S. (2009). Why encouraging more people to become entrepreneurs is bad public policy. *Small Business Economics, 33*, 141–149.

Shannon, C. E., & Weaver, W. (1949). *The mathematical theory of communication.* Urbana, IL: University of Illinois Press.

Shaviro, S. (2014). *The universe of things: Notes on speculative realism.* Minneapolis, MN: University of Minnesota Press.

Shepherd, G. J., St. John, J., & Striphas, T. (2006). *Communication as . . . : Perspectives on theory.* Thousand Oaks, CA: Sage.

Sigman, S. J. (Ed.). (1995). *The consequentiality of communication.* Mahwah, NJ: Lawrence Erlbaum.

Siles, I., & Boczkowski, P. (2012). At the intersection of content and materiality: A texto-material perspective on the use of media technologies. *Communication Theory, 22*, 227–249. doi:10.1111/j.1468–2885.2012.01408.x

Simon, H. A. (1997). *Administrative behavior: A study of decision-making processes in administrative organizations* (4th ed.). New York: The Free Press.

Skeggs, B., & Loveday, V. (2012). Struggles for value: Value practices, injustice, judgment, affect and the idea of class. *British Journal of Sociology, 63*(3), 472–490. doi:10.1111/j.1468–4446.2012.01420.x

Slack, J. D. (1989). Contextualizing technology. In B. Dervin, L. Grossberg, B. O'Keefe, & E. Wartella (Eds.), *Rethinking communication: Paradigm exemplars* (Vol. 2, pp. 329–344). Newbury Park, CA: Sage.

Slack, J. D. (2006). Communication as articulation. In G. J. Shepherd, J. St. John, & T. Striphas (Eds.), *Communication as . . . : Perspectives on theory* (pp. 223–231). Thousand Oaks, CA: Sage.

Smith, D. E. (1990). Femininity as discourse. In D. Smith (Ed.), *Texts, facts, and femininity: Exploring the relations of ruling* (pp. 159–208). London: Routledge.

Sonnenburg, S. (2007). *Kooperative Kreativität: Theoretische Basisentwürfe und organisationale Erfolgsfaktoren.* Wiesbaden: Deutscher Universitäts-Verlag.

Sørensen, B. M. (2008). 'Behold, I am making all things new': The entrepreneur as savior in the age of creativity. *Scandinavian Journal of Management, 24*, 85–93. doi:10.1016/j.scaman.2008.03.002

Spender, J.-C. (1996). Making knowledge the basis of a dynamic theory of the firm. *Strategic Management Journal, 17*, 45–62.

Spinello, R. A. (2014). *Global capitalism, culture, and ethics.* New York: Routledge.

St. Pierre, E. A., Jackson, A. Y., & Mazzei, L. A. (2016). New empiricisms and new materialisms: Conditions for new inquiry. *Cultural Studies <—> Critical Methodologies, 16*(2), 99–110. doi:10.1177/1532708616638694

Star, S. L., & Strauss, A. (1999). Layers of silence, arenas of voice: The ecology of visible and invisible work. *Computer Supported Cooperative Work, 8*(9), 9–30. doi:10.1023/A:1008651105359

Stark, D. (2009). *The sense of dissonance: Accounts of worth in economic life.* Princeton, NJ: Princeton University Press.

Stewart, K. (2007). *Ordinary affects.* Durham, NC: Duke University Press.

Storey, J., Salaman, G., & Platman, K. (2005). Living with enterprise in an enterprise economy: Freelance and contract workers in the media. *Human Relations, 58*, 1033–1054.

Stout, L. (2012). *The shareholder value myth: How putting shareholders first harms investors, corporations, and the public.* San Francisco, CA: Berrett-Koehler.

Suchman, L. (2000). Organizing alignment: A case of bridge-building. *Organization, 7*(2), 311–327.

Suchman, L. (2007). *Human-machine reconfigurations: Plans and situated actions*. Cambridge: Cambridge University Press.

Suddaby, R., Cooper, D. J., & Greenwood, R. (2007). Transnational regulation of professional services: Governance dynamics of field level organizational change. *Accounting, Organizations and Society, 32*(4–5), 333–362.

Szulanski, G. (2003). *Sticky knowledge: Barriers to knowing in the firm*. Thousand Oaks, CA: Sage.

Tapscott, D., & Williams, A. D. (2006). *Wikinomics: How mass collaboration changes everything*. New York: Penguin.

Tarde, G. (1895/2012). *Monadology and sociology*. Melbourne, Australia: re.press.

Taylor, J. R. (2011). Organization as an (imbricated) configuring of transactions. *Organization Studies, 32*, 1273–1294.

Taylor, J. R., & Van Every, E. J. (2000). *The emergent organization: Communication as its site and surface*. Mahwah, NJ: Lawrence Erlbaum.

Teece, D. J. (1998). Capturing value from knowledge assets: The new economy, markets for know-how, and intangible assets. *California Management Review, 40*(3), 55–79.

Terranova, T. (2000). Free labor: Producing culture for the digital economy. *Social Text, 18*(2), 33–58.

Thomas, K. (1999). Introduction. In K. Thomas (Ed.), *The Oxford book of work* (pp. xiii–xxiii). Oxford: Oxford University Press.

Thompson, E. P. (1963). *The making of the English working class*. New York: Random House.

Thompson, J. D. (1967). *Organizations in action*. New York: McGraw-Hill.

Thompson, P., & Harley, B. (2012). Beneath the radar?: A critical realist analysis of 'The Knowledge Economy' and 'Shareholder Value' as competing discourses. *Organization Studies, 33*, 1363–1381.

Thompson, P., Warhurst, C., & Callaghan, G. (2001). Ignorant theory and knowledgeable workers: Interrogating the connections between knowledge, skills, and services. *Journal of Management Studies, 38*, 923–942.

Thrift, N. (2005). *Knowing capitalism*. London: Sage.

Toffler, A. (1980). *The third wave: The classic study of tomorrow*. New York: Bantam.

Tomaskovic-Devey, D. (1993). *Gender & racial inequality at work: The sources & consequences of job segregation*. Ithaca: ILR Press.

Totaro, P., & Ninno, D. (2014). The concept of agorithm as interpretative key of modern rationality. *Theory Culture and Society, 31*(4), 29–49.

Totaro, P., & Ninno, D. (2016). Algorithms and the practical world. *Theory Culture and Society, 33*, 139–152.

Treem, J. W. (2012). Communicating expertise: Knowledge performances in professional-service firms. *Communication Monographs, 79*, 23–47.

Tweedie, D. (2013). Making sense of insecurity: A defence of Richard Sennett's sociology of work. *Work, Employment & Society, 27*, 94–104.

Vallas, S. P., & Cummins, E. R. (2015). Personal branding and identity norms in the popular business press: Enterprise culture in an age of precarity. *Organization Studies, 36*, 293–319. doi:10.1177/0170840614563741

Valliere, D., & Peterson, R. (2009). Entrepreneurship and economic growth: Evidence from emerging and developed countries. *Entrepreneurship and Regional Development, 21*, 459–480.

Vásquez, C. (2013). Spacing organization (or how to be here and there at the same time). In D. Robichaud & F. Cooren (Eds.), *Organization and organizing: Materiality, agency, and discourse* (pp. 127–149). New York: Routledge.

Vásquez, C., Brummans, B. H. J. M., & Groleau, C. (2012). Notes from the field on organizational shadowing as framing. *Qualitative Research in Organizations and Management*, 7(2), 144–165. doi:10.1108/17465641211253075

Vatin, F. (2013). Valuation as evaluating and valorizing. *Valuation Studies*, 1, 31–50.

Vollmer, H., Mennicken, A., & Preda, A. (2009). Tracking the numbers: Across accounting and finance, organizations and markets. *Accounting, Organizations and Society*, 34, 619–637. doi:10.1016/j.aos.2008.06.007

Vosselman, E. (2014). The 'performativity thesis' and its critics: Towards a relational ontology of management accounting. *Accounting and Business Research*, 44, 181–203. doi:10.1080/00014788.2013.856748

Watt, P. (2016). The rise of the 'dropout entrepreneur': Dropping out, 'self-reliance' and the American myth of entrepreneurial success. *Culture and Organization*, 22(1), 20–43. doi:10.1080/14759551.2015.1104682

Watzlawick, P., Bavelas, J. B., & Jackson, D. (1967). *The pragmatics of human communication: A study of interactional patterns, pathologies, and paradoxes*. New York: Norton.

Whelan, G., & O'Gorman, C. (2007). The Schumpeterian and universal hero myth in stories of Irish entrepreneurs. *Irish Journal of Management*, 28(2), 79–107.

Whitehead, A. N. (1920). *The concept of nature: Tarrner lectures delivered in Trinity College, November, 1919*. Cambridge: Cambridge University Press.

Whittle, A., & Spicer, A. (2008). Is Actor Network Theory critique? *Organization Studies*, 29, 611–629.

Wile, R. (2016, March 29). Harvard economist: All net U.S. job growth since 2005 has been in contracting gigs. *Fusion*.

Williams, C. L., & Connell, C. (2010). 'Looking good and sounding right': Aesthetic labor and social inequality in the retail industry. *Work and Occupations*, 37, 349–377.

Willis, P. (1977). *Learning to labor: How working class kids get working class jobs*. New York: Columbia University Press.

Winthrop-Young, G. (2011). *Kittler and the media*. Cambridge: Polity Press.

Wittgenstein, L. ([1953] 2009). *Philosophical investigations* (G. E. M. Anscombe, P. M. S. Hacker, & J. Schulte, Trans. 4th ed.). New York: Blackwell.

Witz, A., Warhurst, D., & Nickson, D. (2003). The labour of aesthetics and the aesthetics of organization. *Organization*, 10, 33–54.

Wood, A. J. (2016). Flexible scheduling, degradation of job quality and barriers to collective voice. *Human Relations*, 69(10), 1989–2010. doi:10.1177/0018726716631396

Wood, M., & Brown, S. (2011). Lines of flight: Everyday resistance along England's backbone. *Organization*, 18, 517–539. doi:10.1177/1350508410387961

Woolgar, S., Coopmans, C., & Neyland, D. (2009). Does STS mean business? *Organization*, 16(1), 5–30. doi:10.1177/1350508408098983

Zaloom, C. (2006). *Out of the pits: Traders and technology from Chicago to London*. Chicago: University of Chicago Press.

Zorn, T. (2002). Converging within divergence: Overcoming the disciplinary fragmentation in business communication, organizational communication, and public relations. *Business and Professional Communication Quarterly*, 65(2), 44–53. doi:10.1177/108056990206500204

Zwick, D., Bonsu, S. K., & Darmody, A. (2008). Putting consumers to work: 'Co-creation' and new marketing govern-mentality. *Journal of Consumer Culture*, 8, 163–196.

Index

Printed in the United States
by Baker & Taylor Publisher Services